DIVERSIFYING THE COURTS

Diversifying the Courts

Race, Gender, and Judicial Legitimacy

Nancy Scherer

NEW YORK UNIVERSITY PRESS
New York

NEW YORK UNIVERSITY PRESS
New York
www.nyupress.org

© 2023 by New York University
All rights reserved

References to Internet websites (URLs) were accurate at the time of writing. Neither the author nor New York University Press is responsible for URLs that may have expired or changed since the manuscript was prepared.

Please contact the Library of Congress for Cataloging-in-Publication data.

ISBN: 9781479818709 (hardback)
ISBN: 9781479818723 (paperback)
ISBN: 9781479818754 (library ebook)
ISBN: 9781479818747 (consumer ebook)

New York University Press books are printed on acid-free paper, and their binding materials are chosen for strength and durability. We strive to use environmentally responsible suppliers and materials to the greatest extent possible in publishing our books.

Manufactured in the United States of America

10 9 8 7 6 5 4 3 2 1

Also available as an ebook

In memory of my Aunt Rozzy and Uncle Allen, my biggest fans

CONTENTS

Preface: The Sonia Sotomayor Nomination   ix

Introduction: Why Do U.S. Presidents Pursue (or Not Pursue) the Goal of Diversity to Choose Federal Judges?   1

1. A Brief History of Diversity on the Federal Bench   11
2. Why Democrats Support Diversifying the Courts   25
3. Why Republicans Oppose Diversifying the Courts   41
4. Sitting Judges Discuss Diversity   58
5. Diversity, Party Identification, and Political Legitimacy   73
6. Legitimacy and Gender Diversity on the Bench   88
7. Legitimacy and Racial Diversity on the Bench   104
8. Legitimacy and Descriptive/Substantive Representation   118
9. Legitimacy and Party Identification   126

Conclusion: The Legitimacy of the U.S. Courts Is under Attack   139

Acknowledgments   149

Appendix A: Methods   151

Appendix B: Mock Newspaper Articles   157

Appendix C: Full Regression Models   173

Notes   185

References   199

Index   217

About the Author   223

PREFACE

The Sonia Sotomayor Nomination

For centuries, dating back to the George Washington presidency, politicians have used federal court nominations to advance the political causes that they and their allies hold dear (Maltese 1995).[1] In the twentieth and twenty-first centuries, it has fallen largely to the judiciary to resolve the highly divisive political issues surrounding race, ethnicity, and gender (Rosenberg 1994). In an environment where judges rule on these crucial policy debates, fierce partisan battles over who will sit on the federal courts are inevitable. The Sotomayor story illustrates this state of affairs quite effectively because it highlights the acrimonious and partisan nature of diversity appointments to the federal courts. The Sotomayor confirmation proceedings provide a good illustration of what the confirmation process looks like for minority and female nominees.

Only three months into his presidency, Barack Obama had his first opportunity to name a Supreme Court justice when, on April 20, 2009, Justice David Souter announced he would retire. As occurs with most Supreme Court vacancies, speculation immediately began among legal and political elites about whom the president might choose as Souter's replacement. Although initial statements from the White House suggested the president would not be ready to name Souter's successor until October (Associated Press 2009b), President Obama reached a decision much sooner. On May 26, 2009, he announced that he would nominate Sonia Sotomayor. If confirmed, she would be the first Hispanic American to serve on the Supreme Court.

During the 2008 presidential campaign, Obama had made clear what criteria he would apply in choosing a nominee. He said he would look for judges who were "empathetic"—meaning, he indicated, that they had struggled in life: "We need somebody who's got the heart, the empathy, to recognize what it's like to be a young teenage mom, the empathy to understand what it's like to be poor or African American or gay or disabled or old—and that's the criterion by which I'll be selecting my judges" (Whelan 2008, quoting Obama). In other words, Obama sought people who, unlike many elite legal professionals, had faced adversity because of their personal background, and therefore had been exposed to the world in which most Americans live.[2]

It was not immediately apparent how President Obama planned to identify nominees with empathy. His campaign statement, however, suggested that members of marginalized groups would be the key to his appointment strategy, as they are more likely to have struggled in life, making them better situated to understand the plights of diverse citizens who come before the courts. Sotomayor clearly fit the bill. In praising her qualifications for the Supreme Court, President Obama emphasized Judge Sotomayor's experience with hardship: "Experience being tested by obstacles and barriers, by hardship and misfortune; experience insisting, persisting, and ultimately overcoming those barriers.... It is experience that can give a person a common touch and a sense of compassion; an understanding of how the world works and how ordinary people live. And that is why it is a necessary ingredient in the kind of justice we need on the Supreme Court" (*New York Times* 2009a, quoting Obama). The White House also noted that Sotomayor would serve as an outstanding "role model of aspiration, discipline, commitment, intellectual prowess and integrity for her ascent to the federal bench from an upbringing in a South Bronx housing project" (*New York Times* 2009b).

Sotomayor's parents hailed from Puerto Rico. They left the island during World War II and eventually settled in New York City, where Sonia was born. Her father died when she was nine years old, and she was raised by her single mother in the public housing projects of the South Bronx. Though she dreamed, as a child, of one day becoming a police detective, her affliction with type 1 diabetes forestalled that possibility (Stolberg 2009).[3] Through hard work and perseverance at her studies, Sotomayor managed to escape the projects at age 18, attending Ivy League institutions of higher education (earning a B.A. from Princeton University and a J.D. from Yale University Law School) (Federal Judicial Center, biographical database; (hereafter fjc.org). Her educational pedigree alone suggests Sotomayor was among the best and the brightest of her generation.

Sotomayor's professional experience was equally impressive. Following law school, she worked in both the public and private sectors, as a criminal prosecutor in the Manhattan District Attorney's Office and as a corporate lawyer in private practice (fjc.org). It was her judicial experience, however, that prompted some to pronounce Sotomayor the *best-qualified* appointee to be nominated to the U.S. Supreme Court.[4] If confirmed, Sotomayor would become the only individual to have served as a U.S. District Court judge (appointed by President George H. W. Bush to the Southern District of New York), a U.S. Court of Appeals judge (appointed by President Bill Clinton to the Second Circuit), and ultimately a Supreme Court justice. It seemed no arguments could be made against Sotomayor concerning her qualifications.

But the discussion surrounding Sotomayor's appointment did not center on any aspect of her distinguished career. Instead, Democrats and Republicans alike focused mainly on her personal characteristics. First, there was Sotomayor's ethnicity. Republicans had tried, during the George W. Bush administration, to name the first Hispanic American to the Supreme Court, and now the Democrats were upstaging them.[5] Both parties coveted the honor of making the first Latino appointment to the high court as part of a political strategy to secure long-term electoral support from this fast-growing ethnic population. Second, there was Sotomayor's gender. In 2006, when President Bush had replaced Justice Sandra Day O'Connor with a white man, Samuel Alito, the number of women on the Court dropped to one. By appointing Sotomayor, Obama would be able to restore the number of women on the Court to two.

Democrats and affiliated interest groups lauded the president for appointing a highly qualified Latina. Many Hispanic leaders expressed great pride in the Sotomayor nomination—a feeling widely shared throughout Hispanic communities, not only among political elites (Solano 2009). Sotomayor, some suggested, could transform Hispanic Americans' opinions about the U.S. government, by showing that its halls of power are open to people like them. Maria Cardona, a founding member of Hispanics for a Fair Judiciary, stated: "President Obama has demonstrated bold leadership in nominating the first Hispanic to the Supreme Court. Justice Sotomayor will serve as a role model to all Latinos, especially those entering the legal profession, knowing that their own aspirations to serve our country in the highest positions of the judicial branch can be achieved" (Cardona 2009).

Women's groups also had effusive praise for Obama; they were pleased that he recognized the injustice of having but one woman on the Court at a time when women constituted nearly half of American law school graduates (Catalyst 2012) and more than half of the nation's population. The president of Emily's List, Ellen R. Malcolm, noted that "Judge Sotomayor will help add balance to the court and her unique perspective will help ensure that women's rights are protected" (Malcolm 2009). The president of the National Association of Women Lawyers, Lisa Horowitz, concurred: "We encouraged President Obama to appoint a woman for Supreme Court Justice to promote diversity amongst the Supreme Court and are pleased he has done so" (Hutzler 2009). Even Laura Bush, wife of the president who allowed the number of women on the Court decline from two to one, expressed how proud she was, as a woman, to see another woman join the Supreme Court (Oakland Press 2009).

Women's groups and Hispanic groups also believed that Sotomayor's presence on the Court could influence the other justices, making them more likely to heed the voices of Latinos and women.[6] As Henry Solano, interim president and general counsel of the Mexican American Legal Defense & Education Fund, put it: "This is a historic, significant and meaningful nomination. At a time when the Hispanic community is at the heart of a number of highly politicized issues and faces attacks on our civil liberties, having a Latino on the Supreme Court provides a crucial perspective that will inform the court's consideration of such cases" (Solano 2009).

Ironically, the same two identity characteristics that so pleased the Democrats and their affiliated groups—Sotomayor's gender and ethnicity—became the focal points of attacks by Republicans and their affiliated pundits, newspaper editorial pages, and radio hosts.[7] Amid the cacophony of complaints about Sotomayor, one talking point stood out: Sotomayor is not qualified to sit on the Supreme Court. According to Patrick Buchanan, "No one has brought forth the slightest evidence she has the intellectual candlepower to sit on the Roberts Court" (Buchanan 2005). To further undermine Sotomayor's legal credentials, Buchanan alleged that she had never even read a law review article (ibid.).

Radio host Michael Savage assailed Sotomayor's qualifications based on his presumption that, as a product of affirmative action, she lacked the intellectual chops of the white men who then sat on the Court, like Chief Justice Roberts: "I don't even think she could've passed law school without affirmative action" (Scherer 2011).[8] Other conservatives pejoratively compared Sotomayor to Jennifer Lopez, the famous singer and actress of Puerto Rican descent, but who, like Sotomayor hails from the Bronx. For example, one conservative commentator, Debbie Schlussel, remarked: "Sonia Sotomayor, like singer and actress Jennifer Lopez, is a Latina woman from a modest background. So it is pretty much exactly like nominating Jennifer Lopez, whose nickname, for a time, was J-Lo, to the highest court in the land. They are both Puerto Rican, and so therefore they are both extremely stupid and undeserving of their success" (Media Matters 2009).

Republicans attacked Sotomayor for being nothing more than a pawn in the Democrats' game of identity politics (Washington Times, June 9, 2009). In the 2008 presidential election, both parties had made concerted efforts to capture the support of Hispanics, the fastest-growing segment of the U.S. population; ultimately, Obama won 67 percent of the Hispanic vote. Republicans likely feared that Sotomayor's nomination would cement the relationship between Latinos and the Democratic Party. In this vein, Obama was accused of nominating Sotomayor solely because she was a Hispanic woman, thus creating a new "Hispanic seat" on the Court: "The Democrats managed to link the Sotomayor nomination to a referendum on Hispanics in America" (Editorial, *Washington Times* 2009). In addition, by purposely choosing a Latina, Obama was accused of trying to fill another quota: the two "female" seats on the Court that had existed for the 11 years prior to George W. Bush's replacement of Justice O'Connor with Justice Alito.

Many of Sotomayor's critics seized upon a statement she made in a speech in 2001, in which she suggested that a "wise Latina woman with the richness of her experiences would more often than not reach a better conclusion than a white male who hasn't lived that life" (Savage 2009a). This remark prompted accusations that Sotomayor was doubly unqualified to serve on the Supreme Court. According to her detractors, not only was she a product of identity politics (meaning she had received the nomination based on her gender and ethnicity rather than her ability), she was also an advocate of identity politics on the bench (meaning she was biased against white men).

In the end, after three months of partisan debate, Republicans were unable to mobilize their mass base (as opposed to party elites) to rally against Sotomayor. With no reelection incentive for mobilizing the Republican base, she was confirmed by the Senate on August 5, 2009, by a vote of 68–31 (Savage 2009b).

* * *

Nowhere do politics and law intersect more clearly than in the selection of federal court judges and justices. With the president choosing nominees, the Senate advising and consenting (or not consenting), and the confirmed nominees going on to decide cases of great political import, all three branches of government are implicated in the process. Such inter-branch interaction has periodically led to partisan and ideological schisms over the appointment and confirmation of federal judges. For centuries, dating back to the George Washington presidency, politicians have used Supreme Court nominations to advance the political causes that they and their allies held dear (Maltese 1995). In the twentieth and twenty-first centuries, it has fallen largely to the judiciary to resolve the highly divisive political issues surrounding race, ethnicity, and gender (Rosenberg 1994). In an environment where judges rule on these crucial policy debates, fierce partisan battles over who will sit on the federal courts are inevitable. The Sotomayor story illustrates this state of affairs quite effectively. More important, for purposes of this book, it highlights the acrimonious and partisan nature of diversity appointments to the federal courts.

Diversity on the federal bench, this book will show, has been a normative goal of U.S. presidents for centuries, but the meaning of "diversity," and its theoretical underpinnings, have evolved over time. Despite all the rhetoric about judicial diversity, however, its real-world implications for the American public remain poorly understood. Can it deliver the benefits that its proponents promise? Might it be harmful, as its opponents warn? These are among the central questions this book sets out to answer.

Introduction

Why Do U.S. Presidents Pursue (or Not Pursue) the Goal of Diversity to Choose Federal Judges?

Scholars have long recognized that the judicial appointment process is fraught with party politics (e.g., Steigerwalt 2010; Martinek, Kemper, and Van Winkle 2002; Scherer, Bartels, and Steigerwalt 2010; Scherer 2005). One such aspect of the appointment process—seating more women and minorities on the federal courts—is also part of that politicization.

The focus of this book is to answer the question: Why diversify the federal courts? There are myriad reasons why diversifying the U.S. courts is good policy. One reason is that such strategy may raise legitimacy for the courts among people previously marginalized in the justice system because of gender, race, or ethnicity. These people tend to have lower legitimacy levels for the courts than whites and white men. The main political theories about raising legitimacy levels are descriptive and descriptive/substantive representation, most often cited by Democratic presidents as the avenue by which to raise legitimacy levels. Related to this main question are some subsidiary ones. How did diversity on the bench become such a partisan fight? Do the legitimacy levels of Blacks and women (or any other member of a disadvantaged group) go up when that group is properly represented in the U.S. courts? And, pursuant to the diversity dilemma, I also pay special attention to the legitimacy levels of the courts accorded by whites and white men. According to the backlash theory, does the legitimacy of the courts decline among these groups when diversity rises?[1]

Then I must consider the issue around the party affiliation of individuals in the population. Does the presumed liberalness of women and minorities drive these partisans' legitimacy scores rather than levels of diversity? What if Republicans think that minority and female nominees are more "liberal" than whites and white men? Their legitimacy scores might decrease in the face of diversity not because the nominees seem to be part of an affirmative action plan, as the first set of questions will examine, but because Republicans believe that women and minorities will make the courts more liberal and thus adverse to their policy needs. On the other end of the spectrum, women and minorities may have increasing legitimacy scores under conditions of diversity, but what Democrats are really reacting to is their belief that more Democrats means more liberal courts, who will be closer to their policy views than white male Republican judges would.

Descriptive Representation, Substantive Representation, and Legitimacy

Descriptive representation is a normative theory which posits that, in a democracy, the composition of political institutions should reflect that of the populace (Birch 1993; Griffiths and Wollheim 1960; Mansbridge 1999; Pitkin 1967; Williams 1998). Descriptive representatives are said to "stand for" or be "sufficiently like" those constituents who are members of the same racial, ethnic, gender, or other identity group (Pitkin 1967, 80–82). For an institution to be truly descriptive, it would mirror the demographics of our nation.

The idea that our American political institutions should reflect our population's diverse makeup is as old as the United States: As James Madison stated: "It is *essential* to [a republican] government, that it be derived from the great body of the society, not from . . . a favored class of it[.]" (E. H. Scott 1898, quoting James Madison, Federalist Paper No. 39).

Or, as John Adams put it: "A representative legislature . . . should be an exact portrait, in miniature, of the people at large, as it should think, feel, reason and act like them." Descriptive representation is said to serve both instrumental and symbolic purposes. For example, instrumentally, descriptive representation may translate into better substantive representation for marginalized groups. Or, it may lead to more support among women for Supreme Court nominees who share descriptive characteristics with the group, even though the women lack ideological congruence with the nominated justice (Badas and Stauffer 2018). Descriptive representation also leads to greater knowledge about a Supreme

Court nominee among the group that is being descriptively represented (Evans, Franco, Polinard, Wenzel, and Winkle 2017).

Symbolically, a descriptive representative and a descriptive/substantive representative send signals to under-represented groups that "certain features of one's identity do not mark one as less able to govern" (Mansbridge 1999, 651). I use the term descriptive/substantive representative to mean only those who can provide a particular group with a representative who is both a substantive representative (agreement on ideas) and a descriptive representative (a person who is of the same minority or gender group for which she stands). A white person or a man, no matter how liberal he or she may be, does not meet the requirements of descriptive/substantive representation if representing the Black community.

Such representatives may also serve as role models for members of historically marginalized groups, signaling that they, too, can achieve success at the highest levels of our government (Burrell 1996; Chen 2003; Lawless 2004; Lazos 2008). Because women constitute the majority gender in this country, political theorists argue that an institution dominated by men is contrary to "simple justice" (Reinhart 1993; Verba, Burns, and Schlozman 1997). This is exactly the type of inequity that descriptive gender representation is thought to correct, thereby enhancing the institution's political legitimacy.[2]

Legitimacy is a normative goal of every modern nation. It has been described as a "reservoir of favorable attitudes or good will that helps members to accept or tolerate outputs to which they are opposed or the effects of which they see as damaging" (Easton 1965, 273) that builds institutional loyalty; it is a willingness of a citizen to stand behind an institution's continued existence even when one disagrees with its specific decisions (Klein 2015). Political legitimacy assumes not only the right to govern, but the recognition by the people of the right to govern (Coicaud 1997). It is particularly vital to democracies, like ours, where partisanship leads to outcomes with winners and losers (Clawson and Waltenburg 2009). Legitimacy is similar to the idea of institutional loyalty, the willingness of a citizen to stand behind an institution's existence even when one disagrees with its decisions (Gibson and Nelson 2019). Legitimacy is particularly vital to democracies, such as ours, where partisanship creates a situation with a winner and a loser in most political policy debates (Clawson and Waltenburg 2009). Without high levels of legitimacy, an institution cannot guarantee the people's acquiescence in its decisions (Gibson, Caldeira, and Spence 2005).

And, as the "least dangerous branch" (for its lack of purse and sword), the Judiciary is especially dependent on institutional legitimacy to ensure self-execution of its decisions (Hamilton 1788).

Political legitimacy assumes not only the right to govern, but also, and more important, the recognition *by the people* of the right to govern (Coicaud 1997).

> It is the degree to which the state is viewed and treated by citizens as rightfully holding and exercising political power.... [L]egitimacy concerns evaluations of the goodness and justness of political power ... States that lack some minimal degree of legitimacy, no matter how powerful either coercive apparatus or how appealing their economic performance, have been unable to withstand citizen desires to be willing subjects of the political order in which they live. (Gilley 2006, 31)

The Parties' Competing Arguments

Democrats have principally relied on three arguments to justify their claim that diversity on the bench is imperative to raise the legitimacy of the institution. All involve increasing minorities' and women's presence on the bench: (1) remedying past systemic discrimination perpetrated by the legal profession and the all-white male Senate; (2) making the courts look like America by raising the number of members in groups that have been historically under-represented on the bench (descriptive representation); (3) through descriptive representation, minority and female judges can also provide the voices of people from all walks of life (descriptive/substantive representation).[3] Republicans, nonbelievers in a diversity strategy, also rely on three basic arguments in opposition to a diversity strategy, all of which mimic conservatives' arguments in opposition to "affirmative action": (1) affirmative action, by definition, "favors" members of identity groups—those socially constructed to further the substantive rights of minorities, women, and other marginalized groups—over white men; (2) diversity candidates are less qualified than white males, chosen only for the color of their skin; (3) affirmative action hurts, rather than helps, minorities and women; judicial appointees made pursuant to diversity initiatives are forever branded with badges of inferiority when compared to their white male peers. While the parties' means to this common end of legitimacy could not be more opposite,[4] when one parses through their rhetoric, they nonetheless share a singular end: using the appointment process to build the legitimacy of the courts.[5]

The Diversity Dilemma

There are myriad ways for political institutions to enhance their legitimacy. Descriptive and descriptive/substantive representation are two theorized methods that Democrats use to justify diversifying our institutions. But, as far as the judicial branch of government is concerned, these two theories remain just that—theories. Understanding diversity's true impact on the legitimacy of the bench is paramount to understanding our democracy and the ability of these normative theories to explain legitimacy.

The federal bench is a particularly good institution within which to test theories about descriptive and descriptive/substantive representation. First, the president has wide latitude to mold the gender and race composition of the federal judiciary; the courts thus lack the barriers of entry that women face for elected offices (Lawless and Fox 2008). And, unlike the elected branches, control over the gender or racial makeup of the federal bench lies principally with the president, rather than the electorate. Moreover, as the only branch of government associated with fairness and justice, it would make more sense that people expect descriptive and descriptive/substantive representatives in the U.S. courts to give them the appearance of fairness.

In devising a judicial selection strategy, the parties' opposing choices for achieving legitimacy raise a thorny political dilemma—the same one we encounter when arguing about affirmative action. If one buys into the theory of descriptive representation, then they would expect the Democrats' diversity strategy to raise legitimacy levels for marginalized groups (like women or minorities). But, if one does not believe in the theories of descriptive or descriptive/substantive representation, such diversity strategies could have a negative impact on whites', men's, or white men's legitimacy levels (Scherer and Curry 2010).

The Republicans' strong preference for white men to fill judicial vacancies, its "color-blind" approach, would seem to suffer the same problem as the diversity approach. By dismissing diversity and promoting whiteness, legitimacy levels of minorities and women may decline. Such an approach signals to members of diversity groups that their own are being bypassed for judicial seats, thus reinforcing the privileged status of white men. At the same time, white men's legitimacy levels would be expected to be higher than they would be under a diversity plan, as "color-blindness" promotes more appointments for whites, men, or white men, thereby preserving the white male bastion of the federal courts. I characterize this political conundrum as the "Diversity Dilemma," and it is at the heart of this book.

The diversity dilemma has grave implications. It suggests that party politics in the United States prohibits universal legitimacy for the U.S. justice system, so long as we remain in a highly charged partisan political state, one that leads the parties to press for appointment strategies that are polar opposites.[6] It suggests that judicial appointments cannot serve as legitimacy-builders. Courts cannot shore up their legitimacy through diversity appointments since just as many Republicans will lose legitimacy for the courts as more minority and female candidates are appointed to the courts. As the only unelected branch of the federal government, the federal judiciary is more reliant on its reservoir of good will from the electorate than are the elected branches; unlike the elected branches, the Judiciary's reservoir does not get replenished with each election cycle (Caldeira and Gibson 1992). And, without the power of purse or sword, the Judiciary is further crippled because it relies on voluntary compliance with its orders.

Lacking high levels of legitimacy, the rule of law may be jeopardized. Tyler (1990) and Gibson, Caldeira, and Spence (2003) have shown that greater legitimacy for the legal system produces more voluntary obedience with the law. Thus, if there is an inherent distrust by the races (Black and Hispanic versus white, for example) and genders (male versus female) over appointment strategies, the diversity dilemma may also result in greater disobeyance of the law among whichever demographic group feels that the federal bench reflects a political order where they are second-class citizens.

Book Structure

In all of American history there has never been such an aggressive assault on the U.S. courts as is under way right now. No president has ever attacked the legitimacy of the judicial branch of government the way former president Donald Trump has.[7] This book could not be more timely, as it concerns an important issue facing this nation: presidential hostility for the courts and attempts to undermine the legitimacy of the courts. Losing legitimacy is especially problematic for courts because they rely on self-execution of their orders, lacking purse and sword. I conclude that greater diversity on the bench raises diversity levels for women and African Americans. But, as minorities' and women's legitimacy levels rise, those of whites and white men go down. There is no easy solution to this problem.

The remainder of the book will be organized as follows. I divide the book into three parts. In part I, I elaborate on each political party's stated justifications for pursuing or opposing a diversity appointment strategy, and discuss how these justifications are connected to legitimacy. Chapter 1 provides a brief history of diversity on the bench. Chapter 2 details the principal arguments made by Democrats in favor of diversity strategies for judicial appointments, and chapter 3 examines the Republicans' arguments rejecting a diversification strategy in favor of color-blindness. Chapter 4 summarizes a number of exclusive face-to-face interviews I conducted with sitting district court judges, most of whom were diversity appointments themselves. I did this because, in order to obtain descriptive and substantive representation, there must be a "motivation to represent." The interviews provide important information on how the diversity representatives on the bench feel about representing members of their gender or race.

In part II, I turn my attention to the empirical results of three experiments/surveys I designed and conducted for purposes of this book project. The surveys/experiments were intended to ascertain respondents' levels of legitimacy, their long-term support for the courts (also known as diffuse support), and their short-term support for a specific judicial decision (specific support) based on varying conditions of diversity. I focus on these two types of support for the courts because prior research suggests that each is inextricably tied to the other, and so each may engender greater willingness of the people to support judicial institutions in the face of unpopular decisions, the very definition of political legitimacy.

Chapter 5 sets forth the details of how the three experiments were conducted. In this chapter, I also discuss the data collected from post-experimental surveys, and the methods I shall use to analyze these data. Finally, I provide coding for the independent variables used in all of the models I create. I then turn to the findings of the two experiments. Chapter 6 looks at the descriptive gender representation experiment and results; chapter 7 looks at the descriptive race representation experiment and its results. And, chapter 8 reviews the third experiment, which measures descriptive/substantive representation and whether a decision by a Black judge garners more support for the decision than had the decision been made by a white judge. Finally, chapter 9 takes on the possibility that legitimacy levels of the experimental subjects are really being driven by party identification combined with the experimental treatments, and not the treatments alone. How do Democrats react to the treatment versus Republicans? Does their support rise, ebb, or remain static?

In part III, with empirical findings in hand, I turn to the conclusion. I argue that there has never been a time in which legitimacy of the courts and its judges has been so severely under attack as it was under Donald J. Trump. I also consider if diversity efforts on the bench, whether tied to legitimacy or not, nonetheless serve other important functions and thus, provide a policy to continue. Democrats have principally relied on three arguments to justify their claim that diversity on the bench is imperative to raise the legitimacy of the institution: (1) increasing minorities' and women's presence on the bench remedies past systemic discrimination perpetrated by the legal profession and the all-white male Senate; (2) minority and female appointments serve as an important democracy-building measure for members of groups who have been historically under-represented on the bench; and (3) through descriptive representation, minority and female judges can also provide the voices of people from all walks of life, judges with empathy who understand the plight of the people better than a white or male figure, even if they have the same ideological leanings as minorities and women. I use the term descriptive/substantive representative to mean only those who can provide a particular group with a representative who is both a substantive representative (agreement on ideas) and a descriptive representation (a person who is of the same minority or gender group for which they stand). A white person or a male, no matter how liberal they may be, does not meet the requirements of descriptive/substantive representation if representing the Black community.

It makes sense for Democrats to push for diversity as a way to curry favor with minorities and women, two key segments of the party's electoral base. Republicans, by contrast, are best served by appointing conservative white men (the bulk of Republican appointments) and women who follow the precepts of originalism in constitutional and statutory interpretation (Scherer 2005). To date, only Democratic presidents—Carter, Clinton, and Obama—have implemented large-scale diversity initiatives for the appointment of federal judges. The lack of a diversity plan has historically resulted in increased white male presence on the bench.

1

A Brief History of Diversity on the Federal Bench

Since the days of George Washington, U.S. presidents have grappled with the diversity of their judicial appointees. The meaning of diversity, however, has changed drastically over time. From the early days of the Republic until the late nineteenth century, a "diverse" bench meant one whose judges hailed from a variety of states and regions (Rehnquist 2002, 56). Presidents adopted this as a goal for both practical and political reasons. From a political standpoint, given the intense regional conflict of this period—largely between North and South, but also between the expanding West and the established Eastern seaboard states (Crowe 2010)—stocking the Supreme Court with justices from different parts of the country appeased presidential allies across the nation. Washington's appointment strategy was to ensure that no two justices from the same state served on the Court at the same time (Marshall 2008, 128).

From a practical standpoint, the Judiciary Act of 1789 required that Supreme Court justices "ride circuit"; this meant each justice was assigned a regional circuit court in which he heard appeals (fjc.gov/riding circuit). It was necessary because Congress created appeals courts with no permanent judges sitting in these courts; local judges and Supreme Court justices would sit alongside one another on appeals of local interest, mostly turning on state law. It was therefore paramount that justices understand the laws of the states in their circuit—a requirement that only local lawyers could fulfill, according to the conventional wisdom. This changed with the Judiciary Act of 1891, which created nine new Circuit Courts of Appeals and accorded these courts permanent staffing. Thus, these new appeals courts obviated the need for Supreme Court justices to serve on regional courts. As the practice of circuit riding ended, so did the norm of geographic diversity. Although Herbert Hoover worried about having too obvious a geographic overlap among Supreme Court justices,[1] more recent presidents have abandoned the idea of geographic diversity. Regional tensions persist today, and many

Americans resent what they consider the outsized political and cultural influence of the Northeast; five of the nine justices hail from that region (Sotomayor, Kagan, Alito, Kavanaugh, and Breyer and his replacement, Justice Brown Jackson). Of course, the idea of geographic diversity applies only to the Supreme Court. District court judges must reside in the state where their district is located; appellate judges must come from one of the states in their circuit, with each state being represented by at least one judge.

Religious Diversity

Catholics

In 1836, President Andrew Jackson appointed the first Catholic to the previously all-Protestant U.S. Supreme Court: Chief Justice Roger Taney. But Jackson was not pursuing any normative goal about religious diversity (Perry 1986; Goldman 2006). Instead, Taney, who was from a wealthy landed ancestry, early settlers in the colony of Maryland, was appointed because he was a close political ally and friend of Jackson's (Tyler 1872). Notwithstanding a wave of anti-Catholic sentiment swelling across the nation (Swisher 1935, 317), the Senate confirmed Taney unanimously.

Not until 1894 did President Grover Cleveland appoint the second Catholic to the high court, Edward D. White. Like Taney, White came from a wealthy old-line family in a majority-Catholic state, in this instance Louisiana (Oyez 2020). Cleveland, like Jackson before him, appears to have had no political agenda in appointing a Catholic justice. The Senate confirmed White unanimously.

However, at the turn of the twentieth century, presidents began to treat Supreme Court nominees' religion as a political issue, realizing that a religious-diversity appointment could shore up electoral support among urban immigrant voters, many of whom were Catholic or Jewish (Goldman 2006; Perry 1986). With this in mind, in 1899, President William McKinley, a Republican, appointed Joseph McKenna to the Court who, unlike his blue-blooded Catholic predecessors on the Court, was the son of Irish immigrants. This appointment required McKinley to walk a fine line. He had to appease the virulently anti-Catholic American Protective Association, which had backed him in the last election, and at the same time send a message that Catholics were welcome in the Republican Party (Abraham 1999, 153). Though anti-Catholic attacks surfaced during McKenna's confirmation hearings, he won unanimous Senate approval (Goldman 2006).

Starting with the appointment of McKenna, each Catholic to leave the Supreme Court (by death or retirement) would be replaced by a Catholic, save during a brief period from 1949 to 1956. Republican and Democratic presidents alike pursued this strategy, both parties recognizing the increasing importance of the Catholic vote. So grew the notion of a "Catholic seat" on the Court. Upon McKenna's death, President William Howard Taft elevated Justice White to Chief Justice.[2] After White's death, President Warren Harding appointed Catholic Pierce Butler to the Court. In 1940, when Butler died, President Franklin Roosevelt appointed another Catholic, Frank Murphy.

When Murphy died in 1949, President Truman chose not to replace him with another Catholic, thus leaving the Catholic seat empty. Much controversy arose among Catholic leaders, but Truman remained defiant (Goldman 2006). Seven years later, President Eisenhower would bring back the Catholic seat. While political considerations factored into his decision (he thought it would help Republicans win over Catholic votes in the 1956 election), Eisenhower was greatly swayed by Cardinal Francis Spellman of New York, whom he knew by virtue of Spellman's service as a military vicar and foreign envoy of President Roosevelt during World War II (Goldman 2006). Eisenhower thus appointed William Brennan as an associate justice, a decision he would later regret.[3] After the election of John F. Kennedy as the first Catholic president, the importance of maintaining a Catholic seat on the Supreme Court waned. Brennan remained the sole Catholic justice until the Reagan administration, when two others joined him: Antonin Scalia, the first Italian American appointed to the Supreme Court, and later, Anthony Kennedy. Today, five Catholics serve on the Court (Roberts, Thomas, Alito, Sotomayor, and Kavanaugh), indicating that religious diversity among the justices is no longer of great concern to presidents.

On the lower courts, President John Adams made the first attempt to appoint a Catholic. Philip Barton Key was one of the so-called midnight judges Adams appointed in the waning moments of his presidency, as part of a reorganization of the courts under the Judiciary Act of 1801.

When President Thomas Jefferson's allies in Congress repealed the Act in 1802, Judge Key left the bench. Nearly three decades later, Andrew Jackson made the first legitimate appointment of a Catholic to the lower courts, Samuel Hadden Harper, to the District of Louisiana. Most subsequent presidents followed Jackson's lead and appointed at least one Catholic, and sometimes as many as four, to the federal bench. It was not until the Franklin D. Roosevelt administration that tokenism for Catholics on the lower federal courts ended. FDR appointed 40 Catholics to U.S. district and appeals courts—30.1 percent of his total lower-court nominations. This trend largely continued after Roosevelt's death (Goldman 2006, 219).[4]

Jews

In 1916, President Woodrow Wilson, a Democrat, famously nominated Brandeis as the first Jewish person to sit on the Supreme Court. During a time of rampant anti-Semitism among the American population (Karfunkel and Ryley 1978, 13–36), Wilson knew his candidate faced an uphill battle getting confirmed.[5] After five months of hearings, the Judiciary Committee gave Brandeis a favorable recommendation, voting along party lines 10–8; he was quickly confirmed by the Democratic-led Senate, 47–22 (Karfunkel and Ryley 1978, 57; Urofsky 2009).

President Herbert Hoover would nominate the second Jew to the Supreme Court in 1932—Benjamin Cardozo—putting two Jews on the Court simultaneously. Beginning midway through Franklin Roosevelt's presidency and continuing until the Clinton administration, there would be only one Jewish justice—creating a "Jewish seat" to go along with the Catholic seat. When Cardozo died in 1938, he was replaced by Felix Frankfurter.[6] Frankfurter was subsequently replaced by Arthur Goldberg, and Goldberg by Abe Fortas. Neither Nixon, Carter (who had no opportunity for a Supreme Court appointment), nor George H. W. Bush appointed any Jews to the Supreme Court. President Bill Clinton had the opportunity to nominate two justices, and he selected Jews both times: Ruth Bader Ginsburg and Stephen Breyer. In the Obama administration, one more Jew, Elena Kagan, would join the Court, bringing the percentage of Jews on the Court to 37 percent;[7] Jews constitute but

1.4 percent of the American population. For the first time in history, no white Protestant men sat on the Supreme Court.

As for Jewish judges on the lower courts, presidents in the early twentieth century followed McKinley's and Taft's lead. They continued to appoint token Jews, and slowly the number began to grow. By the end of the Johnson administration, the appointment of Jews was no longer a focus of diversity, as all eyes turned to the civil rights movement. Indeed, starting with the Nixon administration, there would be no Jews on the Supreme Court until the Clinton administration.

The first Jewish person to sit on the federal courts was not, as many people assume, Louis Brandeis. That distinction belongs instead to Jacob Trieber, given a recess appointment in 1900 by President McKinley and later confirmed by the Senate as a district court judge in Arkansas. Then in 1911, Julian Mack became the first Jewish judge on the U.S. Courts of Appeals, when President Taft, who had appointed Mack to the U.S. Commerce Court in 1910, elevated him to the Seventh Circuit Court of Appeals.[8]

Racial and Gender Diversity

African Americans

Before the civil rights movement gained momentum in the late 1950s, only one African American had ever sat on the federal courts. In 1937, President Franklin D. Roosevelt appointed William Henry Hastie, who had been a lawyer for the Interior Department, to the U.S. Court for the Virgin Islands—an Article I court, formed under Congress's power to create inferior courts, on which judges could serve a single ten-year term (Hastie 1973). President Truman later elevated Judge Hastie to the Third Circuit Court of Appeals, making him the first African American to sit on a more prestigious Article III court, where judges enjoy life tenure (ibid.). The Eisenhower administration, which took a passive approach to civil rights, appointed no new African Americans to the bench and thus, Hastie remained the sole Black judge on an Article III court. Eisenhower did, however, appoint one African American, Scovel Richardson, to an Article I court, the U.S. Customs Court, who was then elevated when the Customs Court became the Court of International Trade, an Article III court.

Under President Kennedy, the number of African American judges began to slowly increase. Kennedy appointed James B. Parsons to the U.S. District Court for the Northern District of Illinois in 1961, making Parsons the first African American to sit on an Article III district court. Two more Black judges earned appointments to the lower courts during Kennedy's abbreviated term in office: Wade McCree to the Eastern District of Michigan, and Thurgood Marshall to the Second Circuit, originally as a recess appointment. Kennedy's choice of Marshall, the longtime chief counsel of the NAACP, sparked fierce opposition from white Southern senators, who fought seating him permanently (Williams 1998, 332–338). The same was true when President Lyndon Johnson chose Marshall as the first African American to serve on the Supreme Court, in 1966. He was ultimately confirmed in 1967. Also in 1966, Johnson appointed the first Black woman to the federal courts, Constance Motley; she served on the U.S. District Court for the Southern District of New York. In total, Johnson would appoint ten Black judges to the federal courts during his five years in office. The pace slackened somewhat under Presidents Nixon and Ford. In the eight years during which they occupied the White House (Nixon from 1969 to 1974, Ford from 1974 to 1977), they appointed nine African Americans to the lower federal courts (six for Nixon, three for Ford), and none to the Supreme Court.

Women

The first female judges reached the federal courts slightly earlier than the first African Americans. In 1928, Calvin Coolidge was the first to name a woman as a federal judge; he appointed Genevieve Cline to the U.S. Customs Court (an Article I court). Six years later, Franklin Roosevelt chose Florence Allen Ellinwood as the first woman on an Article III court, the Sixth Circuit Court of Appeals. Thereafter, however, progress for women was even slower than it was for African Americans. The second woman to be seated on an Article III court would not occur until 1950, when President Truman appointed Burnita Shelton Matthews to the U.S. District Court for the District of Columbia. Presidents Kennedy, Nixon, and Ford each appointed only one woman to the Article III federal courts. Lyndon Johnson appointed three, and Eisenhower none.

LatinX

Among racial and ethnic minorities, Latinos' representation on the federal courts lagged behind all others. Not until 1961 did President Kennedy appoint the first Latino to an Article III court: Reynaldo Garza, who joined the U.S. District Court for the Southern District of Texas. Presidents Johnson, Nixon, and Ford appointed three, two, and one Latino judge(s), respectively, to the federal bench. None were appointed to the Supreme Court.

The End of Tokenism

As the historical record demonstrates, judicial diversity was a nonpartisan issue from the nation's founding through the 1970s. Democratic presidents in the twentieth century showed a slightly greater propensity for appointing judges from under-represented groups, but both parties followed the same basic approach: They made strategic diversity appointments to the Supreme Court, hoping to help the president's party attract more voters (going back to the Jewish seat, Catholic seat, Black seat, etc.); they also used tokenism on the lower courts. All of that would change with President Jimmy Carter's implementation of a wide-scale diversification agenda for the U.S. courts. Just as race and gender had moved to the center of electoral politics and policymaking, the issue of minorities and women on the U.S. courts followed suit.

When President Carter took office in 1977, there were 570 judges on the federal bench (including active and senior status judges). The total included only eight women, five Hispanics, and 20 African Americans. Believing such imbalance jeopardized the integrity and legitimacy of the entire justice system, Carter became the first president to promise, and then implement, a far-reaching appointment strategy with diversity as its cornerstone. In fact, his appointment strategy applied not only to the judiciary but also to all executive-branch agencies. Reflecting Carter's campaign promise, the 1976 Democratic Party platform stated: "All diplomats, *federal judges* and other major officials should be selected on a basis of qualifications. At all levels of government services, *we will recruit, appoint and promote women and minorities*" (Democratic Party Platform 1976; emphasis added). During his four years in office, Carter

TABLE 1.1. Presidential Appointments to the U.S. Supreme Court (1933–2020) Total Number and Percentage of Appointments by Race, Ethnicity, and Gender

	White Men	Women	Blacks	Hispanics	Total Appointments
Roosevelt	9(100%)	0	0	0	9
Truman	4(100%)	0	0	0	4
Eisenhower	5(100%)	0	0	0	5
Kennedy	2(100%)	0	0	0	2
Johnson	1(50%)	0	1(50%)	0	2
Nixon	4(100%)	0	0	0	4
Ford	1(100%)	0	0	0	1
Carter	0	0	0	0	0
Reagan	3(75%)	1(25%)	0	0	4
H.W. Bush	1(50%)	0	1(50%)	0	2
Clinton	1(50%)	1(50%)	0	0	2
W. Bush	2(100%)	0	0	0	2
Obama	0	2(100%)	0	1(50%)	2
Trump	2 (67.7%)	1(33.3%)	0	0	3

appointed far more women and minority judges than all of his predecessors combined: 11 women, nine African Americans, and two Latinos to the appellate courts; he also named 29 women, 28 African Americans, and 14 Latinos to the district courts.[9] Carter had no opportunity to name a Supreme Court justice. Tables 1.1 through 1.3 present the number of white men, minorities, and women appointed by each president, from FDR to Obama, at all three levels of the federal hierarchy. Indicated in parentheses are the percentages of the president's total appointments that each group represents.

Looking at the period encompassing 1977–2020, three modern-day Democratic presidents and their diversity appointments, and the dearth of diversity appointments by Republican presidents in the same period, we see clear partisan lines drawn on diversifying the federal bench. Indeed, the first president to nominate a woman was a Democrat (Roosevelt). The first president to nominate an African American to the federal courts was President Johnson. And, the first Hispanic was appointed by a Democrat (President Kennedy). But, in the patterns that emerge from these data, the biggest spikes in diversity appointments

TABLE 1.2. Presidential Appointments to U.S. Courts of Appeals (1933–2020)
Total Number and Percentage of Appointments by Race, Ethnicity, and Gender

	White Men	Women	Blacks	Hispanics	Total Appointments
Roosevelt	51(98.0%)	1(2.0%)	0	0	51
Truman	26(96.3%)	0	1(3.7%)	0	27
Eisenhower	45(100%)	0	0	0	45
Kennedy	20(95.2%)	0	1(4.8%)	0	21
Johnson	37(92.5%)	1(2.5%)	2(5.0%)	0	40
Nixon	45(97.8%)	0	0	0	46
Ford	11(100%)	0	0	0	11
Carter	34(60.7%)	11(18.6%)	9(16.4%)	2(3.7%)	56
Reagan	75(90.4%)	7(8.4%)	1(1.2%)	1(1.2%)	83
H.W. Bush	31(73.8%)	7(16.7%)	2(4.8%)	2(4.8%)	42
Clinton	34(51.5%)	22(33.3%)	9(13.6%)	7(10.6%)	66
W. Bush	39(63.9%)	16(25.8%)	5(8.1%)	3(4.8%)	62
Obama	17(31%)	24(43%)	9(16.3%)	6(10%)	55
Trump	37(68.5%)	11(20.3%)	0	1(1.8%)	54

TABLE 1.3. Presidential Appointments to the U.S. District Courts (1933–2020)
Total Number and Percentage of Appointments by Race, Ethnicity, and Gender

	White Men	Women	Blacks	Hispanics	Total Appointments
Roosevelt	134(100%)	0	0	0	134
Truman	100(99.0%)	1(1.0%)	0	0	101
Eisenhower	129(100%)	0	0	0	129
Kennedy	98(96.1%)	1(1.0%)	2(1.9%)	1(1.0%)	102
Johnson	115(91.2%)	2(1.5%)	7(5.5%)	3(2.4%)	126
Nixon	172(95.0%)	1(0.6%)	6(3.3%)	2(1.1%)	181
Ford	43(89.6)	1(2.1%)	3(6.2)	1(2.1%)	50
Carter	136(66.7%)	29(14.3%)	28(13.8%)	14(16.9%)	203
Reagan	247(85.2%)	24(18.3%)	6(2.1%)	13(4.5%)	290
H.W. Bush	108(73.0%)	29(19.6%)	10(6.7%)	6(4.0)	148
Clinton	159(52.1%)	87(28.5%)	53(17.4%)	18(5.9%)	305
W. Bush	176(67.4%)	53(20.3%)	18(6.9%)	27(10.3%)	261
Obama	102(38.0%)	103(41%)	50(18.6%)	27(10.0%)	268
Trump	110(63.2%)	44(25.2%)	9(5.1%)	8(4.6%)	154

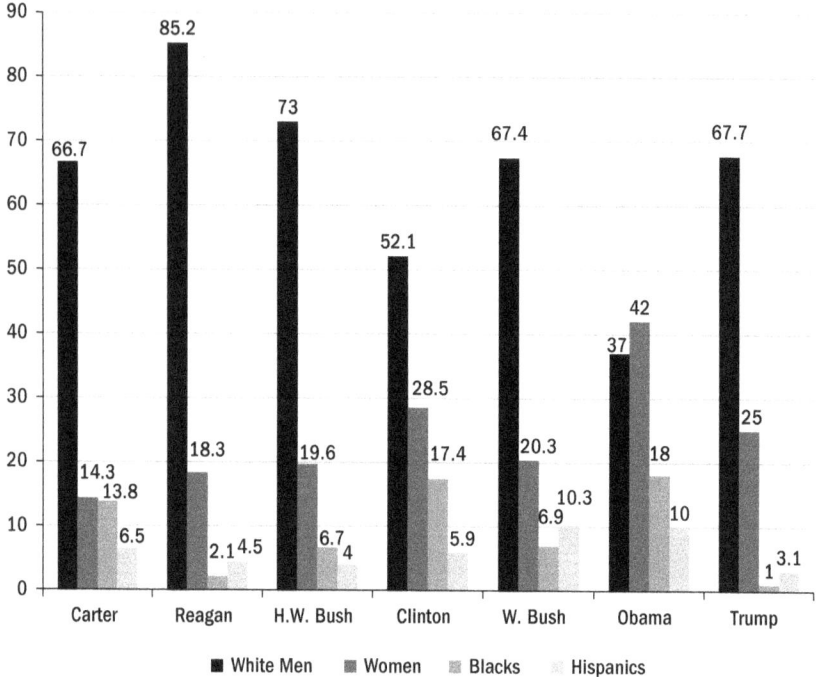

Figure 1.1. Presidential Appointments to All Levels of Federal Court (1977–2020)

occur as we move from Republican president to Democratic president in the years 1977–2019.

Whereas Democratic presidents have followed Jimmy Carter's lead in their attempts to achieve judicial diversity, Republican presidents have mostly maintained the position of Carter's successor, Ronald Reagan, who disavowed all of Carter's measures to increase diversity on the bench. From that point forward, the diversity debate would be waged along party lines. Viewed from the perspective of electoral politics, this is to be expected. The parties have opposing stances on affirmative action and claim entirely different demographic groups as part of their respective bases.

As discussed in chapter 3, Republicans instead advocate a "colorblind" system for awarding government benefits and jobs, which they claim is based on individualism, and not group membership. In practice, this approach tends to perpetuate the "old boys'" network on the federal bench. As shown in figure 1.1 and tables 1.1 through 1.3, no under-represented group made gains in the judiciary during the Reagan administration. Although President Reagan appointed Sandra Day O'Connor to become the first female Supreme Court justice, the number of women on the high court remained static for the next 11 years of Republican control of the White House. Further down the judicial hierarchy, Reagan named seven women to the courts of appeals (8.4 percent of his total appointees) and 24 women to the district courts (18.3 percent). President Reagan appointed no African Americans or Hispanics to the Supreme Court, one African American (1.2 percent) and one Hispanic (1.2 percent) to the appellate courts, and six African Americans (2.1 percent) and 13 Hispanics (4.5 percent) to the district courts.

President George H. W. Bush did not improve much on Reagan's diversity record. Although neither of his Supreme Court nominees was a woman, H. W. Bush did name one African American, Clarence Thomas. Thomas would replace Justice Thurgood Marshall, thus keeping intact the one "Black seat" on the Supreme Court.[10] Of H. W. Bush's appointments to the courts of appeals, 16.7 percent were women (all of them white), 4.8 percent African American, and 4.8 percent Hispanic. He appointed similar proportions of women and minorities to the district courts: 19.5 percent women, 6.8 percent African Americans, 4.0 percent Hispanics.

The younger President Bush, George W., appointed a slightly greater proportion of female judges than did his father (26.1 percent of appellate nominees, 20.3 percent of district court nominees), although he fell short of the percentage of women Clinton and Obama appointed. Nor did he replace Justice O'Connor with another woman on the Supreme Court (although he tried).[11] Similarly, he appointed minorities to the lower federal courts at a rate only marginally higher than his father. On the appellate courts, 8.1 percent of George W. Bush's judges were African American and 4.8 percent were Hispanic; on the district courts, 6.9 percent were Black and 10.3 percent were Hispanic.

For a good illustration of the partisan battle over diversity on the bench, one need only look at the diversity efforts of Obama versus Trump. Trump appointed a total of 229 judges and justices to all levels of the federal hierarchy. 63.3 percent of these appointments were white men, compared to 37.0 percent of Obama's total judges appointed. Only 24.0 percent of Trump's appointments were women, while women made up 42 percent of Obama's appointees. Racial and ethnic diversity also decreased significantly from Obama to Trump. Blacks were 18.1 percent of Obama's appointments and 10.5 percent were Hispanic. Trump's appointments of minorities, however, lagged far behind. Trump appointed only nine African Americans (3.9 percent) and nine Hispanics (3.9 percent) to the federal courts (and no blacks and two Hispanics to the courts of appeals).

As these percentages indicate, under Republican presidents, women achieved far better representation on the judiciary than did minorities. This likely stems from the fact that there is a much larger pool of ideologically conservative women from which to choose judges, compared to the pool of conservative minorities. However, women still remain the most under-represented class of individuals on the bench compared to their presence in the population. Consider, for example, George W. Bush's appointees to federal district courts. Hispanics constituted 10.3 percent, near parity with their proportion of the U.S. population in 2000, when W. Bush took office (12.3 percent). But only 20.3 percent of Bush's nominations went to women, who made up more than half of the general population. And, despite the inroads women and minorities have made, white men continue to occupy a much higher proportion of judicial seats than their 31 percent of the U.S. population (see figure 1.2).

Figure 1.2 illustrates just how far the American judiciary would have to go in order to achieve "descriptive representation" or "mirror representation"—that is, for the percentage of judges from each group to mirror their percentage in the general population. This figure presents a snapshot of diversity on the courts as of 2021.

According to the 2019 updated U.S. Census,[12] white men constitute only 31 percent of the U.S. population and yet, in each of the categories set forth in figure 1.2, they make up at least 48.0 percent of the bench and as much as 80.4 percent among senior judges on the courts of appeals. Senior judges are former full-time Article III judges who elect to become semi-retired with a reduced caseload when eligible. Eligibility is based on a combination of age and the judge's years on the bench.[13]

In contrast, women constitute 50.9 percent of the population but reach a high of only 33.3 percent on the Supreme Court. This presents an under-representation of women by 17.6 percentage points. The lower

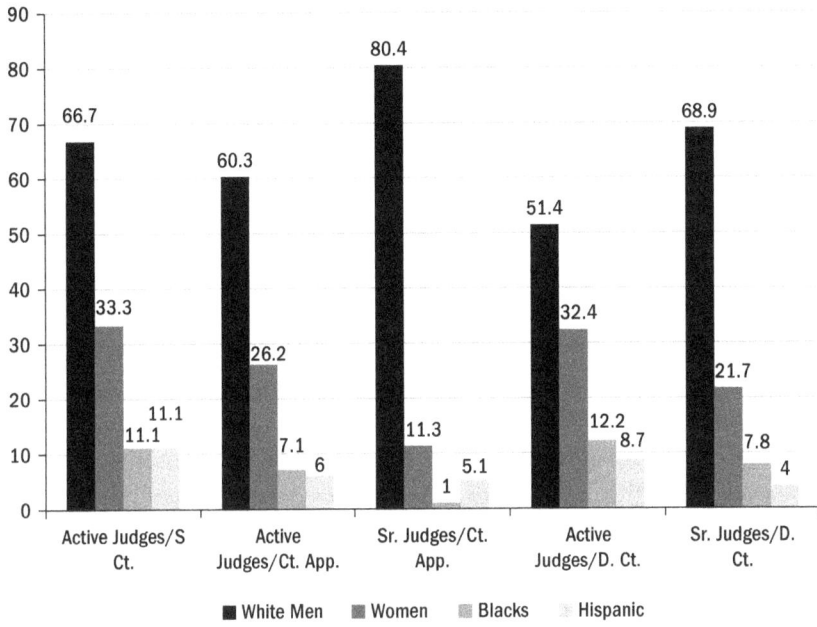

Figure 1.2. All Judges on U.S. Courts, Sitting and Semi-Retired Judges (January 1, 2021)

courts face even greater discrepancies between a group's percentage of the population and percentage on the bench. On the Courts of Appeals, women comprise only 35.8 percent of active judges, compared to their 50.9 percent of the population (a difference of 15.1 percentage points). African Americans comprise 13.4 percent of the general population, but among active judges, their presence is 12.1 percent (a difference of 1.3 percentage points). I note that some may consider this to satisfy goals of descriptive representation, while others believe mirror representation is the only way to satisfy the tenets of descriptive representation for Blacks. Hispanics fare much worse. Active Hispanic judges on the Courts of Appeals make up 6.3 percent of appellate judges, while their presence in the population is 16.7 percent (a difference of 10.4 percentage points). Together, Blacks and Hispanics constitute more than 30 percent of the population but only about 13 percent of active judges on the appellate bench. When one considers that 67.5 percent of all criminal defendants in federal court are African American or Hispanic, and that the federal courts have exclusive jurisdiction over Civil Rights Act claims, this under-representation is particularly striking.

Legitimacy Should Be the Goal of All Judicial Appointments

In the following two chapters I will discuss in detail the Democratic and Republican parties' conflicting stances on diversifying the federal judiciary. In short, Democrats believe presidents should employ an appointment strategy designed to increase diversity, while Republicans consider that approach potentially damaging or counterproductive. These opposing views notwithstanding, the two parties' positions have one common thread: both seek as their ultimate goal to preserve and enhance the legitimacy of the U.S. justice system.[14] They pursue this putatively nonpartisan end, however, through partisan means. In the end, if we do see statistically significant results, meaning greater minority or female presence on the bench raises legitimacy levels of minorities and women, then we can say that Democrats' efforts to increase diversity on the bench serves two party goals: enhancing judicial legitimacy and satisfying the thirsts of party elites who spearhead voting efforts and who donate large sums of money to finance campaigns (Scherer 2005). But we may now find another reason diversity is important to the Democratic Party. It enhances its core constituencies' desire for responsive and fair courts by raising their legitimacy levels for the courts. There is, of course, another reality: There may be a backlash by whites, and especially white men in the race study and men and white men in the gender study. This, theoretically, lowers legitimacy levels for whites and white men, certainly not the intended impact Democrats were seeking in an appointment strategy. Under this scenario, one could conclude that increasing diversity could adversely impact the legitimacy of the courts, as it lowers the levels for a significant part of the population.

2

Why Democrats Support Diversifying the Courts

Beginning with Jimmy Carter, all four Democratic presidents in the past four decades have endorsed an appointment strategy for the U.S. courts predicated on increasing the level of diversity. They all concur that at the heart of their diversity efforts is a determination to raise the legitimacy levels of minorities and women. These groups had been marginalized in the selection for law schools, entry into the legal profession, and the selection of judges (for whom legitimacy levels were presumably low). Yet, although Carter, Bill Clinton, Barack Obama, and Joseph Biden shared a belief in this common goal of diversity, they had different ideas about the way to reach that goal. Before we get to what they disagreed on, we must first understand the construct of legitimacy.

Remedying Past Discrimination

As a consequence of the civil rights movement and the feminist movement, courts and political leaders in the 1960s and '70s began facing up to the fact that most of the nation's institutions discriminated against minorities and women.[1] They recognized that they had violated the fundamental principles of equitable jurisprudence: the "root idea of equity . . . [is] that law should be administered fairly" (Holdsworth 1915, 293). To remedy the legacy of discrimination, courts began ordering discriminators to take active, affirmative measures to ensure equal opportunity for all: "In fashioning and effectuating the desegregation decrees, the courts will be guided by equitable principles. Traditionally, equity has been characterized by a practical flexibility in shaping its remedies and by a facility for adjusting and reconciling public and private needs" (*Brown v. Board of Education* 1955, at 299–300; internal quotation marks omitted). These measures included programs now known collectively as "affirmative action."

In 1974, the executive director of the U.S. Civil Service Commission, Bernard Rosen, explained the need for affirmative action and emphasized the panoply of options for implementing it:

> Meaningful response is now being made to the problems of those who have not participated in the competition for public employment, or who even now cannot do so successfully because the system may have been designed and operated without taking them into account. The response has taken a variety of approaches, depending on the nature of the problems of the work force and the needs of the employer. Generally, successful equal employment opportunity programs comprise a full range of affirmative actions. These actions are tailored to the problems of those who, because of past discriminations, are not competing successfully for entry into the system; or who, once on the rolls, are unable to realize their full potential because of gaps in education or skills, also often due to past discrimination. (Rosen 1974, 238)

Affirmative action in its early days took many forms, as Rosen had encouraged. At one end of the spectrum were government-ordered hiring quotas for minority and female job candidates (Gamson and Modigliani 1987; Glazer 1987)—exemplified by the "Philadelphia Plan" that the Lyndon Johnson administration rolled out in 1967. "The plan set specific numerical [hiring] goals for each of the building and construction trades.... Labor Department officials announced that 'because of the deplorably low rate of employment among members of minority groups' in the [construction] industry, they would set up similar plans in other major cities" (Glazer 1987, 374). Such quota-based plans could also be applied for hiring women. President Johnson's Executive Order 11375 (also issued in 1967) fell short of ordering quotas, but it required contractors wishing to do business with the federal government to develop affirmative action plans using "goals and time-tables" to increase the number of minorities and women they employed. At the other end of the continuum from the Philadelphia Plan, the government created task forces charged with examining race or gender inequality, such as the National Women's Business Enterprise Policy (Executive Order 12138, 1979), which issued reports and recommendations but had little real power. Federal affirmative action efforts had an undeniable impact:

In 1984, the Office of Federal Contract Compliance Programs found that government contractors were hiring women and minorities at twice the rate of other businesses.

President Carter, upon taking office, wasted no time in broadening the scope of government-ordered affirmative action. Whereas previous plans had dealt only with employers who contracted directly with the federal government, the Public Works Employment Act of 1977 established that no federal money would be granted to state or local governments unless at least 10 percent of the projects undertaken with the grant money were awarded to minority businesses. Carter's judicial selection strategy fit with his broader philosophy about affirmative action as a means to remedy past discrimination. Margaret McKenna, the Deputy Assistant for the White House Office of Legal Counsel, stated early in Carter's term that the president had a "firm commitment to affirmative action in the judicial selection process and [a] concern that the [judicial selection] panels[2] . . . find and recruit minority groups and nontraditional candidates for the federal bench" (Berkson and Neff 1979). Scholars assessing Carter's diversity initiative generally characterize it as an affirmative action plan (e.g., Goldman 1997; Fowler 1983; Gottschall 1983).

Robert Lipshutz, Carter's White House Counsel, described the president's plan this way in an address to the District of Columbia Bar Association: "The President has two goals in the selection process. Two goals of equal importance. One is to continue to appoint only judges of high quality; the other is to open the selection process to groups, such as minorities and women, which historically have had little representation on the federal bench" (Clark 2003, quoting Lipshutz).[3]

Carter issued three executive orders aimed at remedying the past systemic exclusion of minorities and women from consideration for federal judgeships. First, he set out to dismantle the traditional method of selecting lower-court judges, called senatorial courtesy. Home-state senators (overwhelmingly white men) had the power to bestow appellate judgeships on their favorites (also overwhelmingly white men), which perpetuated the old-white-boys' network (Berkson and Neff 1979; Clark 2003). Carter's Executive Order No. 12059 (1978) wrested that privilege from the senators and awarded it instead to newly created merit selection committees. However, Carter could not persuade senators to cede their senatorial-courtesy prerogative over district court nominations (Scherer 2005, 79). This often led the administration to disregard recommendations from home-state senators who selected white men to fill judicial vacancies over qualified minority or female candidates (Goldman 1997). It also directed the new merit selection committees to make "special efforts" to identify minorities and women for appeals court vacancies: "Each panel is encouraged to make special efforts to seek out and identify well-qualified women and members of minority groups as potential nominees." Carter's third selection-related executive order, No. 12097 (1978), directed his attorney general, Griffin Bell, to make "an *affirmative effort* . . . to identify qualified candidates, including *women and members of minority groups*" for federal judgeships (emphasis added).[4]

Carter characterized his selection strategy as one meant to "redress" the lack of women and minorities on the bench. In signing the Omnibus Judgeship Act on October 20, 1978, Carter explained, "This [A]ct provides a unique opportunity to begin to redress another disturbing feature of the Federal judiciary: the almost complete absence of women or members of minority groups. . . . I am committed to these appointments, and pleased that this [A]ct recognizes that we need more than token representation on the Federal bench."

In venues other than the judiciary, President Carter supported the whole spectrum of equitable remedies, from quotas to task forces. For the federal courts, however, Carter acknowledged that quotas were unfeasible, because of the Constitution's stipulation that the appointment of Article III judges requires the "advice and consent" of the Senate, thus constraining the president's judicial selections. "If I didn't have to get Senate confirmation of appointees, I could just tell you flatly that twelve percent of all my judicial appointments would be Black and three percent Spanish-speaking and 40 percent would be women" (Scherer 2005, quoting Carter).[5]

Although inter-branch politics prevented Carter from imposing strict quotas, he was still determined to meet certain benchmarks for diversifying the courts. He reportedly promised a group of African American leaders from the South that he would appoint a Black judge to every U.S. district court in the former Confederate states (Slotnick 1983). And, as stated above, the administration often ignored the norm of senatorial courtesy to appoint women and minorities instead of recommended white men (Goldman 1997). But the conflict was not just between the Senate and the administration. Carter's White House Counsel's Office was often at odds with Attorney General Griffin Bell, who insisted that the dearth of qualified minority and female lawyers made it difficult to choose them to fill judicial vacancies (Clark 2003, 1138).

The Relationship between Remedying Past Discrimination and Legitimacy

According to the theory of procedural justice, a person's perception of the legitimacy of a court turns not on the *substance* of the outcome of a particular case, but on the perceived *fairness* of the judicial process in that case (Thibaut and Walker 1975). In other words, a person can lose a court case but still walk away from the experience feeling the court has great legitimacy, if the judge treated that person with respect and gave him an opportunity to be heard. In a large body of scholarship, Tom Tyler and colleagues built on Thibaut and Walker's theory. Using empirical evidence, these scholars found that procedural justice leads not only to satisfaction with the resolution of a specific case but also to greater satisfaction and trust in the legal system as a whole (Tyler 1990, 106–107; Tyler 1984; Tyler, Casper, and Fisher 1988).[6] Procedural justice has also been found to enhance the legitimacy of other political institutions, including Congress (Tyler, Casper, and Fisher 1988). Indeed, "court experiences spill over to help define the individual's stance toward government institutions and political life in general" (ibid., quoting Jacob 1969, 129).

Procedural justice relates directly to the goal of remedying past discrimination. Were a court to find that minorities had suffered systematic discrimination but then award a hollow remedy (for instance, an injunction merely ordering the discriminator to stop discriminating but lacking any enforcement mechanism with bite), the victims would certainly consider that court to have acted unfairly. That would undermine the court's legitimacy among the participants in the case.[7] Outsiders' perception of the court's legitimacy might be affected too, even if they were not parties to the litigation (as is often the case in class-action discrimination cases). Of course, this is not purely a hypothetical exercise, as the U.S. courts have prescribed hollow remedies in many discrimination cases. Without equitable remedies to redress discrimination, the courts may well have faced widespread dissatisfaction with the processes, which could jeopardize the legitimacy of the entire system. "[E]valuating a political system's claim to legitimacy depends on the presence of constitutional guarantees of access and equality, properties that can be competently judged by an outside observer" (Weatherford 1991, 251).

Carter would be the only president to rely on this remediative theory of legitimacy to justify a diversity-driven appointment strategy. Neither Clinton nor Obama ever indicated that their diversity plans were intended as remedial actions or that they were "affirmative action" plans. This may be in part because Supreme Court case law in the intervening years began applying a strict scrutiny analysis to benign preferences (those that help marginalized groups); the intermediate scrutiny standard in place during the Carter administration gave the government greater leeway to engage in diversity initiatives.[8] In one key decision, the Court struck down an affirmative action plan where there was only an "amorphous claim that there has been past discrimination in a particular industry."[9]

Descriptive Representation

Descriptive representation is a normative theory which posits that, in a democracy, the makeup of political institutions should reflect the diverse makeup of the populace (Birch 1993; Griffiths and Wollheim 1960; Mansbridge 1999; Pitkin 1967). Descriptive representatives are said to "stand in for" or be "sufficiently like" those constituents who are members of the same racial, ethnic, gender, or other identity group (Pitkin 1967, 80–82). Thus, "Black legislators represent Black constituents, women legislators represent women constituents and so on" (Mansbridge 1999, 629). In theory, if an institution were truly descriptive, it would mirror the demographics of our nation.

The concept that political institutions should reflect the population's diverse makeup is as old as the United States. In *Federalist No. 39*, James Madison opined that a truly representative government should draw from all sectors of the population: "It is *essential* to [a republican] government, that it be derived from the great body of the society, not from . . . a favored class of it" (Madison, quoted in Scott 1898, 60). John

Adams argued even more explicitly in favor of descriptive representation: a representative legislature, he wrote, "should be an exact portrait, in miniature, of the people at large, as it should think, feel, reason and act like them" (Adams, quoted in Pitkin 1967, 60).

While equitable remedies designed to redress past discrimination are purely instrumental in nature (meaning they deliver tangible benefits), descriptive representation serves both instrumental and symbolic purposes. Instrumentally, descriptive representation may directly translate into better substantive representation for under-represented groups (See, e.g., Haider-Markel, Joslyn, and Kniss 2000; Schwindt-Bayer and Mishler 2005; Sanbonmatsu 2003). "When [voter] interests are uncrystallized, the best way to have one's most important substantive interests represented is often to choose a representative whose descriptive characteristics match one's own on the issues one expects to emerge" (Mansbridge 1999, 643). For example, Haider-Markel, Joslyn, and Kniss found that the presence of gay and lesbian legislators led to the adoption of more domestic-partner registration programs (Schwindt-Bayer and Mishler 2005). Thus, many have asserted that only through descriptive representation can we ensure that ours is a government "of the people, by the people, for the people" (Lincoln, the Gettysburg Address, 1863).

Descriptive representation may also have symbolic importance, as it signals to under-represented groups that "certain features of one's identity do not mark one as less able to govern" (Mansbridge 1999, 651). A descriptive representative may serve as a role model for members of their group, demonstrating that they too can achieve success at the highest echelons of government (Chen 2003; Mansbridge 1999; Vargas 2008). And the mere presence of representatives from once-marginalized groups can help undermine the perception that the courts are run by white men (Sapiro 1981).

Descriptive representation, however, is not without its critics, who make three principal arguments against the application of this normative theory to actual political institutions. First, many political scholars contend that identity groups are not necessarily best served by leaders who share their race, ethnicity, or gender; rather, they gain the most from having substantive representatives—that is, representatives who share their policy preferences (e.g., Pennock 1979; Pitkin 1967; Swain 2002; Thernstrom and Thernstrom 1997). These scholars recognize that descriptive representation incorrectly assumes that minorities and women are monolithic groups who all share the same substantive goals (Swain 2002; Young 2000; Mansbridge 1999; Dovi 2002). For example, Dovi (2002) argues that class divisions may make wealthier Black representatives poor substantive representatives of lower-class Blacks. Certainly, it is indisputable that both female and minority leaders lie along the entire ideological spectrum. Consider the ideological divide between Congresswomen Marjorie Taylor Greene (R-FL), who lies on the far right of the ideological continuum, and Nancy Pelosi (D-CA), who lies on the far left—or the ideological distance between Justice Clarence Thomas, on the far right, and Justice Thurgood Marshall, on the far left. Clearly, these individuals do not substantively represent the views of all women, or all Blacks.

Some academics have gone one step further; they argue that efforts to increase descriptive representation in Congress have the unintended consequence of *decreasing* a minority's overall substantive representation within the institution (Cameron, Epstein, and O'Halloran 1996). For example, Cameron and colleagues examined the impact of majority-minority congressional districts—those intentionally drawn to concentrate Black voters, which virtually ensures the election of a Black congressperson in the district—on African Americans' aggregate levels of substantive representation in Congress. They found that districts surrounding a majority-minority district tend to elect more conservative representatives than they would elect if Black voters were dispersed among several voting districts. Similar findings have been made about Latino representation in Congress (Griffin and Newman 2007).[10]

A third group—the most cynical of scholars—mocks the theory of descriptive representation. They argue that it is unreasonable to expect every group to have representation in proportion to their numbers in the population. To make this rhetorical point, they question just how far descriptive representation might go. For instance, should "morons" represent "morons"? (Griffiths and Wollheim 1960).

In sum, descriptive representation looks not at the historical underpinnings of discrimination, but rather at both the present (which identity groups are currently under-represented?) and the future (how might the symbolism of diversity influence future generations?).

Can Appointed Judges Be Descriptive Representatives?

The theory of descriptive representation is most often debated in the context of Congress—should the presence of Black, Hispanic, homosexual, or female congressional representatives, for example, reflect their presence in the nation? Unelected federal judges, however, do not "represent" constituents in the same way that members of Congress do. Behavioral studies on descriptive representation—measuring how the political behavior of Black or female constituents change by virtue of having a descriptive representative—are largely inapposite here. Federal court judges are appointed for life terms, not elected for fixed terms. Thus we have no theoretical basis to believe that the appointment of more Black judges to the federal bench would lead to greater political activity by the Black population.

When discussing descriptive representation in the judiciary rather than in Congress, one must bear in mind several important distinctions. First, the phenomenon that Cameron and other scholars have identified, in which increased descriptive representation can lead to decreased substantive representation, does not apply to the judiciary.[11] Unlike legislative districts, court districts are not gerrymandered to concentrate minority populations; the decision to seat more Black judges, for example, lies largely within the president's discretion. And a president's appointment of a Black judge in one federal court does not affect the ideology of judges appointed in neighboring districts or other courts. Indeed, since presidents appoint federal judges who share their ideological values (Scherer 2005), all judges appointed by the same president should lie relatively close to one another on the ideological spectrum. Furthermore, litigants do not choose their judges the way voters choose their legislators; judges in the federal court system are randomly assigned. Nor do judges perform constituent service or communicate ex parte with litigants or citizens, as a member of Congress might do with a lobbyist or constituent. Thus, a Black judge cannot be politically responsive to the needs of the Black community the way an elected representative can.

Despite these differences between Congress and the courts, the theory of descriptive representation remains applicable to the judiciary because of the symbolic messages sent to under-represented groups. The potential good that can come from marginalized groups seeing some of their members obtain prestigious government positions—most notably, an increase in the government's legitimacy levels among those marginalized groups—would occur whether the institution in question was Congress, the executive branch, or the courts. Accordingly, scholars have applied the theory of descriptive representation with equal force when studying the federal judiciary (Cook 1971; Ifill 2000; Overby et al. 2005; Scherer and Curry 2010; Vargas 2008). At least one scholar has argued that descriptive representation is even more critical in the courts than it is in the elected branches: "Judges have a more direct and irrevocable impact in the lives of many Americans than local or even national legislators. This is particularly true for African Americans, who are disproportionately involved with the judicial system" (Ifill 2000, 407–408).

Bill Clinton was the first president to turn the theory of descriptive representation into actual policy. During his 1992 presidential run, then-Governor Clinton promised to make the cabinet and other appointed positions "look like America" (Third Presidential Debate, 1992). In a campaign speech criticizing the judicial appointments of the two preceding administrations, Clinton repeatedly emphasized the need for the federal judiciary to better "reflect" the racial, ethnic, and gender makeup of the general population—the basic definition of descriptive representation:

> A most troubling aspect of judicial appointments during the Reagan-Bush era has been the sharp decline in the selection of women and minority judges, at the very time when more and more qualified women and minority candidates were reaching the time of their lives where they could serve as judges.
>
> While there are many fine women and minority attorneys all over the country who would potentially be superb federal judges, Mr. [George H. W.] Bush's appointments fail to reflect the breadth and diversity of the bar, much less that of our nation. The narrow judicial appointments of George [H. W.] Bush have resulted in the emergence of a judiciary that is less reflective of our diverse society than at any other time in recent memory. (Clinton 1992)

President Clinton justified his diversity plan strictly on descriptive representation theory. Because of Supreme Court rulings that struck down most quota-based affirmative action plans, Clinton could not cite the remediative theory as a justification without running afoul of the Court's interpretation of the Constitution.

Descriptive Representation and Legitimacy

Some scholars consider descriptive representation the key to establishing the government's legitimacy (e.g., Mansbridge 1999). Others, like Pitkin, gave little weight to this form of legitimacy; Pitkin believed substantive representation was the only meaningful form of representation. Whereas procedural justice is said to promote legitimacy by providing litigants with fair and open processes, descriptive representation promotes legitimacy by creating the appearance that a particular governmental institution is open to people from all backgrounds. The mere act of appointing judges from under-represented groups, according to proponents of descriptive representation, can have a greater impact on the courts' legitimacy than anything judges do in the courtroom. Scholars base this belief on the assumption that descriptive representation will increase legitimacy among under-represented groups (Pitkin 1967). Historically, both women and minorities suffered discrimination in the legal profession: in admittance to law school, access to prestigious law jobs, and as viable candidates for judgeships (handpicked by white male senators through their senatorial courtesy privileges). Accordingly, normative theorists believe increasing the number of women and minorities on the bench is critical to increasing legitimacy levels among these groups.

Legal scholars have also asserted that, if the federal courts are to be perceived as legitimate, "no segment of the nation's diverse population can be excluded from court membership. . . . A court system that does not reflect the membership of society breeds increasingly higher levels of disaffection and disillusionment" (Maule 2001). Justice O'Connor agreed, in her opinion in *Grutter v. Bollinger*: "In order to cultivate a set of leaders with legitimacy in the eyes of the citizenry, it is necessary that the path to leadership be visibly open to talented and qualified individuals of every race and ethnicity."[12]

Descriptive/Substantive Representation

The normative theory of substantive representation holds that those who represent the public should be responsive to the policy views of their constituents, meaning "acting for others, an activity on behalf of, in the interest of, as the agent of, someone else" (Pitkin 1967, 113). Judges are not agents for litigants the way congresspersons are agents of their constituents. However, the attitudinal model tells us that the judges and justices vote to further their own personal policy preferences (Segal and Spaeth 2002). But the judges' interests may be the same as those seeking legal relief. Though substantive representation turns on agreement with policy issues, we also have to consider descriptive attributes. Thinking about substantive representation this way is not enough to find the best representative. There is a descriptive aspect to substantive reputation. There is now a second goal to reach beyond policy agreement. A president must consider whether he thinks Blacks with similar views as the community are better substantive representatives than are whites. Why, for example, could not a white male Democrat substantively represent the views of the Black community?

To answer that question, one must recognize that minorities and women experience the world differently than white men. This is the case among judges as well as among the general population (e.g., Edwards 2002; Martin 1990; Scherer 2004). For instance, Edwards (2002) describes how the realities of segregation and racial discrimination affect Black judges' views. Martin (1990) explains that female judges' life experiences may lead them to deal with cases involving sex discrimination differently than male judges. To the extent that minority and female judges have unique perspectives that influence their decision-making, their presence on the bench is necessary, according to the theory of substantive representation, to ensure that the voices of more Americans are considered in the judicial process. I call this new version of substantive representation "descriptive/substantive representation."

The question of whether true substantive representation requires a descriptive representative has generated much controversy, and three of the six women to sit on the Supreme Court have weighed in on it. Justice O'Connor rejected the theory that gender influences judicial decision-making, stating that a "wise old man and a wise old woman will reach the same conclusion" (Barrett and Bash 2009). Justice Ginsburg expressed mixed views on the subject, agreeing with O'Connor's observation about wise men and wise women, yet also maintaining that "women bring to the table their own experiences, which inform their decision-making" (Totenberg 2010, paraphrasing Ginsburg).

Justice Sotomayor, on the other hand, initially embraced the notion that a judge's gender or ethnicity can, and perhaps should, influence the judge's thinking. In a speech during her years as an appeals-court judge, Sotomayor said,

> Justice O'Connor has often been cited as saying that a wise old man and wise old woman will reach the same conclusion in deciding cases. I am . . . not so sure that I agree with the statement. First . . . there can never be a universal definition of wise. Second, I would hope that a wise Latina woman with the richness of her experiences would more often than not reach a better conclusion than a white male who hasn't lived that life. (Sotomayor 2002)

This statement put a lot of political pressure on Sotomayor during her confirmation proceedings, and she was forced to clarify this statement:

> It is clear from the attention that my words have gotten and the manner in which it has been understood by some people that my words failed. They didn't work. The message that the entire speech attempted to deliver, however, remains the message that I think Justice O'Connor meant, the message that prior nominees including Justice Alito meant when he said that his Italian ancestry he considers when he's deciding discrimination cases. (CNN.com, quoting Sotomayor 2009)

Like Presidents Clinton and Carter before him, President Obama has sought to transform a normative theory into political policy. In stressing the need for judges who can adjudicate cases with a true understanding of the needs of ordinary litigants, Obama is the first president to rely on the theory of descriptive/substantive representation to justify his diversity policy for the federal courts.

It is likely that Obama moved away from President Clinton's position—pure descriptive representation—because of its association with quotas or preferences for women and minorities. The public has overwhelmingly rejected such forms of affirmative action (Quinnipiac University Polling Institute 2009). However, some studies have found that public support for diversity efforts changes depending on the wording of poll questions. Americans respond more favorably to questions about "affirmative action" if there is no mention of preferences or quotas (Plous 1997; Shelton and Minor 1995). This ambiguity in public opinion allowed Obama to press for diversity on the bench while distancing himself from justifications that were either unpopular (descriptive representation and the dreaded quotas often associated with it) or unconstitutional (remediative efforts meant to redress past discrimination).

How would Obama strike this delicate balance? During his campaign for president, then-Senator Obama emphasized the need for more judges with "empathy" (Hooks and Parsons 2009). Rather than bluntly stating his desire to see more minorities and women on the courts, as his Democratic presidential predecessors had done, Obama shifted the focus away from identity politics and toward a neutral standard of empathy. This did not diminish Republican objections to Obama's diversity strategy; Senate Republicans used procedural tactics to stall his lower-court nominees from the beginning of his presidency (Shapiro 2009). Yet former President Obama's approach to judicial selection strategy may have gained traction with the public. One study, conducted during his time in office, found that 68 percent of Americans believe a judge's ability to "empathize with ordinary people" is very important (Gibson 2010).

Though Obama framed his diversity strategy in terms of empathy, in practice he seemed to pursue an approach strikingly similar to that of Carter and Clinton. He acknowledged that he used race, ethnicity, and gender characteristics to help identify "empathetic" judges (see preface). He argued that judges from marginalized groups are likely to possess a greater capacity for the empathy he finds so valuable, and his first two appointees to the Supreme Court were members of groups currently under-represented on the bench: Sonia Sotomayor, a Hispanic female, and Elena Kagan, a white female. President Obama also appointed women and minorities to the lower federal courts in far greater numbers than any previous president (see figures 1.1 through 1.3).

Descriptive/Substantive Representation and Legitimacy

At first glance, substantive representation would seem to engender only short-term policy agreement between an institution and the public: People hear about a new law or court decision that aligns with their interests, and they are satisfied. However, by garnering public support for its actions one by one, over time, an institution can fill its reservoir of good will sufficiently to protect it when, inevitably, it makes an unpopular move. As research has shown, "The Court's support is derived from 'the total impressions made by the Court over a long period of time'" (Mondak and Smithey 1997, 1123, quoting Petrick 1968; see also Grosskopf and Mondak 1998; Mondak 1992; Tanenhaus and Murphy 1981). Moreover, with its descriptive component, legitimacy may be said to derive from the same sources as it did from descriptive representation: better substantive representation for minorities because one of their own has risen to the halls of power. However, there are some scholars who have found that diffuse support, or long-term support, is more tied to specific support than previously imagined (Bartels and Johnston 2013; but see also Gibson and Nelson 2015). While the Bartels and Johnston study found that specific support drives people's long-term support for the Court, Gibson and Nelson suggest that the Bartels and Johnston study incorrectly measured ideological agreement with the Court, the basis for specific support. They re-ran the models using different national data and found that long-term support was not contingent on specific support.

Maintaining legitimacy among minority groups has been a complicated issue for democratic governments throughout history, even when the government and its constituents were homogenous. In the early American republic, everyone except adult white men were disenfranchised, but the Founders worried about making ideological minorities feel represented, lest the voices of the majority drown them out. James Madison feared such a situation as he drafted the Constitution: "[M]easures are too often decided, not according to the rules of justice, and the rights of the minor party, but by the superior force of an interested and overbearing majority" (Madison, *Federalist Paper No. 10*, in Scott, ed., 1898). When a minority group has no say in an institution's decision-making process, that group may perceive the institution as illegitimate. (Today, for instance, vegans might consider the U.S. Department of Agriculture illegitimate, because it encourages raising animals for food.) Legal scholars have argued that substantive representation can resolve this "tyranny of the majority" dilemma by ensuring that racial and ethnic minorities' interests (as well as those of other marginalized groups) are at least considered in the decision-making process of any given institution. "If the law has not only rejected [minorities'] view of social reality, but has refused even to permit the articulation of it . . . those who disagree lack any resources for understanding the law as theirs" (Kahan, Hoffman, and Braman 2009).

Conclusion

In conclusion, there are three prevailing theories that U.S. presidents have used to justify efforts to diversify: equity, descriptive representation, and substantive representation. Though Supreme Court precedents have made it difficult for presidents to publicly base their diversification strategies on equity or descriptive representation, substantive representation has not yet been shut down. The key word for those who advocate substantive representation is empathy: Does the nominee have empathy for the people whose cases he or she will decide? Can the nominee walk in a defendant's shoes? Here, however, diversity can become a proxy for ideology. Liberals and Democrats tend to like judges with a lot of empathy, while conservatives and Republicans are content with judges whether or not they possess empathy for the poor and downtrodden—a similar stance to their broader ideology, as the next chapter will show.

3

Why Republicans Oppose Diversifying the Courts

When it comes to diversity on the bench, Republican presidents have to pull off a tough balancing act. In the long term, they must satisfy their party's conservative white male base, which opposes anything resembling affirmative action or identity politics. In the short term, however, they need some measure of support from women and minorities in order to win elections. This balancing act stands in stark contrast to the Democrats, who can achieve both goals—satisfying the base and courting identity groups—through a diversity strategy. Beginning with Ronald Reagan, Republican presidents have also used a three-pronged approach to seek electoral support from key interest groups without alienating their base.

First, they publicly oppose affirmative action, characterizing it as an unfair system of quotas and preferential treatment. They argue that such a policy rewards minorities and women without any consideration of merit, preventing more qualified candidates (presumably white men) from filling important government jobs. For example, the 1984 Republican Party platform stated: "We will resist efforts to replace equal rights with discriminatory quota systems and preferential treatment. Quotas are the most insidious form of discrimination: reverse discrimination against the innocent" (Republican Party Platform, 1984). Instead, Republican presidents advocate a "color-blind" standard for awarding government benefits and jobs (Laham 1998, 73).[1]

Second, upon taking office, Republican presidents immediately dismantle the diversity plans of their Democratic predecessors; as with public statements denouncing affirmative actions, this helps to appease the party's base. For example, early in his first term, Reagan issued an executive order abolishing the merit selection committees that Jimmy Carter had created and ordered to make "affirmative efforts" to identify qualified women and minorities for judgeships (Executive Order No. 12059, May 5, 1981). Similarly, George W. Bush wasted little time undoing

Bill Clinton's diversity efforts. His Justice Department switched the United States' legal position in a ground-breaking affirmative action case involving the admissions process at the University of Michigan.[2] While the Justice Department supported the university under Clinton (claiming that race may be used as a factor in higher education admissions decisions), the same department under Bush argued the university's policy violated the Equal Protection Clause of the Fourteenth Amendment, and that only a color-blind admissions process was constitutional.

After establishing their principled opposition to diversity programs, Republican presidents move on to the third phase of their approach: making special efforts to appoint minority and female judges—the very tactic for which they criticize Democrats. During his 1980 presidential campaign, Reagan told the American Bar Association (ABA) that he would not choose judicial candidates on the basis of race, ethnicity, or gender (Lopez 2008): "[W]e will never select individuals just because they are men or women, whites or Blacks, Jews, Catholics or whatever. I don't look at people as members of groups; I look at them as individuals and as Americans" (Goldman 1997, 329, quoting Reagan). During the same campaign, however, Reagan promised the American public that he would appoint "the most qualified woman he could find" to become the first female Supreme Court justice (Hogan 1990, 147). He did appoint the first woman to the Court, Sandra Day O'Connor. But although O'Connor was well-respected in her home state of Arizona, where she had served as majority leader of the state senate before becoming a judge, few believed that she was the most qualified woman for the job (Goldman 1997, 329).

President George H. W. Bush used one of the highest-profile Supreme Court nominations in history to engage in identity politics. When Justice Thurgood Marshall, the first African American to sit on the Court, announced his retirement, the president chose another African American, Clarence Thomas, to take his seat. This created the appearance of a "Black seat" on the Supreme Court, hearkening back to the days of tokenism when Catholics and Jews were each allotted one spot. President Bush proclaimed that race had nothing to do with his decision, and that he chose Thomas simply because he was the "best person" for the job (Yang and LaFraniere 1991). Many observers were dubious, asserting that Thomas lacked the intellectual capacity to sit on the Supreme Court. As one conservative legal consultant told a reporter, "The fact is, Clarence Thomas is a hard worker, but he's not an erudite scholar" (Feldmann 1991, quoting Fein). The editorial board of the *Syracuse Post Standard* (1991), discussing the Bar Association's appraisal of Thomas, concurred:

> Now the ABA has come up with a lukewarm split decision [of qualified versus unqualified] that at the very least punches holes in the Bush contention he picked the best man for the job. It is ever more apparent his nominee was named primarily because he's a Black conservative, not because he'll bring anything close to a superior intellect or significant judicial experience to the bench.

President George W. Bush faced a similar dilemma when Justice O'Connor announced her retirement in 2005—should he appoint another woman to take that seat? Even First Lady Laura Bush engaged in conjecture, publicly admitting she hoped her husband would nominate a woman to replace O'Connor (Tarr 2010). And so he did. By choosing White House Counsel Harriet Miers to fill the vacancy, Bush gave the appearance that he was maintaining a designated "female" seat on the Court (Fletcher 2005). However, the Miers nomination did not proceed smoothly. Despite her close association with the Republican President Bush, many prominent conservatives opposed Miers, calling her unqualified (Babington and Edsall 2005; Baker and Balz 2005; Stolberg 2005). Democrats largely remained silent on the issue. When the outcry against her continued, Miers withdrew from consideration. Forced to choose a different nominee, Bush settled on someone sure to please the Republican base: Samuel Alito, a white man with strong conservative credentials.

As a Texan, George W. Bush recognized the growing importance of Hispanic American voters, and he hoped to win them over to the Republican Party. He peppered Spanish into some of his speeches, and he appointed Alberto Gonzales attorney general, the highest-ranking cabinet position any Latino had ever attained. This strategy extended to Bush's judicial nominations as well. His first group of appellate court nominees included Miguel Estrada, chosen for the Washington, D.C., Court of Appeals (Goldstein 2001). If confirmed, Estrada would have been a frontrunner to become the first Hispanic Supreme Court justice

(Editorial, *New York Times* 2003). Mindful of Estrada's compelling personal narrative—an immigrant who overcame poverty and eventually graduated from Harvard Law School—Democrats in the Senate hoped to avoid giving the president and the Republicans an electoral opportunity with Hispanic voters by confirming Estrada (ibid.). After Democrats stalled his nomination for more than two years, Estrada withdrew his name from consideration.

Bush seemingly made greater efforts to diversify the federal courts than any previous Republican president, for he did not restrict those efforts to high-profile nominations for the Supreme Court and appellate courts. Republican presidents clearly believe that diversity appointments can help them win support from identity groups that usually vote Democratic (women, Hispanics, African Americans). Why else would they contravene their "color-blind" principles to nominate candidates such as Sandra Day O'Connor, Clarence Thomas, and Harriet Miers, whose qualifications did not match those of most Supreme Court justices? However, Republicans have little to show for their attempts to curry favor with identity groups. Despite an initially positive response to Reagan's appointment of Justice O'Connor, his approval ratings among women remained low throughout his presidency (Mann 1983). Nor did George H. W. Bush's nomination of Clarence Thomas improve his standing with Black voters—only 11 percent of them voted to reelect Bush in 1992 (Bolce, DiMeio, and Muzzio 2002). And, despite George W. Bush's solid record of appointing women to the lower federal courts (see figures 1.1 and 1.2),[3] female voters continued to favor Democrats in both the 2004 and 2008 presidential elections (Bennett 2004; U.S. News and World Report 2008). Bush's efforts to increase the representation of Hispanics among the federal bench judges—he appointed 30 to Clinton's 23—similarly failed to pay dividends for the Republican Party, which garnered only 31 percent of the Hispanic vote in 2008 (Lopez 2008).

There are two main explanations for why Republicans' diversity appointments to the courts have not translated into electoral gains among under-represented groups. First, most voters base their choices on other factors, such as the candidates' personalities and policy positions. Second, voters who follow the appointment process usually seek not only a descriptive representative (who comes from their identity group) but also a substantive representative (who will advocate for their interests).

This explains why George H. W. Bush's appointment of Clarence Thomas, a staunch conservative who opposed affirmative action, to replace the civil rights champion Thurgood Marshall, earned him scant support from African Americans (Edsall 1991). Presidents from both parties choose judges with ideologies similar to their own. Any woman or minority judge a Republican appoints, therefore, will likely adhere to originalism as their method of constitutional interpretation—a method that often results in decisions that go against the interests of minority groups and women's groups.

In sum, despite the Republicans' hard-line opposition to affirmative action and diversity appointment strategies when Democrats occupy the White House, Republican presidents have also engaged in identity politics, using the judicial appointment process to further party efforts to win over certain groups of voters. Conservatives outside of the executive branch often oppose such efforts, putting their core ideals about individualism and color-blindness above potential electoral gains.

Although they have not always remained faithful to their color-blind philosophy, all three Republican presidents since 1980 have articulated their opposition to diversity initiatives in remarkably similar ways. They rely on three core arguments, which are identical to the arguments Republicans marshal against affirmative action more generally: (1) it leads to the appointment of less-qualified judges; (2) it stigmatizes female and minority judges; and (3) it discriminates against potential white male judicial candidates. I now turn to these arguments in detail.

Less-Qualified Judges

The judicial appointment process has never been based *strictly* on merit. Beginning with George Washington, presidents have always chosen judges from their own party, and in recent years, from their own ideological wing of the party (Epstein and Segal 2005; Scherer and Miller 2009; Scherer 2004, 49–73). Epstein and Segal (2005, 26) state that "the simple reality is that both the Senate and the president take into account nominees' partisanship and ideology, in addition to their professional qualifications, when they make their decisions, and they always have." Moreover, when patronage appointments ruled the day for lower courts, judges were chosen through the "old boys' network," in which personal connections with a home-state senator mattered more than qualifications (Scherer 2005, 77). Yet when Carter implemented the first diversity initiatives for the federal courts, conservatives expressed concern that adding more minorities and women would damage the overall quality of the bench. As one Republican senator remarked, "Race or sex has nothing to do with . . . [the appointment process]. Carter has gone too far in trying to impose quotas. The whole approach is off base. . . . We like the principle of merit selection. We applaud that. . . . Yet are they doing that?" (Slotnick 1980, 117). This argument presumes that whenever race, gender, or ethnicity becomes a factor in the appointment process, merit, by definition, is no longer considered the standard for choosing federal judges.

> The precepts of merit selection dictate that only those possessing the most illustrious credentials will be recommended, without regard to political considerations. However, it is claimed, affirmative action is, by its nature, a political goal, and one which directly contravenes the very thrust of merit selection. It submerges quality in order to redress past race and sex discrimination (Berkson and Carbon 1979, 4). (citation in original)

This, of course, assumes that merit was ever the primary consideration of senators when exercising their home-state senatorial courtesy privileges and naming judges to the lower federal courts (Slotnick 1983).

Since Justice O'Connor's retirement, Republicans have attacked all female nominees to the Court (except Justice Amy Coney Barrett) as unqualified. Pat Buchanan had this to say about Harriet Miers:

> [H]er qualifications for the Supreme Court are non-existent. She is not a brilliant jurist, indeed, has never been a judge. She is not a scholar of the law. Researchers are hard-pressed to dig up an opinion. She has not had a brilliant career in politics, the academy, the corporate world or public forum. Were she not a friend of Bush, and female, she would never have even been considered. (Buchanan 2005)

Another popular Republican pundit, Ann Coulter, claimed that George W. Bush, if he wanted to pick a woman to fill O'Connor's seat, should have been able to find someone more qualified than Miers:

> The only sexism involved in the Miers nomination is the administration's claim that once they decided they wanted a woman, Miers was the best they could do. Let me just say, if the top male lawyer in the country is John Roberts and the top female lawyer is Harriet Miers, we may as well stop allowing girls to go to law school. (Coulter 2005)

Manuel Miranda, former aide to then-Senate Majority Leader Bill Frist (R-TN), questioned Miers's qualifications because she had never served as a judge:

> The reaction of many conservatives today will be that the president has made possibly the most unqualified choice since Abe Fortas, who had been the president's lawyer. The nomination of a nominee with no judicial record is a significant failure for the advisers that the White House gathered around it. (Miranda, quoted in Curry 2005)[4]

When Barack Obama nominated Elena Kagan, the former dean of Harvard Law School and a high-ranking Justice Department official, conservatives also attacked her as being unqualified to sit on the Supreme Court; like Miers, Kagan had never served as a judge. Writing in *National Review*, Ed Whelan, president of the Ethics and Public Policy Center, claimed:

> Kagan may well have less experience relevant to the work of being a justice [than any nominees] in the last five decades or more. In addition to zero judicial experience, she has only a few years of real-world legal experience. Further, notwithstanding all her years in academia, she has only a scant record of legal scholarship. Kagan flunks her own "threshold" test of the minimal qualifications needed for a Supreme Court nominee. (Whelan 2010)

Senator John Cornyn (R-SC), a member of the Judiciary Committee, believed that even Harriet Miers "was eminently more qualified" than Kagan was (Frumin 2010, quoting Cornyn). Similarly, Rush Limbaugh declared: "This woman is worse than Harriet Miers. Intellectually, she's a lightweight" (Meyers 2010, quoting Limbaugh).

Conservatives have also launched ad hominem attacks against African American judicial nominees, focusing on an alleged lack of qualifications. Thurgood Marshall suffered this fate. Despite his many years litigating landmark civil rights cases before the Supreme Court (including *Brown v. Board of Education* [1954]), the ABA labeled Marshall "unqualified" when President Kennedy nominated him for a seat on the Second Circuit Court of Appeals (Reske 1994).[5] Some conservatives have gone so far as to argue that Blacks are genetically less intelligent than whites (Herrnstein and Murray 1994).[6]

Because questions about their qualifications plague female and minority judicial candidates, several empirical studies have tested the hypothesis that minority and female nominees are less qualified than their white male peers (Haire 2001; Lindgren 2001; Slotnick 1980; Vining, Steigerwalt, and Smelcer 2012). One early study on President Carter's diversity appointees found that, when quality is measured as graduation from an elite law school, there is no difference between minority and women judges (when treated as a single group) versus white male judges (Slotnick 1980).[7] Yet, when Slotnick used the ABA's ratings to measure judges' qualifications, minorities and women appeared less qualified than white male judges (ibid.). This was the result from the ABA's ranking criteria, which emphasized the nominee's number of years of legal experience (Vining et al. 2012). Because of historic barriers of entry to law school for women and minorities, and the subsequent difficulty they had obtaining prestigious legal jobs, President Carter's diversity nominees rarely had the 15 years of legal experience required to attain a higher ABA rating (ibid.). Thus, one could argue that historical discrimination led the ABA to rate minorities and women lower than white men.

Three more recent examinations of judges' qualifications, all based on ABA ratings, also tested how minorities and women measure up to whites and males. Haire (2001) found that minorities and women received lower ABA ratings than white men, even after controlling for all other indicia of quality. But her data included only the nominees of Carter, Reagan, and George H. W. Bush. Since historical discrimination kept most of Carter's diversity appointees from meeting the ABA's 15-year legal experience requirement, and since Reagan and H. W. Bush appointed too few minorities and women to make the sample large enough for meaningful analysis, Haire's findings suffer from the same sample-selection problems as Slotnick's. Two other studies (Lindgren 2001; Vining et al. 2012), both of which included Clinton nominees, reached the opposite conclusion, finding no statistically significant difference (at $p < .05$) between the ABA scores of minority versus white judges or female versus male judges. The claim that minorities and women are less qualified for the bench than white men, therefore, appears specious.[8]

Stigmatization

Political theorists have long debated the place of shame and stigma in a democratic polity (Tarnopolsky 2004). According to this body of scholarship, a democratic government, like a tyrannical government, can engage in a "politics of shame" (ibid., 469–470). Shaming occurs when the ruling class singles out a minority group (meaning a group that has no voting majority) and treats it as the "other" because it poses a threat to prevailing social norms (ibid., 470). At certain times in U.S. history, both minorities and women have been shamed by the white male ruling class. In essence, shaming is a form of discrimination.

Republicans in recent decades have turned the tables on the politics of shame. Today, when the *government tries to increase the presence of minorities and women in government institutions*, Republicans maintain that the government *further shames and stigmatizes* these groups (Eastland 1996; Thomas 2007; Limbaugh 2010). Extending this argument to the judicial appointment process, Republicans claim that the Democrats' diversity initiatives for the bench stigmatize the nominees who benefit from such programs. Because of their connection to an "affirmative action" program, these minority and female appointees are supposedly perceived as unqualified by the broader (presumably white male) public. In this argument, Republicans do not claim that the minority and women candidates are unqualified, but that the public presumes them to be unqualified, whether or not that is the case. This damages the reputation not only of the minority or female nominees, but of the entire bench.

Perhaps the most vocal advocate of this position is Justice Clarence Thomas. In his autobiography, he describes his anger at realizing that his white peers viewed his admission to Yale Law School and his successes there as tainted or unmerited (Thomas 2007, 74–75). Thomas later expressed that anger in several of his opinions, most notably his concurrence in *Adarand Constructors, Inc. v. Peña* (Thomas, J., concurring in part and concurring in the judgment). Ruling on this case, which dealt with the federal government's use of benign preferences (those meant to help under-represented groups) to award contracts, Thomas stated:

> [T]here can be no doubt that racial paternalism and its unintended consequences can be as poisonous and pernicious as any other form of discrimination. So-called "benign" discrimination teaches many that because of chronic and apparently immutable handicaps, minorities cannot compete with them without their patronizing indulgence.... These [affirmative action] programs stamp minorities with a badge of inferiority.[9]

Justice O'Connor made similar observations in *City of Richmond v. Croson*,[10] another case about the use of benign preferences. Writing for the plurality, she asserted that "classifications based on race carry a danger of stigmatic harm. Unless they are strictly reserved for remedial settings, they may in fact promote notions of racial inferiority and lead to a politics of racial hostility." Around the time of the *Adarand* decision, Glenn C. Loury, an African American economist and social critic, argued that the time had come to rethink traditional affirmative action programs that use benign preferences: "I am convinced that the long-term interests of African Americans will be helped, not harmed, by a rational reassessment and reform of current preferential policies" (Loury 1996).

Republicans and their sympathizers believe that those who are *most* injured by affirmative action programs are the well-qualified minority and female hires, contractors and appointees who are stamped with a "badge of inferiority." Justice Thomas's concurrence in *Grutter* poignantly expresses this view:

> When Blacks take positions in the highest places of government, industry, or academia, it is an open question today whether their skin color played a part in their advancement. The question itself is the stigma—because either [reverse] racial discrimination did play a role, in which case the person may be deemed "otherwise unqualified," or it did not,

in which case asking the question itself unfairly marks those Blacks who would succeed without discrimination.[11]

Other prominent conservatives have reached the same conclusion as Thomas. Radio commentator Rush Limbaugh has argued that, in order to avoid a badge of inferiority, minorities should try to shun any association with affirmative action: "Affirmative action was a lowering of standards. This is why people really didn't want to be considered affirmative action babies 'cause [sic] it was a stigma. You didn't get there on merit if affirmative action got you there. You got there because the way was paved for you" (Limbaugh 2010). Conservatives believe that the same stigmatization attaches to women who are hired (or appointed) through a diversity initiative. According to Diana Furchtgott-Roth, the chief economist at the U.S. Department of Labor in the George W. Bush administration, "not even a woman would choose a female brain surgeon for delicate surgery if she knew that the surgeon was a product of affirmative action. Giving preferences to a few women sows seeds of doubt that reflect on all" (Furchtgott-Roth 2010).

There is some empirical evidence to support the "badge of inferiority" argument. Studies show that whites assume other whites to be qualified for a particular job, while they perceive minorities with similar credentials to be unqualified for the same position; whites simply assume that minorities got their jobs because of affirmative action (Nacoste 1990; Summers 1991). The same is true of women in high positions, who are presumed to have been hired through a concerted diversity program (Nye 1998). At least one journalist has argued that Sarah Palin, having been chosen as John McCain's running mate specifically because she is a woman, suffered from the same stigma with which Justice Thomas believes he is burdened (Lithwick 2008).

Claims of Stigmatization and Incompetence May Delegitimize the Federal Courts

If the white public perceives minority and female judges as less qualified than white men—whether or not this is true—then a diversity strategy could undermine whites' (or white men's) trust in the judicial process. Given some whites' misconceptions about minority and female hires generally and judicial appointees specifically, one could imagine a scenario in which a white male litigant appears before such a judge, loses his case, then feels that he has not received a fair hearing because he perceives the judge as unqualified. Extending this one litigant's dissatisfaction to white male litigants across the country, trust in the judicial process may decline as the number of diversity appointees rises. Moreover, if a decision by a female or minority judge in a high-profile case were to contradict white male public opinion, then this segment of the population might suffer the same loss of trust as an actual litigant appearing before a female or minority judge. In short, there would be a crisis of confidence in the judicial process.

As explained in the introduction, the widespread perception that the judicial process is unfair jeopardizes the legitimacy of the entire legal system. Empirical research based on the theory of procedural justice has shown that when the public perceives a political institution to be operating incompetently, levels of trust and confidence in that institution decrease (Hibbing and Theiss-Morse 2002). Another study concluded that government's failure to live up to citizens' expectations also plays a large role in the public's loss of satisfaction with the government (Orren 1997). Under these conditions, Republicans could argue that diversity initiatives in the judiciary jeopardize the legitimacy of the institution by creating the appearance that the bench is stocked with unqualified minority and female judges. Regardless of whether these judges are actually unqualified, the same de-legitimization process would take place.

Reverse Discrimination and Backlash

Republicans claim that any consideration of race, ethnicity, or gender in the government's awarding of jobs or benefits amounts to "reverse" discrimination, violating the Equal Protection Clause in the Fourteenth Amendment. Basing decisions on group traits, rather than an individual's merits, they contend, runs counter to both the spirit and the letter of the law. And as Justice Thomas has warned, those who feel victimized by reverse discrimination will lash out at those they believe are receiving unfair advantages: "Inevitably, such [diversity] programs . . . provoke resentment among those who believe that they have been wronged by the government's use of race."[12] Justice O'Connor has also expressed fear of racial backlash from affirmative action programs, stating that race preferences "contribut[e] to an escalation of racial hostility and conflict."[13]

According to Gregory Rodriguez of the New American Foundation, white male backlash:

> won't take the form of a chest-thumping brand of white supremacy. Instead, we are likely to see the rise of a more defensive, aggrieved sense of white victimhood.... [O]ne can hear evidence of white grievance in many corners of the country. And it's not coming just from fringe bloggers.... [E]ven though [whites] are still the majority and collectively maintain more access to wealth and political influence than other groups, whites are acting more and more like an aggrieved minority. (Rodriguez 2010)[14]

Even President Obama recognized the existence of white backlash resulting from opposition to racial policies; he believes it stems from whites' feelings that they are being punished for the wrongdoing of their ancestors through diversity initiatives that give preference to minorities (Obama 2008).[15]

White backlash to liberal racial policies emerged at the same time as affirmative action itself, in the early 1970s (Swain 2002, 156). Cases involving constitutional claims of reverse discrimination, like *Regents of the University of California v. Bakke*,[16] *DeFunis v. Odegaard*,[17] *City of Richmond v. J. A. Croson*,[18] *Adarand Constructors, Inc. v. Peña*,[19] *Grutter v. Bollinger*,[20] *Parents Involved in Cmty. Schs. v. Seattle Sch. Dist. No. 1*,[21] *Hopwood v. Texas*,[22] and *Fisher v. Texas*[23] stemmed largely from white backlash to affirmative action (Brooks 2005; Vargas 1999; McNeil 2003). Scholars have also viewed white voters' defection from the Democratic Party as a manifestation of white backlash against liberal racial policies (Thernstrom and Thernstrom 1997, 171–77).

More recently, some have suggested that the predominantly white Tea Party movement is rooted in white voters' disapproval of the government's civil rights agenda (NAACP 2010). One member of the Congressional Black Caucus, Andre Carson (D-IN), made an impassioned speech in which he equated Tea Party members with Southern whites in the Jim Crow era: "Some of these folks in Congress would love to see us [African Americans] as second-class citizens. Some of them in Congress right now of this Tea Party movement would love to see you and me ... hanging on a tree" (Reeve 2011, quoting Carson). Carson and other Black leaders likely based their allegations on comments from Tea Party figures such as Mark Williams, who referred to President Obama as an "Indonesian Muslim turned welfare thug" (Graham 2009).

The virulence of many conservatives' opposition to affirmative action suggests that something deeper than political calculations (diversity does not help Republicans electorally) or normative goals (diversity breeds mistrust in the courts) could be at work. Indeed, the psyches of white men in America may be driving their opposition to diversity appointments. A number of psychological theories suggest that subconscious fears play a greater role than political affiliation in shaping white men's attitudes about affirmative action.

The most widely accepted psychological explanation holds that white men view efforts to increase diversity in any work environment or government institution through the lens of hostility: "out-groups" are threatening white men's formerly privileged "in-group" status (Blalock 1967; Conover 1988; Johnson 1980). Whites and men may see government benefits as a zero-sum game—if women and minorities gain ground, according to their logic, white men must lose ground. As one researcher put it, "[a]n increase in minority percentage should result in an increase in discrimination [against minorities] both because of heightened perceived competition and an increased power threat" (Blalock 1967, 154). Some psychologists, alternatively, refer to this phenomenon as "entitlement disorder" (Hall 2004). Others have suggested that white men distrust diversity initiatives because the procedures used to award government jobs or benefits are not transparent; no one knows how much influence race, gender, or ethnicity (versus qualifications) has in the decision-making process (Nacoste 1990).

Some scholars offer a simpler, more basic explanation for white men's opposition to affirmative action: racism. Fanon (1967) contends that the racism is patent: "There is a fact: White men consider themselves superior to Black men." Others see racism as more subtle, characterizing it as either "symbolic racism" (Sidanius, Pratto, and Bobo 1996) or "new racism" (Augoustinos, Tuffin, and Every 2005). This latter group of scholars claims that, because society no longer tolerates patent racism, white men frame their opposition to diversity initiatives in secretive code language, more acceptable to general society. These merely provide pretexts for their underlying racism. Some empirical studies support this view (e.g., Kinder and Sanders 1996; Sidanius et al. 1996), while others reach the opposite conclusion, finding evidence that suggests there is no embedded racism behind the "principled objections" to affirmative action (e.g., Feldman and Huddy 2005).

It is entirely possible that neither psychological forces nor principled beliefs fuel the conservative backlash against diversity initiatives; it is all politics. Especially when discussing presidents, senators, and opinion makers, one must consider the potential political ramifications were a Republican to support a diversity platform. His white male base may disappear come election time, part of a white male backlash to diversity. On the other hand, were they to oppose diversity strategies, they can exploit white male backlash and provide the Republicans with electoral gains and an effective means of consolidating their political base (Krugman 2007).

Reverse Discrimination May Delegitimize Political Institutions

Republicans also allege that diversity initiatives delegitimize political institutions because they discriminate against whites, particularly white men. As such, they violate a sacrosanct principle of all modern liberal democracies: that discrimination by the government is an illegitimate act (Gardner 1989). Under this reasoning, a discriminatory judicial appointment process could delegitimize the entire U.S. court system. Even if a diversity policy does not give rise to any actionable legal claims by white candidates passed over for a judicial appointment, the white public's *perception* that the process is discriminatory toward white judges would lead them to view it as unfair and illegitimate. Therefore, as Republicans claim, only a color-blind appointment strategy, based on the principle of individualism, can maintain or enhance the legitimacy of the government, including the federal courts.

Scholars do not all share the same interpretation of the relationship between color-blind hiring and legitimacy. Some scholars reject the notion that a color-blind approach is the only way to act in accordance with the Constitution and thus legitimate the government. Several claim that the Fourteenth Amendment's Equal Protection Clause was enacted specifically to treat the races differently (Iijima 1994; Fine, Powell, and Wong 1997; Kull 1992; Lawrence and Matsuda 1997; Skrentny 1996; Siegel 1998). As Strauss maintains (1986, 100), the discrimination prohibition in *Brown v. Board of Education*[24] is not color-blind but the opposite, "deeply race-conscious." Still others criticize color-blindness as a method that subtly facilitates the use of "government power against Black power" (Steele 1990, 7–9).

Also opposing a color-blind approach, some scholars have argued that whites come into any selection process with "white privilege"—the "pervasive, structural, and generally invisible assumption that white people define a norm the 'other,' dangerous, and inferior" (Law 1999). "White skin privilege," as Baldwin has termed it, produces a "social construction which creates a racial bureaucracy where whites exist at the top and African-Americans are at the bottom" (Baldwin 2009). Because of white skin privilege, a so-called color-blind process only perpetuates inequality between the races.

More conservative scholars argue that a color-blind interpretation of the Fourteenth Amendment is consistent with the normative argument that a liberal government's attempt to engage in distributive justice is illegitimate, as it amounts to coercion (Nozick 1974). Other scholars maintain that a process (appointment or otherwise) intended to increase the presence of one race or gender over another constitutes unlawful discrimination, thus undermining the legitimacy of the entire process (Kahlenberg 1996, 116). Kahlenberg (1996) proposes an alternative approach that would increase the presence of formerly marginalized groups in government institutions without running afoul of the Constitution. He suggests that the government use color-blind class-based preferences, which would still aid many members of minority groups, yet would avoid the pitfalls of race-based preferences. This theory itself has been criticized as hypocritical (Cimino 1997).

Conclusion

As this chapter and the previous one have shown, scholars, pundits, judges, senators, and presidents advocate two distinct positions regarding the legitimacy-conferring power of diversity-driven appointments. The arguments break down along partisan lines. Most observers grudgingly accept that, as long as the nation remains deeply divided on race issues, the opposing sides of the diversity debate will remain poles apart. As one scholar cautioned:

> One product of categorically rejecting color-blindness and likening it to racism is a debate that becomes polarized, with each side entrenched in its own position, unwilling to acknowledge the legitimacy of opposing arguments. The opposing camps do not talk to each other so much as they talk past each other. Lost is the opportunity for persuasion and the identification of common ground. What this means as a practical matter for race and law scholars is that our [pro-diversity] preaching may be well received by the choir, but will likely fail to convert the broader population. One is unlikely to persuade people whose positions one has vilified as racist. (Banks 2009)

But despite the profound differences between people on opposite ends of the political continuum, most actually agree on one critical point regarding judicial appointments: *a president's judicial appointment strategy should strive to enhance and preserve the legitimacy of the court system.* The next three chapters of this book center on empirical analysis that tests the alleged relationship between diversity and legitimacy.

4

Sitting Judges Discuss Diversity

Before I turn to the empirical section of the book, I thought it would be helpful first to get the opinions of sitting judges on the various claims made by each political party concerning diversity on the courts. This is because, for descriptive and substantive representation to occur, there must be a motivation on the part of the representative to act in the best interest of the represented (Sobolewska, McKee, and Campbell 2018). In this chapter I review interviews I conducted with sitting federal court judges. The interviews provide direct insight into the views of sitting minority and female judges as to the benefits and drawbacks of a judicial selection strategy centered on diversity. They also provide important information on how the diversity representatives on the bench feel about representing members of their gender or race. Unlike congresspersons, whose very being is to represent their constituents, judges do not necessarily sign up to be such representatives when they are confirmed as judges. We need to better understand whether descriptive and descriptive/substantive representative judges believe that diversity fosters legitimacy and that their role is to represent minorities and females.

I interviewed a total of 19 federal district court judges from July through September 2009. The judges sat in one of three northeastern district courts, including five separate divisions among these three districts. These jurisdictions were purposely chosen because of the diversity of the judges who sit on these courts. All minority judges and female judges in these five divisions were contacted first by written letter, and then by a follow-up telephone call.

Of the ten minority males contacted, four agreed to interviews (40 percent response rate). Six minority female judges were contacted and two were interviewed (33.3 percent response rate). Fourteen white women were contacted and nine were interviewed (64.2 percent response rate). In addition to these diversity appointees, 30 white male judges (equaling the number of females plus minorities contacted) from these five district court divisions were contacted in the same manner as described above. Five white male judges agreed to interviews (13.3 percent response rate). I asked each judge to sit for an interview so that I could gain a judge's perspective about how diversity on the bench may impact the legitimacy of the federal judicial system.

Admittedly, this is not a random sample of all district court judges across the nation. Participants were those judges willing to sit for interviews, not those chosen by random sampling techniques as would be true of a survey. I also purposely oversampled minority and female judges because they were the focal point of the research project. Since minority judges in particular tend to be located in urban and suburban populations, I chose one such region of the country, the Northeast, to conduct my interviews. Although these findings cannot be generalized across all judges sitting on the federal bench, I think the interview testimony nonetheless makes a significant contribution to this study. First, I do not intend to use the interviews to draw broad generalizations about attitudes of all federal court judges on issues concerning diversity on the bench. Instead, the interview testimony is used only to aid me in formulating theories about the relationship between diversity on the bench and legitimacy of the courts; a random national sample is not essential for this purpose. Similar uses of qualitative evidence are common in the social sciences (Auerbach and Silverstein 2003). Second, the interviews provide a chance to gain a completely different perspective on the diversity issue than that obtained through my experiments. While the latter allowed me to assess the public's feelings about diversity on the bench, the former allowed me to ascertain whether the judges appointed by various presidents with the hope of increasing levels of legitimacy among under-represented populations on the bench, themselves believed they were accomplishing the presidents' goals.

The interviews were all in-depth face-to-face meetings that took place in the judges' offices. The interviews were semi-structured and conducted by me with the aid of my research assistant. All interviews were recorded by audiotape, and detailed interview notes were also taken by my assistant, when she was in attendance, or by me, in her absence. Although I had a set of questions that served as an interview protocol, the interviews were flexible, more like conversations. They also veered in many different directions depending on the flow of the interview. And, although question ordering was sometimes altered, I did ask each of the interview protocol questions to each of the interviewees. On the whole, the interviews each lasted about 45 minutes, with the shortest lasting 15 minutes and the longest, two hours.

Before each interview began, I had the judges sign confidentiality forms. Among other things, these agreements prohibit me from citing the judges' names in any published work. Accordingly, I cannot state the judges' names in citations used herein. Instead, I assign to each judge a letter of the alphabet (from Judge A through S). Moreover, the agreements also prohibit me from using any other information about the judge that would allow someone to identify them. Accordingly, I do not disclose the specific jurisdictions from which the judges hail. I collectively refer to these jurisdictions as "Northeastern districts." I also do not identify judges specifically by their race or ethnicity because of the dearth of such judges in most jurisdictions, particularly Hispanic judges. I collectively refer to these judges simply as "minority" judges. Judges are, however, identified as white and also by their gender since both identifiers are prevalent in most district courts.

How Do Today's Judges Feel about Diversity as a Remedy?

White judges (male and female) interviewed for this project uniformly dismissed the notion that diversity appointments should be made in the twenty-first century to remedy racial discrimination in the 1960s that was the product of the Jim Crow era. Notably, of the white female judges interviewed, none were aware of the remediative theory ever having applied to women, but they acknowledged it had affected racial and ethnic minorities. As for giving women judgeships equal to their percentage in the population, Ruth Bader Ginsburg suggested that such a remedy in the twenty-first century would be illogical: "With women in law schools in the fifty-percent range, one need not worry about the numbers. Women hold up half the sky and they will do so in our courts. They need no favors" (Ginsburg 2003). One white female judge even argued that minorities today enjoy an advantage over whites in garnering federal judicial nominations. Commenting about past discrimination, the judge stated, "I think it's time to stop feeling guilty. Today, it is just the opposite. If you are a well-qualified minority then you are sought after [for a judgeship]" (Interview with Judge A 2009).

A few minority judges concurred that the time for remedying past discrimination has passed, including one minority male judge who explained, "I am not worried historically about what happened—I'm worried presently what will happen in the future" (Interview with Judge B 2009). But a majority of African American and Hispanic judges interviewed (both male and female) were not so quick to dismiss the remediative approach. When asked about how to address the current under-representation of minorities and women on the federal bench, a minority female judge pointed out that any discussion about achieving diversity today must first acknowledge past systemic discrimination, such as the practice among many law schools to bar or heavily curtail the admission of minorities (Interview with Judge C 2009). A male minority judge put it this way:

> We are not a fair and just society if we have a portion of the population that is excluded [from government]. . . . Because there had historically been outright discrimination against certain parts of the population, we were not a just society. . . . Remedying past discrimination creates a just society—recasting [the courts] . . . so people do not feel excluded. (Interview with Judge D 2009)

One judge I interviewed, however (a minority woman), suspected that a desire to remedy past discrimination might also have motivated Clinton, as a white progressive from the South:

> I think when you . . . are from the South, you cannot help but think about the inequities from the past and try and right them. . . . [I]f you were just alive [during the Jim Crow era] and had some inkling of law, it is hard not to be cognizant about *Brown* [*v. Board of Education*] and what it did to the South[,] . . . [t]he recalcitrance of most [white] folks to any kind of enforcement of the [*Brown* decision]. With regard to Carter and Clinton, I think that [remedying past discrimination] is part of [their justification for diversity appointments]. (Interview with Judge E 2009)

Judges' Views on Descriptive Representation

When asked about the notion that presidents should strive to make the racial, ethnic, and gender composition of the bench reflect the demographics of the population, most of the judges interviewed responded favorably, although they did not support specific hiring goals (or quotas). For example, Judge G stated it this way: "I'm of the opinion that certainly efforts should be made whenever possible and without the quality being lowered to embrace diversity. I'm a believer of that" (Interview with Judge G 2009). Judge J also wanted to see more diversity on the bench: "If you're asking me whether I think that having increased diversity on the bench is a good idea, I think that it is. I think the more diversity on the bench, the better off we are from the standpoint of different life experiences and perspectives that are brought to the bench" (Interview with Judge J 2009; see also Interview with Judge O 2009; Interview with Judge Q 2009).

Several of the white female judges I interviewed supported descriptive representation on the bench specifically because of its powerful symbolism, citing Justice Sotomayor as an example.[1] As one white female judge said, "[I]f you work hard, you can achieve. Sotomayor has set an example and created an opportunity for other Hispanics" (Interview with Judge A 2009). Another white female judge echoed these sentiments, describing Sotomayor's appointment as "incredibly important" because, for the federal judiciary "to have legitimacy, people have to be able to see it as a place they can aspire to [join], that it is to some extent reflective of the democratic society" (Interview with Judge F 2009).[2]

Minority judges also tended to focus on the symbolism of descriptive representation, though none directly referenced Justice Sotomayor. One minority male judge stated:

> I think it [descriptive representation] is a laudable goal, but more important, it's a realistic goal that is important for the country to see. . . . [I]magine how the country shortchanges itself when it, for instance on gender, says to half the population, we don't believe you can be in [the U.S. courts]. . . . I can tell you that in the minority community, we were really very proud of Judge [X], the first Black and first woman to sit [in this jurisdiction]. . . . [S]he was really . . . a paragon. (Interview with Judge M 2009)

A minority female judge saw descriptive representation in similar terms:

> The courts are supposed to be for the people . . . and when the community has a certain representation, the bench needs to at least reflect that in some degree because, you know . . . I think the public deserves that, quite honestly. It's not some bastion of elitism that no one can get to except if you are a white male. So I think it's important for the community and for what we're supposed to be here for, which justice is. So it should be for one and for all. So it has to be done by one and all. (Interview with Judge E 2009)

Descriptive representation, in the view of one white male judge, "just enhances the ability of the populace to feel that [judges] are more *believable* if our makeup is such that it is more similar to what the populace is" (Interview with Judge G 2009). Another white male judge stated that increased diversity on the bench "instills *confidence* in the system" (Interview with Judge H 2009). Some judges took a more limited view of descriptive representation's potential advantages, saying the benefits would accrue only to minorities. A court system with more diverse judges, they believed, would be "*fairer*" (Interview with Judge I 2009), more "satisfact[ory]" (Interview with Judge K 2009), or "friendlier" (Interview with Judge J 2009) in its dealings with minority litigants and issues that primarily affect minority communities.

Two white male judges, however, expressed only conditional support for descriptive representation. One believed that characteristics other than race, ethnicity, or gender should be considered in striving for a bench that mirrors America: "The community in my view should want on the judiciary people who they can look up to and also identify with. And that means taking account of a lot of different factors" (Interview with Judge L 2009). The other judge, while acknowledging that descriptive representation aided minority communities, worried about white backlash:

> Without question public confidence [in the courts] is important. It does [exist] in some communities and it does not in others. Communities where it lessens their confidence in the courts may believe that affirmative action candidates [for the bench] have an agenda. But [increasing diversity] is very important for minority communities. (Interview with Judge R 2009)

It was also eye-opening to learn that during the W. Bush administration, efforts were made to appoint more African Americans to the bench. One district court judge I interviewed said the George W. Bush administration sought diversity candidates for the bench in his jurisdiction. Prior to his appointment, this judge recalled, an administration official asked him to suggest some possible names for district court nominations. The official instructed the judge "to start with minority and women candidates" (Interview with Judge P 2009).

Finally, two white female judges (Judges A and S) rejected the premise that the composition of the federal bench should resemble that of the general population. A better form of descriptive representation, they suggested, would use the demographics of the nation's law students to determine the appropriate level of minority representation among federal judges.[3] This objection deserves special attention.

The problem with this interpretation of descriptive representation becomes clear when one considers a hypothetical situation. Only 7.3 percent of law students nationwide are African American, so if this restricted formulation of descriptive representation were to be employed, only 7.3 percent of all U.S. district court judges would be African American. Suppose there was a district court with 20 seats, located in a jurisdiction where Blacks made up 25 percent of the population. According to the approach that Judges A and S espouse, this jurisdiction should have only one Black judge (7.3 percent of 20, rounded to the nearest integer).[4] Under the traditional view of descriptive representation, that same jurisdiction would have five Black judges. On a nationwide level, assuming a bench with 600 district court seats and a population that is 13.5 percent African American, the restricted view of descriptive representation would recommend having 44 Black judges, while the traditional method would translate to 81 Black judges. Naturally, all appointees must be qualified to sit on the bench, but it is hard to imagine a scenario in which a president could not identify five qualified Black judges in a heavily Black jurisdiction, or 81 qualified Black judges across the nation. Using the law school population as the basis for determining the diversity level of the courts would only perpetuate the under-representation of minorities, given that they are also under-represented in law schools (Kidder 2003).

Judges' Views on Substantive Representation

The Attitudinal Model states that judges vote according to their personal policy preferences, and not according to prevailing law or method of constitutional interpretation (Segal and Spaeth 2002). The judges interviewed for this book generally acknowledged that their personal backgrounds play a role in their decisions. Only two judges, a white woman and a white man, completely rejected the notion that a judge's race, gender, or ethnicity could influence their decision-making (Interview with Judge L 2009; Interview with Judge N 2009). The white female judge, echoing Justice O'Connor's famous remark about wise men and wise women, asked, "What does gender have to do with judging?" Judge L, a white man, explained his skepticism about substantive representation by describing the inconsistencies between his background and some of his high-profile rulings (Interview with Judge L 2009).

One judge, a white woman, questioned Obama's premise that empathy is critical to judging: "Does empathy play out? Yes. . . . [Y]ou have to say that you understand [the party's position] but in the end you must do what the law requires. You don't want judges who won't apply the law because of empathy" (Interview with Judge F 2009). The remaining 16 judges interviewed, men and women of different ethnicities and races, agreed that a judge's background plays some role in decision-making, but they differed on the magnitude of that role.

Some judges wholly embraced the theory that descriptive representation leads to better substantive representation. One white female judge explained:

> Who you are does affect your decision-making. . . . Your gender informs your decisions. Your race informs your decisions. So clearly the experiences people bring to the bench affects [sic] their decisions. In a discrimination case where a woman is testifying about being excluded from lunch invitations, golf outings, et cetera, I'll relate to that. . . . We identify with those experiences. (Interview with Judge O 2009)

Another white female judge expressed a similar view, adding that even Justice O'Connor, despite her "wise woman/wise man" remark, appreciated the importance of judicial diversity:

We all have our backgrounds and it all impacts on how we perceive events, facts—Justice Sandra Day O'Connor, I remember, actually wrote something about how she benefited from having Thurgood Marshall as a colleague. Everybody does it and that's not a bad thing. (Interview with Judge E 2009, referencing O'Connor 1992)

Striking the same chord, a male minority judge stated, "I think the more diversity on the bench, the better off we are from the standpoint of different life experiences and perspectives that are brought to the bench" (Interview with Judge K 2009). According to him, additional minority judges "are going to bring different perspectives that are not represented across the board at the present time" (Ibid.).

Other judges emphasized that the presence of minority and female voices in the judicial process could lead to better decision-making by white men.[5] A minority male judge explained:

> I do know that there is a value to having different people at the table. . . . My perspective is it has just got to be better for the decision-making process if you have input from different perspectives. I mean, I can't tell you over the course of my lifetime as a [minority] man in America, how many white guys have said, as we discussed whatever, "I never thought of that," or "I never looked at this simple situation that way." (Interview with Judge M 2009)

A white female judge put it this way: "I think everybody is applying the same law but you [as a minority or female] may be able to see more angles. The more angles, the better the decision" (Interview with Judge Q 2009).

Other judges, however, cautioned against attributing too much weight to race, ethnicity, or gender in the decision-making process. One minority male judge suggested that minority identity may yield "insights that could inform [a judge's] thinking, but it is not going to play a major role" (Interview with Judge D 2009). Another white male judge pointed out that other background factors, such as "being a parent," may influence a decision just as much as race or gender would (Interview with Judge P 2009).

One minority male judge, although he supported Democratic presidents' diversity efforts, deplored the Democrats' failure to appoint ideologically diverse judges—specifically, more unabashed liberals. He focused his criticism on President Clinton:

> He made it [the judiciary] diverse in the context of race, but he didn't make it diverse as far as ideology is concerned. . . . He should have had some screaming liberals in his mix. I resented that he was chicken. . . . And I have a feeling that the new president [Obama] is chicken in this regard. . . . I don't call for just ethnic and racial and gender diversity, I call for intellectual diversity. . . . [B]ut, unfortunately, the Democrats are chicken and the Republicans are not with regard to ideology. (Interview with Judge B 2009)

Still others have voiced similar complaints about a lack of liberals on the courts. Left-wing groups criticized Obama for appointing Elena Kagan to the Supreme Court, claiming that the president should choose justices with established liberal records to counterbalance the conservative justices appointed by George W. Bush (Baker and Zeleny 2009).

Judges' Views on How Diversity Efforts Impact the Quality of the Bench

None of the minority judges I interviewed believed that the quality of the courts suffers when a president pursues a diversity appointment strategy. These judges presumed all minorities and women chosen for the federal bench were as qualified as white men on the bench. Most white judges, male and female, agreed with their minority peers, dismissing the notion that diversity appointees are less qualified than white males.[6] One white male judge observed, "The people that I see coming on the bench, especially at the caliber of the federal bench, merely because they are . . . a minority or a female . . . aren't any less qualified" (Interview with Judge G 2009).

A few of the white female judges, however, tempered their responses by emphasizing that "qualifications" must be considered first and foremost. These judges worried that the legitimacy of the federal courts would suffer if unqualified minority candidates were selected. For example, a white female judge stated: "There are some people who are chosen for diversity and not qualifications, but that actually diminishes the public's trust of the courts" (Interview with Judge S 2009). Another white female judge echoed that sentiment: "[I]n striving for diversity you have to be careful not to dilute the quality. I don't think we should engage in real affirmative action. It is unfair to our public if we can't service them" (Interview with Judge O 2009). A third white female judge expressed concern that the appointment of unqualified minority and female candidates would lead to white male backlash, further undermining legitimacy: "If someone is chosen simply to create diversity and they are not as good or up to the task, everyone else figures it out in short order, and it could cause resentment. I don't think that is good for society. I start on the assumption that minorities are not immutably unqualified" (Interview with Judge A 2009).

In sum, while none of the judges believed their minority and female colleagues on the bench to be unqualified, some intimated that a diversity program for the federal courts *could* result in the appointment of unqualified judges, if race, ethnicity, and gender were given greater weight than a candidate's qualifications.

Judges' Views on Stigmatization

One of the judges I interviewed, a minority male, gave credence to the notion that whites assume successful persons of color are beneficiaries of affirmative action: "A significant portion of the white population . . . if they went to two service providers [one a minority, one white] in any sub-category—for example, medicine, law—would say that the service provider [who] was . . . a minority . . . would provide inferior service" (Interview with Judge M 2009). He acknowledged that most whites he meets evince a similarly skeptical attitude toward him. "[T]hey almost invariably ask me, 'Where did you go to school?' That's the first question. Instead of reacting, 'Wow, that's really cool. You're a judge. I don't know any judges. In fact, I've never met a federal judge.' What do you do?" (Ibid.).

Two white female judges I interviewed agreed with the claim that diversity programs stigmatize minorities. One of them echoed Justice

Thomas's belief that diversity initiatives hurt qualified minorities: "[T]here is an unspoken perception that the minority appointee had lower qualifications and was pushed through, even when it is not true" (Interview with Judge N 2009). The other concurred that a stigma attaches to qualified minorities when a diversity program is in place (Interview with Judge F 2009). She also noted that white male nominees sometimes face the same problem if people assume their political connections contributed to their appointment:

> I think there is always that risk. When your criteria are not who [are] the best qualified but something else. . . . I think you make these appointments [subject to] questions about competency. It is up to the person to prove his or her competency. . . . I think white males have a different issue on how they got there. If they are the cousin of "X" or gave a large campaign contribution, people in the know are going to say, "Hmmm . . . that's interesting." I don't think because you are white and male exempts you from [having to] prove competency. (Ibid.)

Yet again, neither of these female judges saw stigmatization as a problem for women appointed under diversity initiatives. The vast majority of judges interviewed (male and female, minority and white) disavowed the notion that a president's use of a diversity initiative to fill federal court vacancies stigmatizes minority or female judges simply because they are appointed under such a policy.

Judges' Opinions on White Male Backlash

Republicans claim that a judicial appointment strategy predicated on diversity, like diversity initiatives in other contexts, will lead to white male backlash. The judges interviewed for this book had differing opinions about this notion. Some refused to answer the question; others seemed outraged by the premise. Asked whether diversity appointments could lead to white male backlash, one white female judge responded, "No, I don't think that and I don't care" (Interview with Judge Q 2009). Referring to white men, she stated, "Let them be alienated" (Ibid.). Another white female judge expressed her frustration with claims of white male backlash this way: "[W]hite males are alive and well and thriving [on the federal bench]. I don't think anyone could say that the white male is getting the shaft" in the appointment process (Interview with Judge F 2009). One white male judge dismissed the notion that Democrats' diversity efforts would create a backlash: "I think it would be pretty difficult [to make that argument] because when you look around . . . the majority [of judges] is still white men" (Interview with Judge G).

Several white female judges, on the other hand, speculated that diversity programs for the federal bench could cause white male backlash (e.g., Interview with Judge A 2009; Interview with Judge F 2009; Interview with Judge P 2009). Another judge, a minority woman, agreed, referencing the fight about identity politics that raged during Justice Sotomayor's confirmation proceedings: "I think the Sotomayor hearings illustrated the tension that seems to exist between the historically dominant subjects of our population and those who have been historically excluded from the bench" (Interview with Judge C 2009). Another judge, a white male, believed that a certain amount of backlash was inevitable, and understandable:

> A white middle-class or even a white working-class person who feels that they [sic] are not obtaining what they should obtain on the merits because of affirmative action . . . is going to feel a resentment that is not without justification. . . . I mean, it's all well and good to say to that person, "[W]ell, this is for the greater good of society," but he is going to say, "[W]ell, it's my life, you know." (Interview with Judge L 2009)

One minority male judge, however, observed that white backlash can stem from racism rather than from any justifiable sense of grievance. When asked why white males view diversity as a threat, he replied:

> Because I think they are hiding under, dare I say . . . a cloak of racism. Racism and gender bias. It's a question of people having been used to the way [the bench] was, for most of the critics are [in] the majority. . . . I've met a judge [who said to me], "It's about time a white guy got nominated." And I had to remind this person, who I think very highly of, "This court was founded back in the 1700s and I think that, until recently, the court had only three to four Black males as judges." (Interview with Judge B 2009)

At the opposite end of the spectrum, a white female judge validated the notion of reverse discrimination, stating that she knew many people, "including some who have been on the wrong end of identity politics in the appointment process, who are anything but prejudiced. But they do resent being on the wrong end of identity politics" (Interview with Judge R 2009). She concluded, "I don't think you should discriminate against white males to increase diversity" (ibid.). One minority male judge sounded a hopeful note, predicting that white backlash would end within a generation:

> Some white men are going to have some negativity about diversity, but I also think that that is generational. . . . People of my son's generation don't assume that when a Black man gets a job, it's because of some affirmative action policy. Particularly when you look at the Black men who are out there now . . . [like] Barack Obama. (Interview with Judge M 2009)

Testimonial evidence from other sitting judges supports this view. For example, one of the female judges interviewed for this project told me: "I was the first attorney [where I worked] who was pregnant. . . . I came back to work in three weeks after my son was born and four weeks after my daughter was born. I was a pioneer and I believed I behaved in such a way to open doors for others" (Interview with Judge A 2009). And, as reported earlier in this chapter, the female judges I interviewed generally supported diversity on the bench, but couched their responses strictly in terms of improving racial diversity, making no mention of gender diversity. In other words, like Justice Ginsburg, they did not consider female appointments to the federal courts to be part of a president's concerted efforts to increase diversity on the bench, even though they clearly are part of such initiatives.

Several of the female judges I interviewed were strong supporters of the Sonia Sotomayor nomination to the Supreme Court, not for its symbolic meaning for women, but only for its powerful symbolism for Hispanics. For instance, one female judge stated: "if you work hard, you can achieve. Sotomayor has [thus] set an example and created an opportunity for other Hispanics" (Interview with Judge A 2009).

Another female judge focused not only on the symbolism of the first Hispanic appointment to the Supreme Court, but also on the message to Hispanics given by Sotomayor's distinguished legal pedigree: "This [Sotomayor] nomination was positive in two ways. First, there is now someone in a high position who represents Hispanics. Second, she [Sotomayor] is someone who went to the best schools and she's respected across the board" (Interview with Judge F 2009).[7] In considering the importance of her nomination, women judges simply did not see any benefits for women who may come before the Court.

Consistent with this finding, the male judges I interviewed, in stark contrast to the female judges, were more likely to recognize that gender diversity was an essential component, along with racial and ethnic diversity, of a president's appointment strategy predicated on diversity. As one male judge stated: "imagine how the country shortchanges itself when it, for instance, on gender, says to half the population, we don't believe you can be in here [on the bench]" (Interview with Judge M 2009). Another male judge similarly remarked, "we should consider diversity in every respect, not only ethnic, but racial, gender, age" (Interview with Judge H 2009).

5

Diversity, Party Identification, and Political Legitimacy

Descriptive representation (in which an institution's demographic makeup mirrors that of the population at large) is thought to increase the level of diffuse support (long-term support) for an institution among formerly under-represented groups. Descriptive/substantive representation (in which a group's representative shares that group's political views and race/gender) is thought to increase the level of specific support (short-term support). To account for both of these possible paths toward greater legitimacy levels for the courts, I designed a set of experiments aimed at measuring legitimacy. In the descriptive representation experiments, the experimental manipulation involves the aggregate percentage of Blacks or women on the bench versus their presence in the population. In the descriptive/substantive representation experiment, the experimental manipulation is the race of the judge; it is designed to measure support for a legal decision based on the race of the judge.

Almost all prior empirical studies examining the legitimacy of the American government and its institutions have relied exclusively on mass public opinion surveys.[1] I, instead, use an experimental approach, which for this type of research is optimal. First, experiments are recognized as the optimal research method for establishing causation, as opposed to studies utilizing mass public opinion, which can only demonstrate correlation (McDermott 2002, 334–335; Brewer 2000, 3–16). This causal link results from the random assignment of participants into distinct treatment groups and control groups, leaving no differences between the groups but for the treatment; any difference between the two groups is then presumed to be caused by the treatment (Iyengar and Kinder 1987). In my experiments, the treatments are varying percentages of Blacks and women on the bench (descriptive representation) and varying combinations of the races of the judges and participants (substantive representation).

The second reason I chose an experimental design was that I could control the information the participants possessed about female and minority representation on the bench. This is critical, because most citizens know little about the Supreme Court and close to nothing about the lower federal courts. In a 1989 *Washington Post* poll, 71 percent of respondents could not name any justice on the Court, while only 2 percent could correctly name all nine. Although 9 percent of respondents managed to correctly identify William Rehnquist as Chief Justice of the United States, six times as many respondents (54 percent) offered the name of Judge Wapner, the somewhat less distinguished judge of the television show *The People's Court* (Morin 1989). In 2018, only half of Americans could name a single justice on the Supreme Court (Birnbaum 2018). Accordingly, in the first set of legitimacy experiments (what I will refer to as the "descriptive representation" experiments), participants were informed in the treatments of the percentages of women or Blacks on the bench before answering questions about the legitimacy of the U.S. courts.[2]

A third reason why experimentation is optimal is related to the descriptive/substantive race representation experiment; there, participants were shown a photograph of the judge rendering a specific legal decision about which they would be asked to rate their agreement; this allowed them to see the judge's gender and race.[3] In a traditional telephone survey, it would be impossible to test citizens' different reactions to legal decisions based on the race or gender of the judge without an experiment. In the computer surveys done here, the treatment is not mentioned in the accompanying newspaper article. The participants could see for themselves the race of the judge in their particular treatment. I could introduce the variables of race and gender in a subtle way, without tipping off the participants.

Finally, I use an experimental research design because certain types of political inquiry benefit from the manipulation of information. "True experiments are few and far between in the study of politics" (Iyengar and Kinder 1987, 8). Accordingly, being able to present hypothetical scenarios as true allowed me to obtain immediate purchase on a critical political puzzle we face in the here and now. For example, in the descriptive representation experiments, different treatment groups were provided with different figures for the percentages of women on the bench (three under-representation treatments, one perfect descriptive-representation treatment, and one over-representation treatment). To wait for the actual proportion of women on the federal bench to reach 50 percent (and then to compare legitimacy levels over time) would take years—indeed, it may never happen. Similarly, in the substantive representation experiment, it is hard to imagine a natural setting in which two district-court judges of different races or genders encounter a case that provides the same facts and raises the same legal issues.

My data have the extra bonus that two of the three data sets are national random samples. This means that these experiments have not only internal validity (requiring only a random distribution of the treatments) but also external validity (requiring a national random sample). Both types of experiments tell us a lot about descriptive and substantive representation. But the findings of the national random samples can be applied to the general public (Iyengar and Kinder 1987, 12).

All experiments here test empirically the normative theories of descriptive and descriptive/substantive representation. In order to do so, I propose a series of refutable hypotheses about the expected outcomes of the experiments according to the precepts of each normative theory. I then collect data (the survey responses) and analyze them using regression analyses. These steps allow me to either reject or not reject the null hypotheses (that is, the opposite of what the theory predicts the outcome to be). For example, according to the normative theory of descriptive representation, one would hypothesize that there is a positive relationship between the aggregate percentage of Blacks on the bench and Blacks' perception of the courts' legitimacy. The null hypothesis would suggest the opposite: that there is no relationship between diversity on the bench and Blacks' levels of legitimacy. If the data allow me to reject the null hypothesis (because I did find a relationship), then there remains the possibility that the normative theory (and, by extension, the claims of the Democratic Party) is backed by empirical evidence. However, if the null hypotheses cannot be rejected, that means there might be no causal relationship between legitimacy and diversity, as Republicans claim about affirmative action.

Although the three sets of experiments share certain features (each uses a measure of legitimacy as the dependent variable, each proffers refutable hypotheses, and each is subjected to statistical analyses), they also vary in significant ways. Accordingly, I will discuss separately the details of the three sets of experiments (descriptive gender representation, descriptive race representation, and descriptive/substantive race representation).

Experimental Design

Descriptive Representation Experiments

The descriptive representation experiments (one for race and one for gender) aid me in assessing whether this normative theory can be supported by empirical research. Moreover, they help answer the pivotal question: Can Democrats justifiably rely on the theory of descriptive representation to support increased diversity on the bench? In these two experiments, the subjects' responses to five survey questions measured legitimacy for the courts, the dependent variable in my regression equations. The key independent variables are the experiment's treatments and their interactions with race and gender. The goal is to discover whether there is a statistically significant difference between each treatment group and the control group. Men in one treatment group will be compared to men in the control group, men in another treatment will be compared to the control group as well.

I also added to the models three other independent variables that measure party identification, income, and education. We know that people with greater knowledge of the courts have higher respect for the courts, and so I use education and income as a rough measurement of knowledge about the courts. The party variable is necessary because there may be important differences between Democrats and Republicans in the control group.

Subjects in the treatment groups of the two descriptive experiments were shown a mock newspaper article describing a report issued by the Administrative Office of the U.S. Courts (a real government body that issues reports of this nature). The articles reported the percentage of women (for the gender experiment) or African Americans (for the race experiment) currently on the federal bench and the percentage of women or African Americans in the U.S. population. All versions of the article provided the same figures for the percentages of women or

African Americans in the population (the actual percentage), but they reported varying percentages of women or African American judges on the bench. The articles also informed readers whether the percentages of women or African Americans on the bench had increased or remained the same in the previous three decades. The articles purported to be from the *Chicago Tribune* and were formatted to look as if they had been downloaded from the *Tribune*'s website.[4] However, the mock articles were all created solely for purposes of this study. Copies of these articles (both the gender and race articles) are set forth in appendix B.

For the gender experiment, there were five treatment groups, each of which read a different article. The articles reported that women today compose: 12.0 percent of the federal bench (a very low percentage); 28.1 percent (the actual percentage of women on the bench at the time of the experiment's commencement); 40.0 percent (under-representation, but a relatively high percentage); 51.0 percent (true descriptive representation, which mirrors the percentage of women in the population); or 60.0 percent (over-representation, and a very high percentage). The articles all reported the true percentage of women in the population (51.0 percent), and all other information in the articles remained the same.[5] In the race experiment, I use two treatment groups: one article told the subjects that African Americans constitute 3.0 percent of federal judges (under-representation), and one said the number was 25.0 percent (over-representation). Participants in the gender experiments were randomly assigned to one of six groups (the five treatment groups plus the control group), while those in the race experiment were randomly assigned to one of three groups (two treatments plus the control).

After reading the mock newspaper articles (or, for the control group, upon beginning the experiment), participants immediately answered a battery of survey questions designed to measure their feelings of legitimacy toward the courts. Five of these questions constitute the dependent variable; they are among the same questions used by Caldeira and Gibson in their landmark study 24 years ago (Caldeira and Gibson 1992), which looked at the legitimacy of the Supreme Court. These questions together measure legitimacy of all courts in the U.S. system. They are set forth in the description of the dependent variable later in this chapter.

To further ensure that the subjects had no reticence to provide their true opinions regarding race and gender, I disguised the purpose of the experiment, stating that it was about the American courts, and not specifically about diversity on the bench. In order to ensure that the respondents do not feel tricked, when the true purpose of the experiment (a technique often referred to as a deception study) is disguised, researchers are ethically and legally bound to provide the subjects with a full description of the experiment's true purpose once their participation is complete. I fulfilled this obligation with the debriefing document set forth in appendix A, and I provided my contact information in the event that subjects wished to withdraw from the experiment (no participant chose this option) or to ask follow-up questions about it.[6]

I carefully designed these experiments to avoid certain common pitfalls. First, it was critical that the mock newspaper articles serving as the experimental treatments appeared as if they were obtained from the websites of actual news organizations; this maintains the integrity of the experiment. To this end, I selected well-known newspapers: three experiments used articles purportedly from *The Chicago Tribune*. I inserted the newspapers' titles at the top of the mock articles, using a font similar to what appears on the widely recognizable masthead.[7]

Conducting the gender experiment online helped to prevent two problems that frequently occur with telephone surveys involving questions about sensitive issues such as discrimination and diversity. First, the subject may want to respond in a manner that will be acceptable to the interviewer, causing people to give different answers based on the characteristics of the interviewer (Cotter, Cohen, and Coulter 1982). Another problem involves the social desirability effect, whereby respondents do not reveal their true preferences on race and gender issues, but rather, respond with what they deem socially acceptable; they hide their racist or sexist feelings. One example of the social desirability effect was detected in polls conducted before the 1990 Virginia gubernatorial race, in which one of the candidates was African American. In telephone interviews, whites overstated their support for the Black candidate because they did not want to appear racist (Finkel, Guterbock, and Borg 1991). For the race experiment, students who were helping me pass out surveys to potential subjects in the experiment were instructed to be out of eye sight of the survey taker. Scholars have found that the more privacy respondents are given in answering race-related questions, the more likely that their responses will reflect their true feelings (Dovidio and Fazio 1992; Hurley 1997).

Descriptive/Substantive Representation Experiment

The descriptive/substantive experiment tests the other normative theory on which Democrats generally rely to justify judicial diversity. These experiments allow me to examine whether descriptive/substantive representation produces higher levels of support for a judge's decision. In other words, do people feel that a member of their own race and gender will render a better substantive decision than whites or men? The main inquiry here is: Do African Americans have more confidence in a legal decision involving a race-related issue when they know the judge is Black? Conversely, does support for a decision decline among white men if they know the judge is female or Black, and does it increase if they know the judge is a white man?

In the descriptive/substantive race experiment, subjects were shown one of three mock newspaper articles describing a decision made by a district court judge. One contained a picture of a Black male judge, one a picture of a white male judge, and one with no picture of the judge (the control group). The treatment is thus the race of the judge.

For this experiment, the mock newspaper article concerned a criminal case. The outcome of the case remained constant among the different treatment groups: Regardless of the information provided about the judge's race, each article described the same ruling. In both hypothetical cases, the judge's decision runs in a liberal direction. I chose a liberal direction because most Americans assume that Blacks are Democrats (and thus more liberal than whites) so the decision meets the a priori expectations of the subjects. Additionally, the cases intentionally raise legal issues in which one might expect a female or African American judge to be more sensitive to the claims of an African American party. This sensitivity based on group identity is at the core of the normative theory of descriptive/substantive representation. The criminal decision involves a drug-related search-and-seizure case in a presumably Black neighborhood; the judge rules that the contraband is inadmissible at trial because the police conducted an illegal search. Copies of these articles are set forth in appendix B.

Population Samples

DESCRIPTIVE GENDER REPRESENTATION

The experiment went into the field July 21–August 4, 2010. A random national sample was drawn using YouGov's Polling Point panel, a proprietary opt-in survey panel comprised of 1.08 million U.S. residents who agreed to participate in YouGov's Web surveys. YouGov interviewed 2,140 respondents who were then matched down to a sample of 1,602 to produce the final data set. An over-sample of Blacks was taken in order to get meaningful results on Blacks' feelings of legitimacy toward the courts. The respondents were matched on gender, age, race, education, party identification, ideology, and political interest. YouGov then weighted the matched set of survey respondents to known marginals for the general population of the United States from the 2006 American Community Survey. The marginals are set forth in appendix A2.

DESCRIPTIVE RACE REPRESENTATION

Participants for this experiment were recruited in the following way. In January and May 2007, members of my research team approached individuals in Pennsylvania Station, Bryant Park, and Central Park in New York City and asked if they wanted to participate in a short survey.

Pennsylvania Station is a major transit hub in midtown Manhattan. It serves commuters on the Long Island Railroad and the New Jersey Transit System and New York City subway riders on numerous subway lines. It also provides intercity train service nationwide via Amtrak.[8] Bryant Park and lower Central Park (where participants were also recruited) are public spaces located in midtown Manhattan; both attract people who live and/or work in New York as well as tourists from around the globe. Accordingly, although the majority of our subjects hail from New York and New Jersey (78%), the remainder of our subjects hail from states as far away from New York as California, Arizona, and Oregon.

These individuals were offered $10 in exchange for their participation in a 15-minute study about "American politics." To test the theory of descriptive representation it was critical that I have a survey with a sizable sample of African Americans. Accordingly, I over-sampled the Black population, causing the racial balance to be 89 Blacks and 91 whites. Those who did not identify themselves as "Black" or "white" were excluded from the analysis.

DESCRIPTIVE/SUBSTANTIVE REPRESENTATION

The experiment went into the field July 21–August 4, 2010. A random national sample was drawn using YouGov's Polling Point panel, a proprietary opt-in survey panel comprised of 1.08 million U.S. residents who have agreed to participate in YouGov's Web surveys.[9] YouGov surveyed 1,380 respondents who were then matched down to a sample of 1,200 to produce the final data set. The respondents were matched on gender, age, race, education, political party identification, ideology, and political interest. YouGov weighted the matched sets of survey respondents to known marginals for the general population of the United States from the 2006 American Community Survey. The sampling method used is set forth in appendix A. The weights applied to the socio-demographic variables are also set forth in appendix A.

How to Measure Legitimacy

"Political legitimacy remains a complex, multi-faceted concept whose measurement is difficult and whose sources and implications may vary widely" (Gilley 2006, 31). As discussed in the introduction, legitimacy concerns public evaluations of the trustworthiness in government institutions and a willingness to follow government directives even when one does not agree with them. It is a collective belief by the people that to obey the government is in their best interests.

Political scientists who study American politics have measured legitimacy in a variety of ways. Some studies rely on a single survey question, asking how trustworthy, fair, or deserving of confidence the respondent finds the government (writ large) or a specific institution within the government (e.g., Gay 2002; Tate 2004). Others have deployed a battery of questions designed to determine whether a respondent resists change to the structure of a given political institution even when they do not agree with the institution's substantive policy outputs (Caldeira and Gibson 1992). These scholars claim the single-question approach likely taps into specific support of an institution, rather than diffuse support (e.g., Gibson 2010; Scherer and Curry 2010). In this study, I have chosen to use a battery of questions to test the respondents' willingness to resist fundamental change in the institutional structure of the federal courts even when they do not agree with the courts' substantive outputs.

For purposes of measuring legitimacy, scholars usually make a distinction between a person's long-term support for an institution, even in the face of a decision with which they disagree, and short-term support for an institution, based on agreement with a specific policy output (or, as here, a specific legal decision). The former type of institutional support is often referred to as diffuse support, and the latter as specific support. While specific support may seem too fleeting to affect the broader construct of legitimacy, studies have shown that specific support for an institution's decisions over time raises one's diffuse support for the institution (e.g., Mondak 1992). Therefore, an increase in either type of support for the courts could lead to an increase in the courts' legitimacy.

Dependent Variable

The dependent variable is the level of legitimacy each respondent has for the U.S. courts. Legitimacy is measured on a 1 through 7 scale, with 7 being the highest level of legitimacy. The legitimacy term is comprised of answers to five questions (each one measured on a 1–7 scale in which 1 = strongly disagree and 7 = strongly agree); these five responses are averaged to provide the respondents' legitimacy scores. Each question begins with the phrase, "To what extent do you agree or disagree with the following statement." The statements were as follows: (1) If the courts started making a lot of decisions that most people disagree with, it might be better to do away with the federal courts altogether; (2) The right of the courts to decide certain types of controversial issues should be reduced by Congress; (3) It would not make much difference to me if the U.S. Constitution were rewritten so as to reduce the powers of the courts; (4) People should be willing to do everything they can to make sure that any proposal to abolish the Supreme Court is defeated; and (5) Courts can be trusted to make the right decisions. Responses to these questions were re-scaled, when necessary, so that larger numerical responses would reflect higher levels of legitimacy for the federal courts. The responses were then averaged to create a single "legitimacy" variable.[10] These particular questions were chosen to represent legitimacy because, according to its common definition, legitimacy reflects someone's trust in the institution and keeping the structure of the Supreme Court in tact despite short term setbacks from the Court (Klein 2015; Gibson and Nelson 2015). Gibson et al. (2003) have advised to use a measurement of trust toward the courts as one element of the legitimacy measure. Later he and his colleagues thought a trust question may also tap into short-term policy approval (Gibson and Nelson 2015).[11] The questions I used were culled from Caldeira and Gibson's (1992) original list of questions. I have four questions that ask respondents to stick by the courts even when they are making decisions they might not like—the heart of legitimacy. In addition, I include a measure about trust in the courts doing the "right thing." Finally, the original questions retained have been slightly amended, reflecting my focus on the legitimacy of all courts, and not just the Supreme Court (Caldeira and Gibson 1992).[12]

The descriptive and descriptive/substantive representation experiments also measure whether increasing the presence of minority or female judges on the bench causes support for the courts to decrease among men or white men. Such backlash would suggest that increasing judicial diversity could create a backlash when other groups are over-represented on the bench.

The descriptive representation experiments (one for gender diversity and one for racial diversity) measure legitimacy in terms similar to diffuse support and centered on the theory of descriptive representation. The descriptive/substantive representation experiment measures legitimacy as specific support for a decision.[13] I did not conduct an experiment to test attitudes about diversity as an equitable remedy for past discrimination because the Supreme Court has ruled that to be an invalid justification for diversity initiatives.[14]

Dependent Variables: Substantive Representation Experiments

The dependent variable for the specific support experiment was a single question asking the respondent: "To what extent do you agree with the judge's decision ?" Participants in the descriptive/substantive representation experiment read about a judge's ruling in favor of a Black man against the police in a drug-related investigation. The judicial decisions in all of these cases were intended to run in a "liberal" direction. Respondents chose from one of seven options to rank their level of agreement with the judge's decision, from "strongly disagree" (coded 1) to "strongly agree" (coded 7).

Unlike the continuous variable created for the descriptive representation experiments, which measured the subjects' responses to a series of questions, in the substantive representation experiment, the response to a single question constitutes the dependent variable. Under these circumstances, many would advise the use of Ordered Probit or Logit to analyze the data. Accordingly, I began my analysis this way. However, for presentation purposes, weighted least squares regression, as used in the descriptive representation experiments, is much easier for the reader to understand. It is becoming more acceptable to analyze data based on a seven-point Likert scale using least squares regression when, as here, the distribution of responses resembles a normal curve. I will present in the text the results of weighted least squared regressions. The Ordered Probit results produced substantively similar results, with the same magnitudes, signs, and significance levels.

Methods of Analysis of the Survey Responses

DESCRIPTIVE REPRESENTATION EXPERIMENTS

In most experiments, the number of possible responses to the treatment conditions is binary. For example, if one is seeking to know how to get out the vote, the treatments would be various forms of mobilization efforts, and there would be two potential responses: The person either voted or did not vote. In this type of experiment, the researcher's data analysis would usually begin with traditional t-tests or chi-squared tests; these tests determine, as an initial matter, whether the treatment groups' binary responses differ significantly from the control group's binary responses. In my experiments, however, the dependent variable is continuous, making use of these tests virtually impossible.

The better course is to proceed directly to regression analysis, where whites and Blacks, men and women, can be analyzed "separately" (through interaction terms) in a single model. The unit of analysis is each subject who participated in the experiment. Because the dependent variable is continuous (as described below), I use least squares regression to analyze the data.

Before analyzing the data, I did a manipulation check to confirm that experiment subjects did, in fact, understand the manipulation on which I am focused. Each survey (except for that administered to the control group) asked respondents whether the newspaper article they read reported that women were over-represented, equally represented, or under-represented on the U.S. courts compared to their presence in the population. Respondents were also given the option to answer that the newspaper "article did not say." 83.0 percent of the people originally treated (and excluding the control group) answered the manipulation question correctly. For the race model, 91.1 percent of subjects answered the manipulation question correctly. Clearly, the manipulations "took."

There are three separate models employed for each experiment. First, I test whether, for women, the courts have more legitimacy as the percentage of women on the bench varies (chapter 6) (compared to the untreated group who knows nothing about the levels of diversity on the bench). The same model is used on the race data (chapter 7). For African Americans, does the courts' legitimacy rise or fall as the percentage of Blacks on the bench rises or falls? Therefore, these first two models allow me to directly test the Democrats' claim that increasing descriptive gender or race representation leads to concomitant increases in legitimacy levels for women and minorities.

A second set of models try to assess the Republicans' claims—that diversity efforts are a form of reverse discrimination and cause white or male backlash in response to diversity programs. These models try to isolate the levels of legitimacy for white men and thus, for backlash. Does it fall when women and Blacks are adequately represented on the bench?

A third set of models tests whether political party identification also mediates the subjects' reactions to the different treatment conditions (see chapter 9). Given the central role that the two political parties play in shaping the debate over diversity on the bench, it makes sense that one's party affiliation, alone or in combination with treatment conditions, could influence one's perception of the courts' legitimacy. This model allows me to determine whether subjects see diversity through a political lens. Do Republican subjects assume that greater diversity on the bench is the product of affirmative action, as Republican politicians scornfully claim occurs under Democratic presidents? Do Democratic subjects assume a lack of diversity results from a preference for privileged white men—a preference that Democrats accuse Republican presidents of exhibiting? If only white male Republicans, for example, experience backlash, or only Black Democrats favor diversity programs, then there is evidence that the treatment conditions were viewed at least in part as a political issue, and not wholly as an issue of descriptive representation.

DESCRIPTIVE/SUBSTANTIVE REPRESENTATION EXPERIMENTS

As with my analysis of the descriptive representation experiments, I again present three sets of models. The simple model tests whether race interacted with the treatment conditions to affect a person's level of specific support for the decision at hand. Moreover, the race of the respondent must be interacted with the experimental conditions, just as gender is. The first model interacts race with the treatment condition and the second set of models adds a three-way interaction: *Gender of Respondent x Race of Respondent x Treatment Condition.*

In chapter 9, I interact party identification with the previous interaction terms, producing an interaction of *Race (or Gender) of Respondent x Party Identification of Respondent x Treatment Condition.* In this set of models, I ascertain whether a person's political party identification mediates the impact of the experimental conditions on their specific support for a particular decision depending on whether the judge is white or African American. Here, similar to the descriptive representation Model 3, I want to assess whether subjects assume that the female and Black judges are the products of affirmative action and thus presume them to be "less qualified" to sit on the bench (or in this instance, perhaps, racially biased). The party identification of the respondent interacted with the treatment conditions will show whether the issue is viewed through a political lens whereby the more strongly a person identifies as a Republican, the more likely they are to make such an assumption about a Black or female judge.

6

Legitimacy and Gender Diversity on the Bench

In the 1970s, women began to enter the workforce in larger numbers than ever before. This was due in part to court orders prohibiting employers from engaging in hiring policies and practices that discriminated against women. No longer could women be kept out of the workforce based on antiquated notions that a woman's proper role in society is as wife and mother, known as the "separate spheres doctrine" (Kuerston 2003, 16–17). Beginning in the 1970s, the Supreme Court declared that governmental gender classifications were deemed "semi-suspect" and would be subject to heightened scrutiny by the Court.[1] Under a long line of cases, the Court made clear that the treatment of women as second-class citizens would no longer be tolerated without an "exceedingly persuasive justification,"[2] and any government policy or practice that violated this principle was deemed unconstitutional under the Equal Protection Clause of the Fourteenth Amendment (for state or local governments) or the Due Process Clause of the Fifth Amendment (for the federal government). Affirmative action was one of the remedies available to the courts to redress past gender discrimination in the workplace.

The president also ordered all executive agencies to aid women who wished to start their own businesses. In Executive Order 12138, President Carter created the National Women's Business Enterprise Policy, requiring each government agency to take affirmative action to support women's business enterprises.

Through a historical accident,[3] Congress banned private employers from discriminating against women in the workforce through the passage of the 1964 Civil Rights Act, Title VII. Interpreting Title VII, the Court proceeded to strike down employment policies or practices that punished women in the workplace, if women, for example, had preschool age children;[4] were pregnant or fertile;[5] or did not act feminine "enough."[6] Courts were also empowered under Title VII to order diversity plans designed to hire more women.[7]

Eventually, private employers and government entities began voluntarily implementing affirmative action plans designed to increase the presence of women in the workforce.[8] Public opinion was also in flux regarding affirmative action for women. One early study found that support for affirmative action for minorities and women was highly polarized by gender and race (Taylor 1991).[9] Taylor found that 26 percent of white women, and 53 percent of white men, believed "affirmative action is wrong and should be changed."[10] Later polls also showed signs of gender polarization, but the magnitude of the difference between the genders was much less than that found in the Taylor study. This may be attributable to the fact that Taylor's question was not specifically aimed at gender diversity, but rather, gender and race diversity. In a 1995 Gallup Poll, people were asked their opinions of affirmative action programs for women: 55 percent of women approved of affirmative action for women (only 12 percent with quotas), while 45 percent of men approved (7 percent with quotas) (Gallup 2001).[11] By 2001, Gallup found 57 percent of women and 49 percent of men approved of affirmative action for women (Gallup 2001), and in 2003, 62 percent of women and 56 percent of men approved of such hiring programs (Bowman and O'Neill 2016, citing 2003 Gallup poll).[12]

Two trends emerge from these Gallup Polls: (1) both men and women have become more supportive over time of affirmative action programs for women; and (2) women's support for such programs is approximately 8–10 percentage points higher than men's. That differential remained steady throughout the time period Gallup ran these polls. Notably, by 2003, a majority of men now supported diversity efforts for women. As we will see later in this chapter, polls have shown men to be much more supportive about affirmative action for women than whites for programs aiding minorities.

Aside from poll questions specifically asking about affirmative action, the American National Election Study (hereinafter, ANES) has polled citizens about women's proper role in the workplace, from 1972 through 2008.[13] Though not perfectly analogous to the subject of this study, the ANES question nevertheless provides some indication about how men and women feel about women rising to positions of power in the workplace and in government, a group that would certainly include federal court judges.[14] The responses to this poll question over time are depicted in figure 6.1.

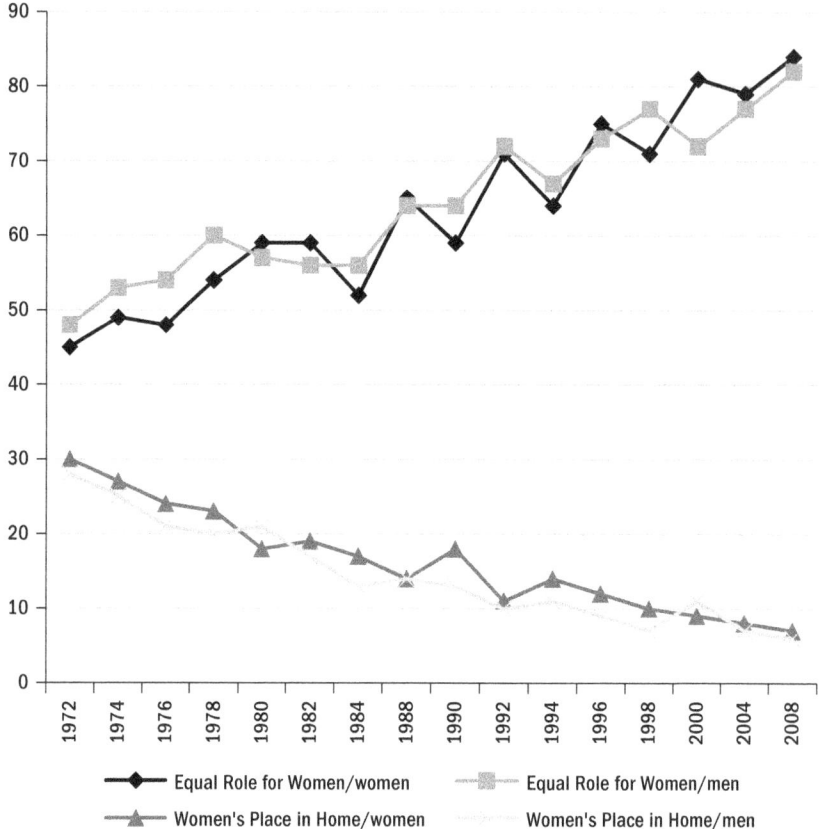

Figure 6.1. Equal Role for Women in Power. Source: American National Election Studies (1972–2008)

The results of the ANES poll indicate that both men and women followed the same trend over time, and had roughly the same percentage of support over time regarding women in positions of power.[15] In 1972, slightly less than half of both men (48 percent) and women (45 percent) believed women should have an equal role in running business and government. By 2008, this number rose to 84 percent for women and 82 percent for men. At the same time, about one-quarter of men (28 percent) and one-third of women (30 percent) believed a woman's place was in the home. These poll numbers are contrary to the polls discussed above, as no gender polarization exists (men and women followed almost exactly the same patterns) on the questions about women's proper and equal role in the workplace, particularly the question of women in power.

Given that the majority of women seem to support affirmative action for women, we now need to examine whether these opinions mean that women support the use of descriptive representation in our government's institutions. To help answer this question, I turn to the political science literature concerning the differences between men and women in a variety of government and electoral situations.

We start with male versus female candidates for office. Although there have been numerous empirical studies about descriptive gender representation, the results are decidedly mixed. These studies predominantly seek to identify whether there are differences in women's attitudes toward female candidates or elected female representatives compared to male candidates or elected male representatives. As for female candidates, one study found that women are more gender conscious than men in their evaluation of candidates, and those women prefer female candidates over male candidates (Rosenthal 1995). However, another study concluded that women's positive feelings toward female candidates are not based on any gender affinity, but instead on policy agreement (Dolan 2008).

The evidence is also ambiguous as to whether women are more likely to vote for a women running for office against a man. Some scholars have found that women are more likely than men to vote for female candidates (Sanbonmatsu 2002; Rosenthal 1995). This is particularly true when women run for office and advocate an agenda more attuned to women's needs (such as sexual harassment, abortion, and child care) (Plutzer and Zipp 1996; Hernson, Lay, and Stokes 2003). But, there are a number of studies finding candidates' genders have no impact on voting decisions (King and Matland 2003; Thompson and Steckenrider 1997; McDermott 1997). Another study found that female candidates enjoy an electoral advantage when their valence scores are higher than the male candidate's (Fulton 2014).[16]

While it is unclear whether women are more likely to vote for a descriptive candidate because of gender (and not issue compatibility), the literature suggests that, at least, women candidates raise awareness among women of all candidates running for office, as women become more interested in learning about the women candidates (Verba, Burns, and Schlozman 1997; Koch 1997; Sapiro and Conover 1997). This type of raised awareness is critical, according to one study. Sanbonmatsu (2003) examined how knowledge about the under-representation of women in Congress affects women's attitudes about descriptive gender representation in the federal legislature. She found that women who are aware of the gender imbalance in Congress are more likely to support increasing descriptive gender representation in the legislature than women without knowledge of women's under-representation in Congress. However, when scholars took the next step—to investigate whether *actual* descriptive gender representation raises women's levels of legitimacy toward various government institutions—these studies found no such connection. Scherer and Curry (2010), using an experimental approach, found that raising the level of female representation on the U.S. courts has no impact on women's levels of legitimacy for the U.S. courts. Two other studies similarly found that women who have a descriptive representative do not exhibit more trust in their own representative or for the legislative body in which the descriptive representative sits (Swers 2002; Lawless 2004).

Further confounding the issue, at least one study has shown that women do not have feelings of linked fate with other women (Gurin 1985). Linked fate is a theory first developed by Dawson (1994), applied to Black voters. The theory holds that Blacks, no matter what their socioeconomic status, believe that policies benefitting the Black community in general are tantamount to benefits for themselves. In contrast, socioeconomic circumstances of white Americans are a significant predictor of whether a white citizen will support policies benefitting the poor. Thus, lacking linked fate, the Gurin study suggests that women should not be expected to have positive feelings of support toward the courts as more women are appointed to the courts.

This lack of sisterhood may be due to what Lani Guinier and colleagues (1997) have termed the "becoming gentlemen" phenomenon. Trying to understand why women overwhelming are ranked at the bottom of their law school classes, and receive fewer prestigious prizes, clerkships and jobs, Guiner et al. found law school socialization to be at the heart of the problem. It was only those women law students who were best able to lose their gender consciousness and instead mimic the habits of their male peers who became successful in their careers. In short, these women did not threaten the white male paradigm of the legal community as did those assuming a gendered voice. Presumably, women judges, as former attorneys at the top of their field, would likely have "become gentlemen" during the course of their legal careers; once on the bench, we would expect these women judges to lack compassion for today's women who seek gender-oriented benefits for themselves.

Psychological Male Backlash

Besides political and normative objections to affirmative action, the psyches of whites, and white men more specifically, in America may also be driving opposition to diversity appointments. Unlike the other explanations for support or opposition to diversity, psychological explanations do not necessarily turn on partisan politics. There are a number of psychological theories that may be at play.

The most widely held psychological explanation for white men's opposition to affirmative action is that they view efforts to increase diversity in any work environment or government institution through the lens of hostility: "out-groups" threatening white men's formerly privileged "in-group" status (Blalock 1967; Conover 1988; Johnson 1980). Under this theory, white men perceive their once-privileged status of superiority being jeopardized by women and minorities. In other words, they see government benefits as a zero-sum game: "An increase in minority percentage should result in an increase in discrimination [against minorities] both because of heightened perceived competition and an increased power threat" (Blalock 1967, 154). Some psychologists alternatively refer to this phenomenon as "entitlement disorder" (Hall 2004). It has also been suggested that white men distrust diversity initiatives because the procedures used to award government jobs or benefits are not transparent; no one knows how much the factors of race, gender, or ethnicity (versus qualifications) play in the decision-making process (Nacoste 1990).

Still others suggest that white men's opposition to affirmative action is a form of racism. Fanon (1967) contends that the racism is patent: "There is a fact: White men consider themselves superior to Black men." Others see the racism as more subtle, characterizing it as either "symbolic racism" (Sidanius, Pratto, and Bobo 1996) or "new racism" (Augoustinos,

Tuffin, and Every 2005). In recognition that society no longer tolerates patent racism, the last group of scholars cited above claims that white men intentionally frame their opposition to diversity initiatives in meritocratic or principled terms (Hughes 1997). But, in fact, their arguments are mere pretexts for their underlying racism. (e.g., Kinder and Sanders 1996; Sidanius et al. 1996).

What do empirical studies tell us about men's feelings toward descriptive representation of women? At least one study has found that men, over time, begin to experience women as less of a threatening out-group than they did in the 1970s—the high-water mark of affirmative action programs for women (Gurin 1985). It seems that theory and reality are not in sync. While public opinion polls report that women support diversity programs *in theory*, it seems that the literature indicates no concomitant uptick in women's support for government institutions with *actual* gender diversity. According to the female judges I interviewed, as well as Justice Ginsburg, women do not seem to believe they need any special diversity initiatives to increase gender diversity on the bench. Instead, they look at the percentage of women attending law school (today, about 54 percent), and claim that women have achieved gender parity with men within the legal profession, including the federal bench.[17] Survey evidence also suggests that men now support affirmative action programs designed to aid women. This contradicts Republican claims that such diversity initiatives cause white men to experience a backlash against those they perceive to be receiving preferential treatment. Given all of the ambiguity about gender diversity, we may find that the experimental approach used here provides greater clarity on the issues.

Hypotheses

Until now, descriptive gender representation theory and reality were not in sync. Public opinion polls report that men and women support diversity programs and believe women should share an equal role with men in running our government. There are, on the other hand, studies showing backlash by whites against Black representatives, suggesting that white men might feel the same way about women on the bench. Another thing to keep in mind is that the courts are somewhat unique among the three federal branches because they enjoy a higher baseline legitimacy level than the elected branches.[18] In addition, since the courts are charged with maintaining justice and fairness for our nation, it may be that citizens are more likely to demand equality on the bench to ensure equality in decision-making.

Wanting to empirically test the theory of descriptive gender representation as it relates to the courts, I hypothesize as follows:

H1: Women *will* confer higher levels of legitimacy for the courts than do women in the untreated (control) group as the percentage of women on the bench rises.
H2: Men *will* confer lower levels of legitimacy for the courts than do men in the untreated (control) group as the percentage of women on the bench rises.
H3: White men *will* confer lower levels of legitimacy for the courts than do white men in the untreated group as the percentage of women on the bench rises.

I now turn to the survey data I collected after execution of the gender experiment. We want to focus not only on women's reactions to gender diversity on the bench (Democratic claims about descriptive representation), but men's reactions as well (Republican claims about backlash).

Empirical Findings
The Control (Untreated) Group

Before turning to the regression models, it is necessary first to ascertain critical baseline statistics to which the treatment groups may be compared. To this end, the survey administered to the control group (who read no mock newspaper article) included two questions not asked of those respondents in the five treatment groups. Specifically, I wanted to establish what the average American believes to be the percentage of women on the courts, and the percentage of women in the general population. These descriptive statistics will aid in determining whether the five experimental treatments contain ratios of women judges to women in the population that are above, equal to, or below those that Americans generally believe such ratio to be.

TABLE 6.1. Baseline Beliefs about Descriptive Gender Representation on the Bench (Control Group Only)

	Men	Women	White Men	White Women	Minority Men	Minority Women	Actual Statistics
% of Women Judges	18	14	20	15	14	12	28
% of Women in U.S.	51	52	51	52	51	54	51

Note: Numbers represent percentages of the U.S. population.

Since the control group received no information about the percentages of women in the population and women on the U.S. courts, I included two questions (what is the percentage of women on the U.S. courts, and what is the percentage of women in the U.S. population) in order to know baseline expectations about gender diversity on the bench. These baseline expectations are given in table 6.1. While both men and women fairly accurately stated the percentage of women in the population (men = 51%; women = 52%), both highly under-estimated the percentage of women judges (men = 18%; women = 14%). In fact, each of these estimations was so low that they are much less than the percentages set forth in the treatment conditions, except for the 12 percent condition. So, for subjects in the treatment groups (except white men in the 12 percent group), the mock newspaper articles report greater representation for women on the bench than the average American would have predicted. Under these conditions, it is possible that the treatment groups' pre-experiment beliefs about women's under-representation may influence their reactions to the treatment conditions, and ultimately their levels of diffuse support.

Regression Models

I now look at the results of a series of regression models that will consider the effect of different levels of descriptive gender representation interacted with different demographic groupings. Because the data were weighted, I use weighted least squares regression.

For simplicity's sake, I do not report here all of the interaction terms between gender, race, and treatment conditions to the extent they do not add to the substantive interpretation of the main variables of interest, be it women as the baseline, men as the baseline, or white men as the baseline. However, all necessary interaction terms between the various independent variables were included in the original model, and the full results of those models are provided in appendix C.

Gender Experimental Treatments

The most direct empirical test of the theory of descriptive representation is presented in the first set of weighted least squares models. Tables 6.2 and 6.3 measure women's, men's, and white men's baseline levels of legitimacy for U.S. courts respectively (see full models in appendix C).

As a point of interest, I note at the outset that men in the survey have higher baseline legitimacy scores for the courts than do women, a historically marginalized group. This is at the heart of the theory of descriptive representation, designed to help raise the courts' legitimacy among groups that had been systemically shut out of the judicial selection

TABLE 6.2 Weighted Least Squares Regression, Legitimacy Levels of the U.S. Courts, by Treatment x Subject's Gender, Women as Baseline

	B	St. Error
Female Subjects in Untreated Group	4.29***	.15
Women x Treatments		
12%	.15	.16
28%	.05	.16
40%	.10	.16
51%	.26*	.16
60%	.09	.16
Men in Untreated Group	.15	.16
Party Identification	−.10**	.03
Education	.16***	.02
Income	.03**	.01
N = 1,186		
(14, 1,171) = 7.69***		
R-squared = .08		

***$p \leq .001$; **$p \leq .05$; *$p \leq .10$ (two-tailed test)
Full model set forth in appendix table C.1

TABLE 6.3 Weighted Least Squares Regression, Legitimacy Levels of the U.S. Courts, by Treatment x Subject's Gender, Men as Baseline

	B	St. Error
Men in Untreated Group	4.44***	.15
Men x Treatments		
12%	.27*	.15
28%	.08	.15
40%	.26*	.15
51%	−.05	.16
60%	−.11	.16
Women in Untreated Group	−.15	.16
Party Identification	−.10***	.05
Income	.03**	.01
Education	.16***	.02
N = 1,186		
F (14, 1171) = 7.69***		
R-squared = .08		

***$p \leq .001$; **$p \leq .05$; *$p \leq .10$ (two-tailed test)
Full model set forth in appendix table C.2

process. Thus, it is appropriate for the Democratic Party to apply the theory in the case of women and diversity on the bench.

The most important finding is that, predicated on the theory of descriptive representation, women have higher legitimacy scores when they are told that the percentage of women on the bench equals women's presence in the general population—both 51 percent. Women's legitimacy scores rise .26 points on the one to seven legitimacy scale, a statistically significant difference compared to the control group. Women, contrary to much of the literature, apparently possess just enough group identity to embrace the motto: what's good for other women (here, seats on the federal bench) is also good for me (female judges providing, for example, better substantive representation and more role models).[19] With race, Blacks have a greater sense of linked fate and group identity than do women (Dawson 1994). In turn, higher levels of linked fate and group identity lead to more trust among Blacks in our legal institutions in the presence of diversity (Scherer and Curry 2010).

The finding here also supports the Democratic Party's belief that descriptive gender representation raises legitimacy levels of the courts among women. Finally, I would highlight the finding that party identification coefficient is a statistically significant predictor of legitimacy levels. The more Republican you get, the less legitimacy you have toward the U.S. courts. In contrast, the coefficient for gender, standing alone, is not statistically significant. In sum, I can reject the null hypothesis that, for women, there is no relationship between gender diversity and feelings of legitimacy for the courts. I will revisit this finding in chapter 9 when I consider the impact of political party affiliation of the mass public on descriptive representation. In addition, I find that education and income are also statistically significant predictors of one's legitimacy. The more educated you are, the higher your level of legitimacy will be. Income also is a positive coefficient, meaning that the higher your income, the higher your legitimacy level.

When men serve as the baseline, and men are compared to the control group (where no levels of diversity were presented to the subjects), there is evidence of backlash against women being amply represented on the bench (see table 6.3). This is because men's legitimacy levels rise when women are under-represented on the bench. This finding suggests that for men, the courts' legitimacy scores go up when their majority status on the federal courts is secure.[20] These findings allow me to reject the null hypotheses for men, that there is no relationship between descriptive gender diversity and feelings of legitimacy. There is a .27 point rise in legitimacy scores for the subjects who received the 12 percent treatment (under which women comprise only 12 percent of the bench) and .26 point rise on the one to seven legitimacy scale when men believe the court is 40 percent women. One thing about these results that is surprising: men's legitimacy scores do not plummet when women are over-represented or mirror-represented on the bench. This may mean that the level of gender diversity can be raised at least to 40 percent without backlash.

Why are men split between two levels of under-representation? It would seem that men see *any* type of under-representation of women as a positive. These findings collectively show that men prefer to keep women in the minority on the bench (that is when their legitimacy scores rise) so that white men maintain their dominant position in the

Judiciary. Here, all three under-representation conditions are positive, though the 28 percent treatment is not statistically significant. Men are clearly threatened by more diversity on the bench, as psychological theory would posit. It is clear evidence of male backlash, a phenomenon that Republicans warn against if diversity strategies are used for the federal bench. Critically, these findings meet the second prong of the Diversity Dilemma (the first being lower legitimacy scores of under-represented groups in the population versus whites or white men). That is because increases in legitimacy under conditions of under-representation, as well as negative values at mirror- or over-representation conditions, constitute male backlash.[21] However, the group that should be most threatened by gender diversity is not all men, but white men.[22]

Gender, Race, and Experimental Treatments

There is reason to believe that not all men, as we tested in table 6.3, experience gender diversity the same way. This is because only white men have historically dominated the U.S. federal courts. Thus, they are the most threatened group of all, as psychological theory counsels. They should feel the most hostile to gender diversity on the federal bench, an out-group. As such, the next model includes an interaction term of variable that teases out the effects of gender diversity on white men only. To test these propositions, I add to the original two models the interaction term of gender × race × treatment condition. The results of this weighted least squares regression model are set forth in table 6.4.

For white men, we see that the coefficients for all three under-representation conditions, the 12, 28, and 40 percent conditions, are positive and relatively the same magnitude. However, only the 12 and 40 percent conditions rise to the level of statistical significance ($p^* \leq .05$ [two-tailed test]). This means that white men who were told that women were under-represented on the bench have higher legitimacy scores than white men in the control group have. White men's legitimacy scores rise .40 (12 percent treatment) and .41 (40 percent treatment) when women are under-represented on the bench. Some may find it encouraging that white men are willing to tolerate a 40 percent level for women on the bench (that is lower than their current percentage), but it still constitutes

TABLE 6.4 Weighted Least Squares Regression, Legitimacy Levels of the U.S. Courts, by Treatment x Subject's Gender x Subject's Race, White Men as Baseline

	B	St. Err.
White Men in Untreated Group	4.30***	.17
White Men x Treatment		
12%	.40**	.18
28%	.26	.18
40%	.41**	.18
51%	.10	.18
60%	.03	.19
Women in Untreated Group	.18	.19
Minority (all minorities) in Untreated Group	.46**	.23
Party ID	−.11**	.04
Income	.03	.01
Education	.16***	.02
N = 1,186		
F(26, 1159) = 5.17***		
R-squared = .10		

***$p \leq .001$; **$p \leq .05$; *$p \leq .10$ (two-tailed test)
Full model set forth in appendix table C.3

under-representation, meanwhile the same white men tolerate their own over-representation.

In figure 6.2, I present post-estimate predictions of legitimacy levels for the three demographic groups which had shown statistically significant differences between the treatment conditions and the control group—men, women, and white men—as shown in tables 6.2, 6.3, and 6.4.

A few things stand out when we look at figure 6.2. First, white men, without experimental stimuli, have lower legitimacy scores than men in the aggregate (4.93). (4.78). Women, however, still lag behind men (4.780). Second, were women to regress to 12 percent of the bench, both men's and white men's legitimacy levels would rise well above their baseline rates (men and white men in the untreated groups). When women are 51 percent of the bench, men's legitimacy levels remain steady, but women's scores go up. Thus, we see a clear picture of the Diversity Dilemma. While

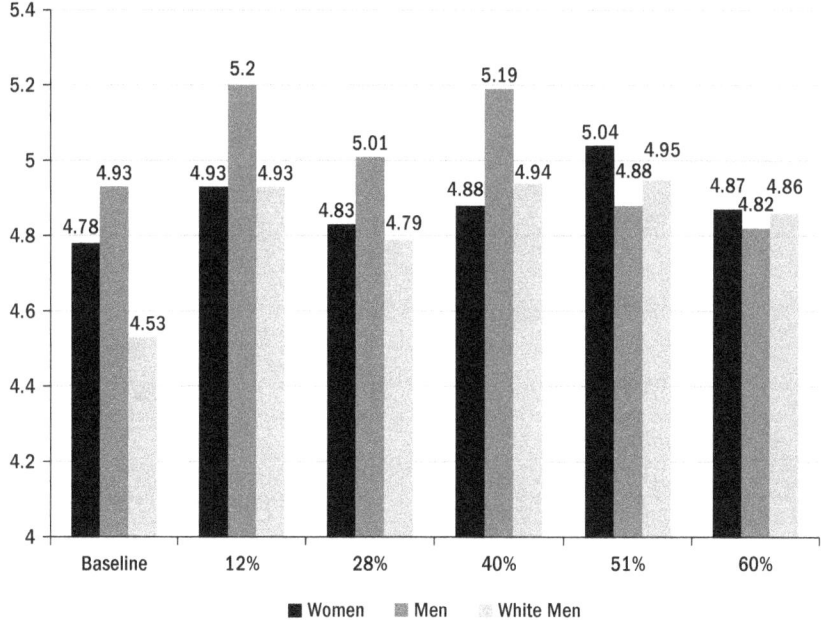

Figure 6.2 Predicted Legitimacy Scores for Men, Women, and White Men
Note: Moderate individuals with some college and $30,000–39,999 income

gender diversity does indeed aid in raising the courts' legitimacy levels among women, at the same time, it also engenders a white male backlash. Is it possible that we can achieve true descriptive representation with no backlash? Should backlash even be an issue to consider because it perpetuates gender discrimination against women?

Conclusion

In this chapter we examined the relationship between descriptive representation and legitimacy for the courts among women, men, and white men as distinct groups. According to the theory of descriptive representation, members of a formerly marginalized group should experience increases in their feelings of legitimacy toward a governmental institution as the presence of that group approaches or goes beyond true descriptive representation. Even though women were a group systemically excluded from the federal and state judiciaries throughout history, I found some evidence that women's diffuse support (i.e., legitimacy levels) for the courts is driven by the percentage of women on the bench. When women see that there is true descriptive representation, that women represent 51 percent of women on the bench just as they are 51 percent of the population, their legitimacy levels for courts in general rise. However, the magnitude of this increase is relatively small. Women also do not view diversity initiatives through the political lens of party affiliation. In other words, for women, reports about gender diversity on the bench are just that: factual reports about diversity on the bench. Women do not make the leap of logic that reports about women's presence on the bench in relation to their presence in the population necessarily mean that an affirmative action program for women, a political issue, is at play.

For men, when viewed as a single group, we see no signs of the gender backlash Republicans believe is an evil by-product of diversity efforts for minorities and women. Men's diffuse support for the U.S. courts remains unchanged (compared to the control group) regardless of over-representation, under-representation, or true descriptive representation of women on the bench. However, when gender and race are interacted, we do see white men's legitimacy levels rise under conditions of under-representation of women on the bench (and, by definition, over-representation of men). White men, it seems, may experience a backlash against diversity efforts once women's percentage on the bench constitutes mirror- or over-representation, diffuse support levels dropped from their heightened levels when women were under-represented on the bench.

Finally, when it comes to gender diversity, white men do not vary their opinions about diversity based on their ideology. Although the treatment conditions (the mock newspaper articles) imply that diversity on the bench may be tied to a quota-based affirmative action plan, when we interact ideology with gender and race, there is no distinction between the way liberal and conservative white men see gender diversity.

7

Legitimacy and Racial Diversity on the Bench

A decade after the Supreme Court ruled segregation in the public school system unconstitutional,[1] Congress began to enact legislation to limit racial discrimination and grant African Americans rights they were historically denied under the law. In 1964, Congress passed the Civil Rights Act, a bill that forbade discrimination on the basis of race in hiring, firing, promoting, and schooling, essentially laying the "basic statutory framework" for affirmative action in both the workforce and the educational system (Dale 2005, 2–3). Title VI of the Civil Rights Act prohibited racial discrimination in all federally funded programs, while Title VII prohibited racial discrimination in the workplace.

However, employers, school districts, and contractors dragged their feet, refusing to voluntarily obey the dictates of the Civil Rights Act. By the late 1960s, judges began to issue court orders to noncomplying companies and states requiring them to hire African Americans, but to do so in the manner dictated by the courts.[2] And many judges, frustrated by the years of stalling tactics, imposed extreme measures in their orders—most controversially, setting hiring quotas for minorities. In 1973, a federal judge went so far as to mandate that half of the new hires in the Bridgeport, Connecticut police department be either African American or Hispanic.[3]

The executive branch also took harsh action against companies that refused to abide by the Civil Rights Act. In 1965, President Lyndon B. Johnson issued Executive Order 11246, requiring nearly all employers working with the federal government to file written affirmative action plans (the order only excused companies with fewer than 50 employees or whose federal contracts amounted to less than $50,000). These plans had to include minority hiring goals and timetables in which the contractors had to commit "good faith" efforts. Thus, by the mid-1970s, quota-based affirmative action had become the norm to ensure minority hiring, at least among the many entities seeking to do business with the government.

These executive and judicial affirmative action practices continued through the Carter administration. However, by the 1980s, public opinion had turned against such aggressive affirmative action programs, and some white employees began to challenge them. They argued that when a government entity used quotas, white men were being denied equal protection under the laws in violation of the Fourteenth Amendment; when a private company used quotas, the argument changed to focusing on Title VI or VII of the Civil Rights Act, because race was being taken into consideration in employers' hiring practices. In *City of Richmond v. Croson* (1989),[4] the Supreme Court ruled for the first time that a government-ordered, quota-based affirmative action plan benefitting minorities violated the Equal Protection Clause. The Court referred to Richmond's policy of setting aside 30 percent of city construction funds for Black-owned firms as "highly suspect." In its essence, *Richmond* and the decisions that followed curtailed the wave of affirmative action policies that had dictated employment practices for nearly two decades. This ushered in a new era of conservatism toward policies aimed at creating greater racial diversity in the workplace.

Any initiative to diversify the federal courts may engender comparisons to an affirmative action program. This is particularly true of the kind of diversity initiative suggested in the mock newspaper articles used in this experiment, in which comparisons are made between the percentage of Blacks on the bench and the percentage of Blacks in the general population. Thus, it is instructive to consider public opinion on the issue of affirmative action before examining the results of the race-based experiment.

Since 1964, the American National Election Survey (ANES) has asked people whether they believe the government should aid Blacks and other minorities. One such time-series question asked whether "the government should make every possible effort to help minorities" or whether "they should help themselves." Figure 7.1 shows the responses to this question from 1970 to 2012.[5]

In figure 7.1, we see that African Americans have shown far greater support for government intervention on behalf of African Americans than have whites. However, support for such measures has declined significantly over time for both races. In 1976, when President Carter was elected and would soon begin his plan to diversify the courts, 60 percent of African Americans supported government intervention to aid Blacks,

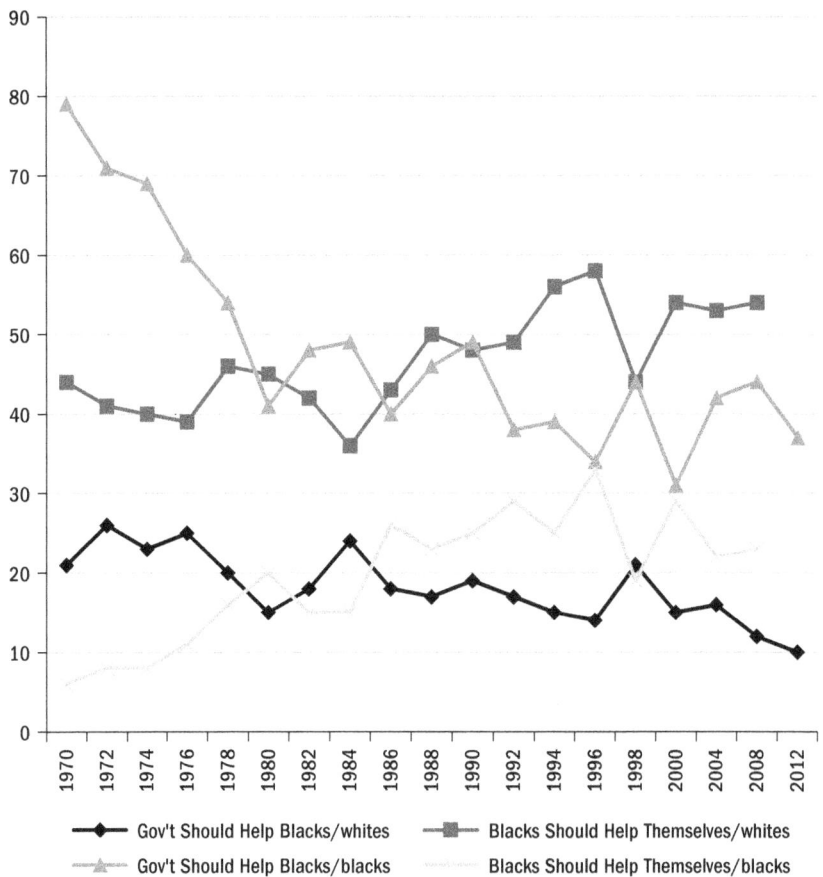

Figure 7.1. Support for Government Aid to Help Blacks and Other Minorities. Source: American National Election Study, 1964–2008

and 11 percent opposed it. In contrast, 25 percent of whites at that time supported such diversity-based efforts, while 39 percent opposed it. By 2008, white support for aiding Blacks fell to 12 percent; at the same time, however, African American support for aiding minorities also declined to 44 percent. Not only did fewer people express support for race-based government intervention, more people consciously opposed it (rather than declining to answer the survey question or saying they had no opinion). In 2008, 54 percent of whites were against the idea (an increase of 38 percent over 1976), as were 23 percent of African Americans (more than double the percentage from 1976).

The ANES has also asked, since 1964, another race-related policy question of particular relevance here: "Should the government in Washington see to it that Black people get fair treatment in jobs or is this not the federal government's business? . . . What do you think?"[6] The results of this poll question are depicted in figure 7.2.

We see the same pattern as previously observed. In 1972, only five years before President Carter would begin his diversity efforts for the

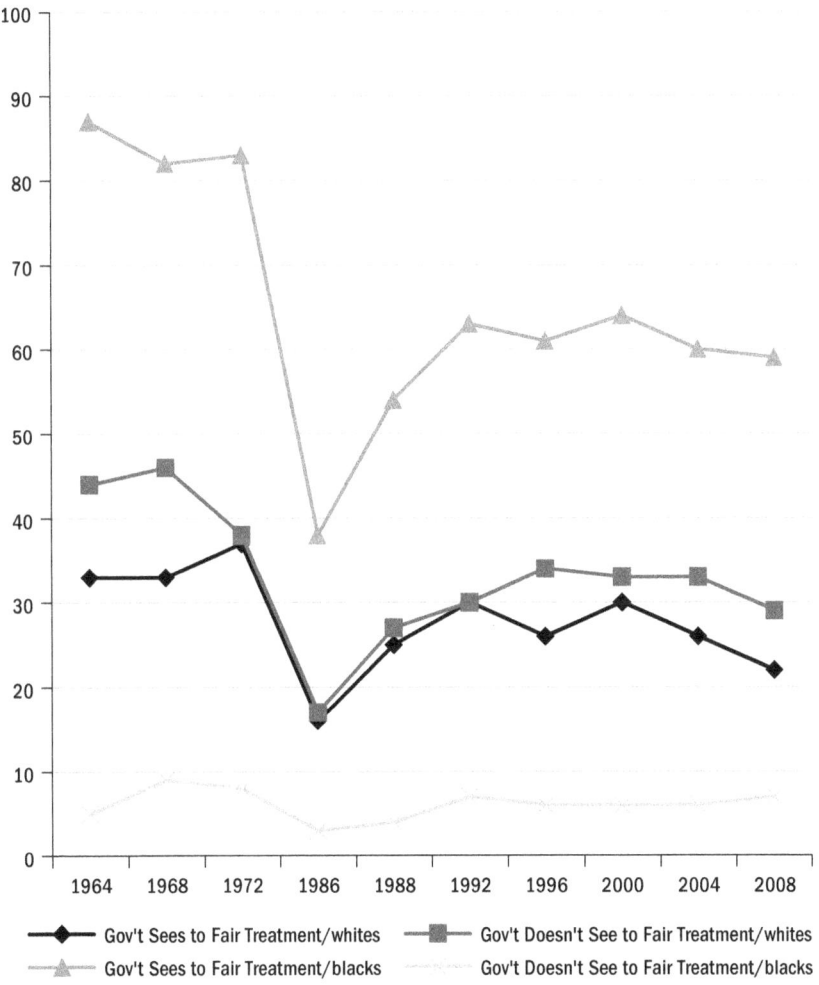

Figure 7.2. Support for Government Intervention to Assure Fair Treatment for Blacks.
Source: American National Election Study, 1964–2008

U.S. courts, 83 percent of Blacks believed the government should intervene to aid Blacks, while only 8 percent disagreed. Among whites, 37 percent supported government intervention compared to 38 percent who opposed it. At this point in time, whites were evenly divided over the question of whether the government should try to ensure fair treatment of African Americans in the workplace. This stands in contrast to the prior question, which showed—throughout the time period in question—far more whites opposing government intervention on behalf of Blacks than whites supporting it. The explanation for these seemingly contrary results is that the first question asked respondents about providing "aid" to Blacks, and they likely interpreted that to mean preferences for Blacks. In the second question, the focus was on simply treating Blacks "fairly" in the workplace, and not awarding any preferences or advantages. By 2008, 22 percent of whites continued to support government intervention to ensure the fair treatment of Blacks (a decline of 15 percentage points from 1972). Surprisingly, Black support also fell, to 59 percent (down 24 percentage points from 1972). However, decreasing support for these policies did not translate into increased opposition. In 2008, 29 percent of whites opposed government intervention in the workplace (9 percentage points lower than in 1972), and 7 percent of Blacks opposed this policy (a drop of only one percentage point).

The bottom line from the ANES polling is this: The races have historically been polarized on the appropriate role for the government in aiding minorities with some type of intervention, whether it be trying to assure workplace equality or awarding preferential treatment. The most recent ANES surveys indicate that this polarization has not diminished.

Another distinguished polling outfit, Gallup, has a time-series question about "affirmative action" in its election polling from 2000 to 2016. Gallup's question is similar to the questions posed by ANES, but it focuses on college admissions—a topic to which many pollsters turned their attention after the 2003 Supreme Court ruling in *Gratz v. Bollinger*,[7] which invalidated the University of Michigan's practice of assigning a certain number of points to applicants based on their racial or ethnic background.

On three occasions between 2003 and 2013, the Gallup Poll asked:

> Which comes closer to your view about evaluating students for admission into a college or university—applicants should be admitted solely on the

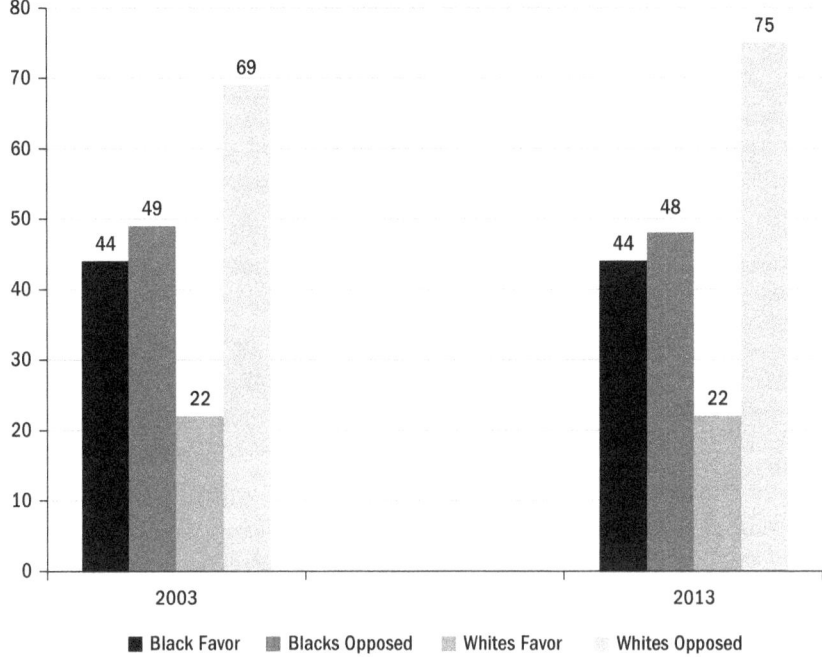

Figure 7.3. Should All Applicants Be Admitted to College on the Basis of Merit?

basis of merit, even if that results in few minority students being admitted, or an applicant's racial and ethnic background should be considered to help promote diversity on college campuses, even if that means admitting some minority students who otherwise would not be admitted?

Gallup's decision to phrase the question in terms of a student being admitted "on the basis of merit" likely contributed to the high percentage of respondents who opposed the use of affirmative action (changing the wording to "solely on the basis of academic qualifications," for instance, might have produced different results).

Figure 7.3 shows the results of the first and last of the three surveys that Gallup conducted on this issue. The only noticeable difference between the two periods is that white opposition to affirmative action grew five percentage points in the ten-year span.

In spite of the lack of support for affirmative action among whites, the United States (mostly Democratic leaders) undertook concerted efforts to secure more positions of power for Blacks in federal and state governments. Private businesses likewise made voluntary efforts to seek out qualified Blacks to place in leadership roles, as Title VII of the Act prohibited private enterprise from continuing discriminatory policies. But have these gains affected Blacks' views about American government and politics more generally? Has the increased presence of African Americans in positions of government power—including the judges with whom this study is concerned—increased Black constituents' feelings of legitimacy for governmental institutions?

There is a significant body of literature on the benefits said to accrue to African Americans by virtue of descriptive representation (meaning representation by someone from your own identity group). Studies have examined not only the relationship between racial diversity and institutional legitimacy, but also a wide range of behavioral and attitudinal changes resulting from descriptive race representation. For example, on the behavioral side, empirical studies have found that, for African Americans, having a Black representative leads to: better communication between representative and constituent (Bullock 1981; Banducci, Donovan, and Karp 2004); greater voter mobilization (Voss and Lublin 2001; *but see* Tate 2004); increased political activism (Harris, Sinclair-Chapman, and McKenzie 2006; *but see* Tate 2004); and increased voter turnout, at the state level (Rocha et al. 2007) and the federal level (Whitby 2007).

Early studies on descriptive race representation showed that African Americans experienced various aspects of the construct of legitimacy when represented by a member of their own race; for example, increased pride in their government when a Black official was elected (e.g., Gurin, Hatchett, and Jackson 1989; Preston 1978). Bobo and Gilliam (1990) found that Blacks living in cities with African American mayors had greater trust in municipal government than Blacks living under white mayors. And, Box-Steffensmier et al. (2003) concluded that Blacks rate the performance of a Black congressman higher than that of a white congressman. Some later studies, however, reached more pessimistic conclusions, but these studies are more about descriptive/substantive representation than they are about descriptive representation. Gay (2002), Tate (2004), and Banducci et al. (2008) all found that being represented by a Black congressman has *no* impact on

Blacks' "trust" in their individual descriptive representative. Questions about trust are generally considered measures of substantive representation, policy agreement with the representatives (Gibson and Nelson 2015).[8] Some have theorized that linked fate, the belief that what is good for my people is good for me, builds a trust between minority constituents and minority representatives; whites, however, do not experience linked fate with white representatives (Casellas and Wallace 2015).

Rather than focusing on whether descriptive race representation by one individual affects Black constituents' feelings of legitimacy toward their representative, three noteworthy studies took a broader view. Specifically, they looked at whether *aggregate* levels of Black representation within a political institution—what Mansbridge refers to as a "critical mass" (1999)—increases support for that institution among African Americans, regardless of whether their particular elected representative is Black (Overby et al. 2005; Tate 2004; Scherer and Curry 2010). However, these aggregate-level studies produced conflicting results.

Overby and colleagues (2005) relied on a random sample of Mississippians in order to test whether Black citizens have higher levels of confidence in the fairness of the state judicial system given the state's fairly sizable proportion of elected Black judges (29 percent).[9] Overby et al. (2005) found no support for their hypothesis. In contrast, relying on a national random sample of African Americans, Tate (2004) found that Black citizens who believe (albeit incorrectly) that Blacks are over-represented in Congress (more than 20 percent of members) have more trust in the institution than those who believe Blacks occupy but a small percentage of congressional seats. Finally, Scherer and Curry (2010), using a sample of convenience (diverse sample primarily from Pennsylvania Station in New York City—"Penn Station"), found that, compared to the control group (who had no information about the percentage of Black judges), African Americans have higher levels of legitimacy for the U.S. courts when informed that Blacks are over-represented on the bench.

As for whites, two studies of descriptive representation—one looking at Congress and one at the federal courts—showed similar results. Both indicated that whites' trust in the institution declined significantly when Blacks were highly visible in positions of power—specifically, when

TABLE 7.1. Baseline Beliefs about Descriptive Race Representation on the Bench

	Whites	Blacks	White Men	Actual
% Judges Black	12.3	7.2	12.3	8.5*
% Blacks in U.S.	26.9	26.3	24.0	13.5*

* These numbers represent the subjects' beliefs about the percentages of Blacks on the bench and Blacks in the population at the time the experiment was administered.

white respondents were represented by a Black congressman (Gay 2002) or when they were told the aggregate percentage of Blacks on the federal bench was 20 percent or higher (Scherer and Curry 2010).

All of these studies inform our expectations regarding the relationship between racial diversity and legitimacy. As the various polls indicate, the experiment's subjects should be racially polarized on the issue of diversity. But the ANES polls also indicate that support for affirmative action is waning among whites *and* Blacks.

The Control Group

Before turning to the hypotheses, as was done with the gender experiment, I wish to review two additional survey questions given to the control group, which establish baseline levels of people's perceptions about the number of Black judges sitting on federal courts. Those assigned to the control group were asked what the percentage of Blacks on the bench is, and what the percentage of Blacks in the population is. The results of these two questions are summarized in table 7.1.

There are two significant patterns in the control group. First, all three demographic groups overestimated the percentage of Blacks in the population by about 10 points. Second, while whites gave fairly accurate numbers for the percentage of Blacks on the bench, Blacks underestimated the figure. This is the exact opposite of the pattern we observed of the control group in the gender experiment (in which all groups seemed to know the approximate percentage of women in the population, but not the percentage of women on the bench). But, as with the gender experiment, all demographic groups believe that Blacks (like women) are under-represented on the bench to a far greater degree than is actually the case. All of the experiment participants were exposed to reports that showed Blacks to be better represented on the bench than they likely predicted before the experiment. In other words, the amount of racial diversity exceeded the subjects' a priori expectations.

Hypotheses

If Blacks' support for the courts does not rise as racial diversity rises, then the theory of descriptive race representation is seriously undermined. Moreover, such a finding would contradict President Clinton's claims that the courts must look like America in order for minorities to feel that the country's judicial institutions are legitimate. On the other hand, evidence that the courts' legitimacy levels rise among Blacks as the percentage of Blacks on the bench rises would support the central hypothesis of this book: that diversity increases legitimacy. We will also look to see whether levels of legitimacy for whites fall under conditions of growing African American representation on the courts. Such a reaction would suggest a white backlash to Democrats' diversity efforts in the judicial appointment process. The lack of such evidence would undermine Republicans' claims that diversity initiatives delegitimize the government.

The mock news articles used in this experiment suggest that judicial diversity may be the result of a quota-based affirmative action plan. This is so because I compare the percentage of Blacks on the bench to the percentage of Blacks in the population, two numbers that would be needed were the president to implement a racial quota. Given the racial divide between support and opposition for affirmative action, I hypothesize as follows:

H1: Whites *will* confer lower levels of legitimacy on the courts (compared to the untreated group) as Black representation on the bench grows larger.
H2: Blacks *will* confer higher levels of legitimacy on the courts (compared to the untreated group) as Black representation grows larger.

Regression Models

I begin with table 7.2, the least squares regression model in which Blacks serve as the baseline—the model that stands as our best direct test of

TABLE 7.2 Least Squares Regression Results, Legitimacy Levels of U.S. Courts, by Treatment x Subject's Race, Blacks as Baseline

	B	St. Error
Blacks in Untreated Group	3.43***	.33
Blacks × Treatment Groups		
Under-Rep	.21	.24
Over-Rep	.60**	.24
Whites in Untreated Group	.94***	.25
Minority (Not Black) in Untreated Group	−.23	.68
Party Identification	−.20**	.09
Income	.01	.05
Education	.15**	.07
N = 186		
F(11, 172) = 3.41***		
R-squared = .18		

***$p \leq .001$; **$p \leq .05$; *$p \leq .10$ (two-tailed test)
Full model set forth in appendix table C.4

the theory of descriptive race representation. If greater racial diversity in our institutions leads to greater legitimacy for that institution among African American citizens, then I would see positive and statistically significant coefficients for the over-representation treatment. I have such evidence here.

Looking at the results, I first note Black respondents in the untreated group have a legitimacy score almost an entire point (.94) less than whites in the control group. This is consistent with the theory of descriptive representation because it shows Blacks to have much lower trust in the courts than do whites, all else being equal. With significantly lower baseline legitimacy levels, there can be little doubt that descriptive representation for African Americans has the potential to equalize baseline legitimacy rates of Blacks and whites. This finding also provides support for the Democrats' argument that descriptive representation is necessary because formerly marginalized groups suffer from low legitimacy levels toward our American institutions. This is exactly the type of result Democrats predicted would occur when Democratic presidents chose an appointment selection method that tries to build legitimacy of marginalized groups.

Also consistent with my hypothesis, Blacks who received the over-representation condition accord significantly higher levels of legitimacy for the U.S. courts than do those in the control group. The magnitude of the coefficient (.60) is more than a half point higher on a one to seven legitimacy scale, or a 7 percent increase in legitimacy levels of the courts. And, the coefficient is statistically significant. As racial diversity on the bench rises, so do the courts' legitimacy levels among Blacks. This finding is consistent with President Clinton's motto that the courts must "look like America" in order to make the courts more legitimate in the eyes of African Americans and other marginalized groups like LatinX, Asians, and women.[10]

It should be noted that party identification, education, and income are all statistically significant predictors of legitimacy levels. As an individual becomes more Republican, the lower his or her legitimacy score

TABLE 7.3 Least Squares Regression, Legitimacy of U.S. Courts, by Treatment × Race, Whites as Baseline

	B	St. Error
Whites in Untreated Group	5.12***	.32
Whites × Treatment Group		
Under-Rep	−.21	.24
Over-Rep	−.59**	.24
Blacks in Treatment Group	−.85***	.24
Minorities (not Black) in Treatment Group	−.92**	.67
Party Identification	−.19**	.09
Education	.13*	.07
Income	.03	.05
N = 186		
F(15,170) = 3.65**		
R-squared = .19		

***$p \le .001$; **$p \le .05$; *$p \le .10$ (two-tailed test)
Full model set forth in appendix table C.5

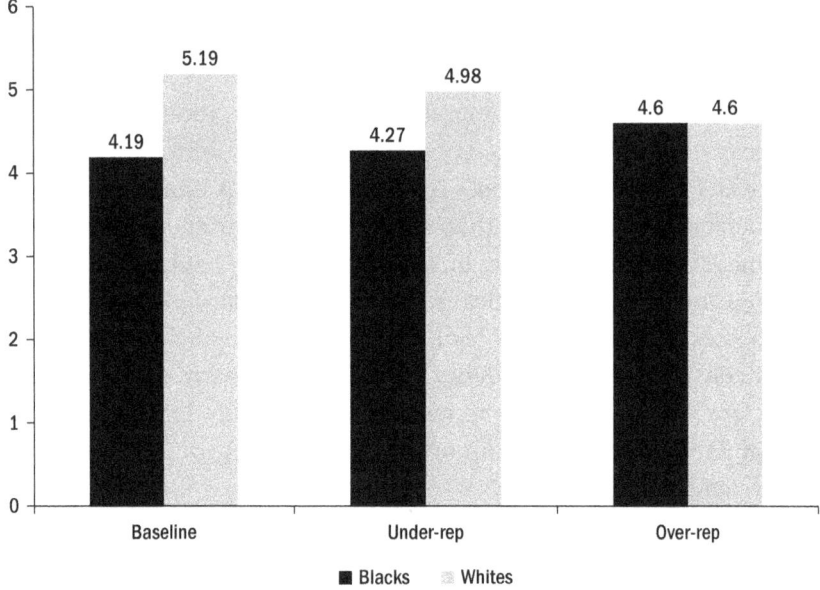

Figure 7.4. Estimated Legitimacy Scores for Blacks and Whites
Note: Moderate individuals with some college and $30,000–49,999 income

would be. For education, the more education one receives, the higher his or her legitimacy score. Similarly, for income, the more one earns, the higher the diffuse support for the courts.

Let us now turn to whites' reactions to a diverse court system in table 7.3, which I predicted would demonstrate decreased levels of legitimacy when Blacks are over-represented on the bench.

As predicted, there is strong evidence of backlash by whites when the courts are diversified and Blacks make up a sizable portion of the bench (23 percent in the experimental condition of over-representation). Based on psychological studies about in-groups and out-groups, it is not surprising that whites would feel threatened when African Americans become over-represented on the bench as it signals the end of white male dominance in the federal judiciary. As such, whites' legitimacy scores drop .59 points on the one to seven legitimacy scale, a 9.8 percent decrease. To the extent that whites are objecting to Blacks' over-representation, they do not appear troubled by their own over-representation on the bench for the past 230 years. Therefore, I would say this is just another avenue for whites to express their fear about too many Blacks being on the bench.

Finally, I want to present post-estimate analyses for the two main demographic groups we study throughout the book. I calculate the courts' legitimacy scores among whites and Blacks including their party identification, income, and education.[11] I set these variables at their medians (for education, the median was "some college"; for income, the median was $30,000–$49,900; for party identification, the median was Independent or moderate). Coding for these variables is provided in appendix A.

In the model with Blacks as the baseline, the condition of over-representation by Blacks on the bench produced a statistically significant and positive increase in legitimacy levels when compared to whites in the over-representation group. A Black person can expect a rise in legitimacy levels of .60 points. The opposite is true for a white person; under the condition of over-representation, legitimacy levels of the courts fall .59 points.

Conclusion

In sum, we have strong evidence that Blacks' legitimacy levels rise when Blacks are over-represented on the bench. This strongly supports the Democratic presidents' calls for racial diversity because it increases legitimacy among Blacks when Blacks are adequately represented on the bench. The findings can be interpreted to support the theory of descriptive representation because Black legitimacy scores rise when Blacks encounter the over-representation treatment. The findings also support the backlash theory, which we can detect by looking at the over-representation of Blacks on the bench and whites' precipitous drops in legitimacy levels. Thus, as was true of the gender data, the case of white and Black judges on the bench encapsulates the Diversity Dilemma.

8

Legitimacy and Descriptive/Substantive Representation

Scholars have theorized that descriptive representation, when coupled with substantive representation, is optimal for minorities and women (Mansbridge 1999). Descriptive representatives often have unique insights about the policy needs of the group to which they belong and are likely to approach decision-making with these insights in mind. The anticipated result is the creation of policies that better reflect the needs of the populace as a whole, and particularly those groups who have been previously marginalized (Pitkin 1967; Mansbridge 1999; Williams 1998). Even absent any evidence, whites believe Black judges and women to be more liberal (Lerman and Sadin 2016).

Empirical studies investigating descriptive representation have largely focused on changes in how people perceive the quality of representation based on the representative's race. For instance, Box-Steffensmeier and colleagues (2003) found that African Americans rate the performance of a Black congressman higher than that of a white congressman. However, two studies found that Black citizens with descriptive representatives do not believe the government to be more politically efficacious than when they are represented by a white representative (Banducci, Donovan, and Karp 2004; Tate 2004). More relevant to this study, Gay (2002) examined whether a descriptive race representative improves Blacks' "trust" in governmental institutions and the people who run them. She found no such relationship.

In recent years, numerous empirical studies have tried to determine whether descriptive representation in Congress leads to better substantive representation for previously disaffected groups. The answer has generally been "yes." For example, Wilson (2010) found that Latino representatives are more supportive of Latino interests than non-Latino representatives in terms of bill sponsorship. Here we can say that the descriptive representative leads to greater policy representation for Latinos (see also Haider-Markel, Joslyn, and Kniss 2000; Schwindt-Bayer and Mischler 2005; Sanbonmatsu 2003; Swers 2002). Mansbridge is very supportive of this theory:

> [T]he best way to have one's most important substantive interests represented is often to choose a representative whose descriptive characteristics match one's own on the issues one expects to emerge . . . [T]he best way to have one's most important substantive issues represented is often to choose a representative whose descriptive characteristics match one's own. (Mansbridge 1999, 634)

Analogizing legal decisions to legislative roll call votes, judicial politics scholars similarly find that, in certain types of cases, female judges vote differently than males, with female judges favoring the "pro-women" position more than their male counterparts (e.g., Boyd, Epstein, and Martin 2010). The example most often cited is when the case involves gender discrimination or sexual harassment; female judges are more sympathetic than male judges to these claims. This is also true of Black judges (Scherer 2004). So, if you are a supporter of descriptive race representation, increases in substantive representation on the bench can contribute to more favorable evaluations of the political institution's policy outputs, as well as of the institution itself, by those who were once marginalized.

Scholars have recognized, however, that evaluations of an institution, as opposed to an individual, may vary in important ways. While citizens may favor the abstract goal of diversifying an institution or seeing women hold elective office, that general support does not always translate into a willingness to vote for a specific female candidate. For example, Sanbonmatsu and Dolan (2008) find that while there is broad support for increased gender descriptive representation, most individuals—men and women—consider the "best government" to be majority male. With respect to descriptive race representation, Gay (2002) finds that, for Blacks, there is not a strong link between descriptive representation and evaluations of people's congresspersons. She also discovered that whites with minority representatives assess their congresspersons less favorably than Blacks do.

With this in mind, I hypothesize that:

H1: Blacks *will* accord greater legitimacy (more agreement with the search and seizure decision) to the courts compared to whites when they see that a Black judge issued the ruling.
H2: Whites *will* accord less legitimacy (less agreement with the search and seizure decision) to the courts compared to Blacks when they see a Black judge issued the ruling.
H3: White men *will* accord less legitimacy (less agreement with the search and seizure decision) to the courts compared to Blacks when a Black judge issued the ruling.

Control Group

To begin, we must compare Blacks' and whites' baseline levels of support for the search-and-seizure decision described in this experiment (the judge excluded evidence against a suspected drug dealer because the police had obtained it via a legally dubious search). The subjects in the control group did not know whether the presiding judge was Black, white, or any other race because their mock newspaper articles did not include a picture, so the subjects' only focus was whether they agreed or disagreed with the substance of the judge's ruling. Figure 8.1 shows the results for each race's specific support levels for the decision. Higher numbers indicate more agreement with the outcome of the case.

Do Blacks have more support for the racially charged decision than whites do? Forty-five percent of whites strongly disagreed with the search and seizure decision compared to only 19 percent of Blacks. At the other end of the spectrum, 20.5 percent of Black participants strongly agreed with the decision compared to 5 percent of whites. Overall, Blacks had more support than whites for the search and seizure decision.

Now I turn to hypotheses testing for the entire sample of subjects. As we can see in table 8.1, the coefficients for the treatment conditions—Black judge and white judge—are not statistically significant.

Therefore, I cannot reject the null hypothesis, which states that there is no relationship between the race of the presiding judge and level of agreement among Blacks. Only the race of the subject, and her party identification, income, and education, are statistically significant

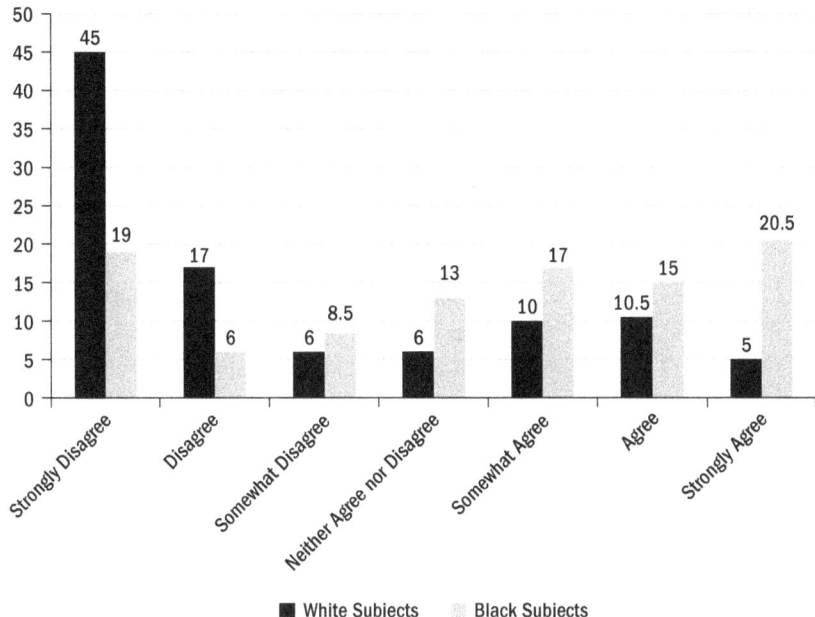

Figure 8.1. Black and White Support for Search and Seizure Decision (Control Group Only)

TABLE 8.1 Weighted Least Squares Regression, Support for Decision Finding an Illegal Search, by Race of Subject × Race of Judge, Blacks as Baseline

	B	St. Error
Blacks in Untreated Group	5.38***	.97
Blacks × Treatment Groups		
White Judge	.12	1.29
Black Judge	−.39	1.65
Whites in Untreated Group	−1.68*	.95
Minority (Not Black) in Untreated Group	−1.24	.97
Party Identification	−.49***	.08
Income	−.05**	.02
Education	.17***	.05
N = 786		
$F(11, 774) = 8.53$***		
R-squared = .11		

Statistical significance: *$p \leq .10$; **$p \leq .05$; ***$p \leq .001$ (two-tailed test).
Full model is set forth in appendix table C.6

predictors of legitimacy levels following a search and seizure decision. More education means higher levels of agreement with the search and seizure decision. For party identification, the more Republican one becomes, the less likely the person will agree with the liberal-leaning decision. For income, more earnings mean less support for the decision. This makes sense because high incomes are usually tied to the Republican Party. In sum, neither of the experimental treatments rose to statistically significant levels. The race of the judge deciding the case was of no moment to African Americans assessing the search and seizure decision.

While the race of the judge has no statistically significant impact on Blacks' support for a racialized case, race of the subject has a large and statistically significant effect on agreement scores. White subjects had lower baseline support for the decision compared to the control group by 1.68 points on the seven-point scale, 28 percent lower than Blacks. Since I hypothesized that the Black judge coefficient would be positive for Black subjects, and the white judge negative, such a result did not occur. In fact, the findings had signs in the opposite direction as hypothesized.

Now we will look at how whites respond to the race of the judge in a search and seizure case. In table 8.2, we see that whites' levels of agreement with the search and seizure decision go down when the presiding judge is Black, once again displaying white backlash against Black judges.

Whites who read about a liberal search and seizure ruling by a Black judge saw their agreement levels drop .35 points below the baseline of 3.65. This means that whites went from "neither agree nor disagree" in the control group (coded four) to "somewhat disagree" under the Black judge treatment (coded five on the one to seven agreement scale). I can thus reject the null hypothesis that there is no relationship between race of the judge and a person's evaluation of the decision.

The treatment with the white judge shows a coefficient with the same negative sign and practically the same magnitude as we saw for the Black judge coefficient; unlike the Black judge coefficient, the white judge coefficient does not rise to the level of statistical significance ($p = .13$). To whites, letting a Black man go free for a violation of his Fourth Amendment rights might seem like the defendant in the criminal case is getting off on a "technicality" and thus, they exhibit lower levels of support for the ruling.

TABLE 8.2 Weighted Least Squares Regression, Support for Decision Finding Illegal Search, by Race of Subject × Race of Judge, Whites as Baseline

	B	St. Error
Whites in Untreated Group	3.65***	.28
Whites × Treatment		
White Judge	−.31	.20
Black Judge	−.35*	.19
Black Subject in Untreated Group	.81**	.32
Minority (not Black) in Untreated Group	.11	.27
Party Identification	−.46***	.08
Education	.17**	.05
Income	−.05**	.02
N= 786		
F(11, 774) = 8.24***		
R-squared = .10		

Statistical significance: *$p \leq .10$; **$p \leq .05$; ***$p \leq .001$ (two-tailed test).
Full model is set forth in appendix table C.7

We now consider how white men perceive Black and white judges when they are ruling in a racialized case such as this one. White male subjects, as we saw in chapter 6, are more susceptible to feelings of backlash when a judge seems to be favoring the out-group compared to the in-group.

Like the previous model, table 8.3 also indicates backlash, but to a much greater degree than we saw in the whites as baseline model. To put it simply, a white man who does not know the race of the judge when reading about a search and seizure case in the newspaper (the baseline group) agrees with the decision at 3.63 points on the one to seven point scale. Simply by finding out that the decision was made by a Black judge lowers white men's agreement levels by .54 points, a 9 percent drop on the one to seven scale. That brings down white men's legitimacy scores from 3.63 to 3.09. This means that white men go from "neither agree nor disagree" with the decision (rounding up the 3.63 level to 4.0), to "somewhat disagree" with the decision (rounding down 3.03 to 3.0). These results are set forth in figure 8.2.

TABLE 8.3. Weighted Least Squares Regression, Support for Decision Finding Police Illegally Searched Alleged Drug Dealer, by Race of the Subject × Race of the Judge, White Men as Baseline

	B	St. Error
White Men in Untreated Group	3.63***	.31
White Men × Treatment		
White Judge	−.06	.28
Black Judge	−.54**	.25
Blacks in Untreated Group	1.06*	.40
Women in Untreated Group	.02	.22
Minorities (not Black) in Untreated Group	.10	.27
Party Identification	−.46***	.08
Education	.16***	.05
Income	−.05**	.02
N = 786		
$F(17, 768) = 5.79^{***}$		
R-squared = .11		

Statistical significance $*p \leq .10$; $**p \leq .05$; $***p \leq .001$ (two-tailed test)
Full model set forth in Appendix table C.8

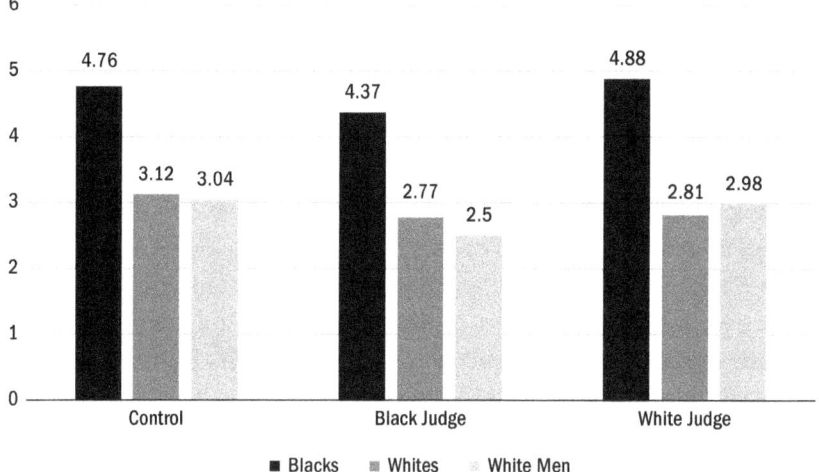

Figure 8.2 Predicted Levels of Support for Decision by Race of Subject and Race of Judge

Figure 8.2 shows predicted values of support for each one of the following groups: whites, Blacks, and white men.

In this figure, we see that Blacks did not respond to the two treatments in the experiment. Apparently, Blacks are more interested in the substance of the decision rather than the race of the presiding judge. Whites, on the other hand, lose trust in the decision when there is a Black judge as opposed to a white judge. Legitimacy scores drop by .35 points on the legitimacy scale. I note that when whites see a white judge make the same substantive decision, legitimacy levels decrease by .31 points on the scale. That finding, however, is not statistically significant. For white men, when they observe a Black judge deciding a pro-defendant case, agreement levels drop .54 points, much more than we saw for whites in the aggregate.

Conclusion

In the descriptive/substantive race representation experiment, the criminal procedure case was highly supported by Blacks whether or not there is a Black judge. This does not support President Obama's claim that minorities need diversity on the bench so that there are "empathetic" voices on the Court. Had the white judge ruled in a conservative manner, then I suspect Blacks' displeasure with the decision would show lower agreement scores. But all that means is that Blacks prefer a substantive-agreeable decision no matter what the race of the judge is. White men, on the other hand, do display backlash for a pro-criminal decision made by a Black judge compared to white judges.

9

Legitimacy and Party Identification

In this chapter, I explore the relationship between an individual's party identification and the legitimacy level they accord the courts. A consideration of this relationship raises two questions: (1) does party identification, as a stand-alone variable, contribute to one's feelings about the legitimacy of our courts?; and (2) does party identification, interacted with the treatment variables, produce different results than those we saw in chapters 6 and 8? In other words, does one's party affiliation, in part, drive legitimacy scores, along with the treatment condition?

The Role of Party Identification in Determining Legitimacy Levels of Mass Public

In *Scoring Points* (2006), I demonstrated that Democratic and Republican *party elites* pay close attention to judicial appointees at all levels of the federal hierarchy. Democratic Party elites demand, among other things, a commitment to *Roe v. Wade*,[1] and that the appointees reflect the diversity of the U.S. population. By committing to diversity on the bench, a Democratic president "scores points" with his party and activist elites who care very much about this issue; they in turn mobilize key Democratic Party constituents on Election Day. These activists are key to the Democratic Party's success at the polls. We also saw in chapters 2 and 3 that Democratic presidents alone prioritize diversity in making judicial appointments. For elites, we need only know the person's party identification to know how that person will react to greater diversity on the bench. As a reminder, Republicans reject diversity as an appropriate goal of judicial selection because it allegedly overtakes merit as a top priority for picking judges; it stigmatizes minorities who are ultimately chosen for the bench; and it amounts to reverse discrimination against whites. But does party identification impact the mass public the same way it impacts party elites? Do Democratic citizens have more support for the Courts when diversity is high? Could it be that the more associated with the Republican Party a person is, the less support he or she will have for the courts when diversity on the bench increases? This would suggest that, along with gender and treatment group, the more Republican a person becomes, the more resentful he or she would be of large percentages of diverse judges on the federal bench, which threaten his or her former status as the majority.[2]

Descriptive Gender Representation and Party Identification

The first set of models I examine uses the same data set I used in chapter 6, only this time the experimental treatment, gender, *as well as* party identification, will be the key variables standing alone and in combination. I want to know how party identification in conjunction with the treatment conditions and gender affects legitimacy scores for the courts.

Gibson and Nelson's (2019) book, which studies aspects of legitimacy of the Supreme Court among Black citizens, provides some insight. They found that party identification is a statistically significant predictor of group identification for African Americans. Another study gives us reason to believe that Democrats are more in favor of achieving gender equity in our political institutions than are Republicans and Independents (Karpowitz, Monson, and Preece 2017). For my study, I would expect to find that, for women and African Americans, party affiliation plays a pivotal role in organizing voters' feelings about diversity, including feelings about affirmative action (Edsall and Edsall 1991).

Hypotheses

Based on the findings reported in Chapters 6, I proffer the following hypotheses:

H1: As one becomes more Republican, he will accord less legitimacy to the U.S. courts.
H2: As a woman becomes more Republican, she will accord less legitimacy to the U.S. courts.
H3: As a man becomes more Republican, he will accord less legitimacy to the U.S. Courts

Before turning to the models with the three-way interaction terms (gender × party identification × treatment), I first want to review some descriptive characteristics about the relationship with the courts' legitimacy. This data set is a national random sample, which allows me to make comparisons to the general population. I first test for any relationship between party identification and legitimacy, without regard to gender, for those subjects in the untreated group.

Table 9.1 shows that party identification has a statistically significant impact on the courts' legitimacy levels among the mass public. As expected, the more Republican one gets, the lower her feelings of legitimacy for the courts. Because party identification has three values (one, two, or three), a Republican's (coded three) legitimacy scores would be .44 points less than a Democrat's (coded one) on the one to seven legitimacy scale.

Tables 9.2 and 9.3 will tell us whether party identification's impact is different for women versus men. In table 9.2, we glean from these results that party identification, as a stand-alone variable, is not a significant factor for women when calculating their feelings of legitimacy about the courts. Party identification impacts Republican women and Democratic women in the same way (.04 point difference).

Let us now look at whether party identification impacts the courts' legitimacy among men. Table 9.3 demonstrates that party identification is a relatively large and statistically significant predictor of legitimacy scores among men. The coefficient for party identification is negative, which tells us that, for men, the more Republican a man gets, the lower the courts' legitimacy levels will be. Republican men will have lower legitimacy levels by .74 points on the one-to-seven scale compared to Democrats [(3 × −.37 for Republicans) and (1 × −.37 for Democrats)]. For Democratic men, the courts' legitimacy drops .37 points on the legitimacy scale, while Republican males drop 1.11 points on the scale, a .74 difference on the legitimacy scale (about an 18 percent decline).

I also want to note that men have higher baseline legitimacy scores than women by .88 points on the one to seven legitimacy scale. This is as expected, since the theory of descriptive representation rests on the assumption that women and minorities, previously marginalized groups, have lower legitimacy levels than men. Introducing descriptive

TABLE 9.1. Weighted Least Squares Regression, Legitimacy Levels of U.S. Courts, by Party Identification, Control Group Only

	B	St. Error
Baseline	5.33**	.19
Party Identification	−.22***	.09
N = 185		
$F(1, 183) = 5.70$**		
R=squared = .03		

Statistical significance *$p \leq .10$; **$p \leq .05$; ***$p \leq .001$ (two-tailed test)

TABLE 9.2. Weighted Least Squares Regression Results, Legitimacy Levels of U.S. Courts, by Party Identification, Control Group Only, Women as Baseline

	B	St. Error
Women in Untreated Group	4.88***	.28***
Party Identification of Women	−.04	.14
Men in Untreated Group	.88**	.38
Party Identification × Men	−.33*	.18
N = 186		
$F(4,181) = 3.80$**		
R = squared = .06		

Statistical significance *$p \leq .10$; **$p \leq .05$; ***$p \leq .001$ (two-tailed test)

TABLE 9.3. Weighted Least Squares Regression Results, Legitimacy Levels of U.S. Courts, by Party Identification, Control Group Only

	B	St. Error
Men in Untreated Group	5.75***	.26
Party Identification	−.37**	.12
Women	−.85**	.38
Party Identification × Women	.33*	.18
N = 185		
$F(3,181) = 3.68$**		
R = squared = .06		

Statistical significance *$p \leq .10$; **$p \leq .05$; ***$p \leq .001$ (two-tailed test)

representation in the institution is said to raise legitimacy scores of these formerly marginalized groups.

I now turn to two models, one in which women are the baseline and one for men as the baseline. The results of these models are set forth in tables 9.4 and 9.5. These models are identical to those set forth in chapter 6, with one big exception. Since there is a chance that subjects' levels of legitimacy as seen in chapter 6 were driven in part by their party affiliation, rather than merely the experimental conditions, there is a possibility that the results would change if I were to interact gender x treatment x party identification. For instance, Republicans may assume that female judges will be more liberal than male judges, and because they want conservative courts, the Republicans do not support descriptive representation for women (Jacobsmeier 2015). We already know that people believe women judges to be more liberal than men (Welch 1985). In other words, it may not be opposition to diversity efforts (seeing them as a quota system), but rather, opposition to more liberal courts that drives legitimacy levels for Republican and Democratic subjects. In the models here we want to look for whether there is a statistically significant coefficient for the party identification interaction term. This would suggest that fluctuations in legitimacy scores are not gleaned entirely from the treatment variable standing alone.

In Table 9.4., the results indicate that party identification does not mediate women's views of the experimental treatments (the coefficient is also negligible at -.07). None of the coefficients for party identification × treatment × gender are statistically significant, indicating that party identification does not change the impact of the treatment coefficients on women's legitimacy levels. Next we review whether men's party identification produces statistically significant results.

Only one of the three-way party identification interaction terms is statistically significant—the 28 percent condition (the bench is comprised of 28% women). This means that when men encounter this treatment, male Republicans' legitimacy scores rise by .26 × 3 (for Republican) or .78 points on the one to seven legitimacy scale. This makes sense, because we saw in chapter 6 that men's legitimacy scores are at their highest when women are under-represented on the bench. For the

TABLE 9.4. Weighted Least Squares Regression Results, Legitimacy Levels of U.S. Courts, by Party Identification × Gender, Women as Baseline

	B	St. Error
Women in Untreated Group	4.24***	.27
Women × Treatment		
12%	−.19	.35
28%	−.15	.34
40%	.01	.34
51%	.01	.34
60%	−.34	.26
Women × Party Identification	−.07	.12
Party Identification × Woman × Treatment		
12%	.20	.17
28%	.12	.17
40%	.06	.17
51%	.13	.17
60%	.15	.17
Men in Untreated Group	.71**	.36
Income	.03**	.01
Education	.16***	.02
N = 1,186		
(25, 1,160) = 5.22***		
R-squared = .10		

***$p \leq .001$; **$p \leq .05$; *$p \leq .10$ (two-tailed test)
Full model set forth in appendix table C.9

most part, however, party identification × gender and × treatment had no meaningful impact on the subjects' feelings about the courts.

Collectively, these gender findings suggest that legitimacy for the courts is driven in part by party identification standing alone. In combination with the treatment and gender, however, party identification adds nothing to the models. These findings are the opposite of what we would expect of elites in the major parties. For elites, knowing one's party affiliation can predict whether the subject supports or rejects greater gender diversity on the bench.

TABLE 9.5. Weighted Least Squares Regression, Legitimacy Levels of U.S. Courts, by Party Identification × Gender, Men as Baseline

	B	St. Error
Men in Untreated Group	4.98***	.26
Men × Treatment		
12%	.14	.37
28%	−.43	.35
40%	−.07	.34
51%	−.02	.39
60%	−.66*	.40
Party Identification	−.37***	.11
Party Identification × Men × Treatment		
12%	.07	.17
28%	.26*	.16
40%	.15	.16
51%	.01	.17
60%	.27	.17
Women in Untreated Group	−.87**	.36
Education	.16***	.02
N = 1,186		
F(25, 1160) = 5.28***		
R-squared = .10		

***$p \leq .001$; **$p \leq .05$; *$p \leq .10$ (two-tailed test)
Full model set forth in appendix table C.10

Descriptive/Substantive Race Representation and Party Identification

I now turn to the descriptive/substantive representation data discussed in chapter 8. As a reminder, I have three experimental treatments: one group received a mock newspaper article about a search and seizure decision with no picture, one received a mock newspaper article with a Black judge presiding over the same case, and one with a white judge presiding. These data also represent a random national sample.

Hypotheses

Based on the findings set forth in Chapter 8, I offer the following hypotheses:

H1: As a white person becomes more Republican, he will have less support for a finding of an illegal search.
H2: If a white person reads about a Black judge finding an illegal search, the more Republican he becomes, the less agreement he will have with the finding of an illegal search.
H3: If a white person reads about a white judge finding an illegal search, the more Republican he becomes, the more legitimacy he will accord the courts.

As I did with the descriptive gender representation data earlier in this chapter, I first want to see how party identification alone impacts the general public's levels of support for the specific decision. I focus only on the control group for this set of regression models.

Table 9.6 tells us that, for average Americans, party identification is a large and statistically significant predictor of substantive support scores (keeping in mind that the subjects in the control group read a mock newspaper story about a criminal decision suppressing evidence of a drug crime). The coefficient for party identification is in the predicted direction. Simply put, as one becomes more Republican, his support for a pro-defendant criminal decision declines. Now we shall look at whether party identification plays a larger role in calculating legitimacy for one race compared to another.

In table 9.7, we see a decline in support scores going from Democrat to Republican when Blacks are the baseline. In fact, support scores drop 1.67 points (or 23.8 percent) on the one to seven support scale when a white person encounters the same search and seizure decision that Blacks read. And, that coefficient is statistically significant at $p < .05$. This means there is a 24 percent decrease in support when comparing Blacks and whites. Party identification, however, is not statistically significant. Next we look at whites in the control group.

In contrast, with white subjects as the baseline, Table 9.8 shows us that, for whites, as party identification goes from Democrat to Republican,

TABLE 9.6. Weighted Least Squares Regression Results, Support for Decision Finding an Illegal Search, by Party Identification, Blacks as Baseline, Control Group Only

	B	St. Error
All Subjects in Untreated Group	3.32***	.41
Party Identification	−.55***	.14
Education	.17**	.08
Income	.03	.03
N = 302		
F(3, 298) = 8.21***		
R = squared = .08		

Statistical significance *$p \leq .10$; **$p \leq .05$; ***$p \leq .001$ (two-tailed test)

TABLE 9.7. Weighted Least Squares Regression, Support for Decision Finding an Illegal Search, by Party Identification × Race, Blacks as Baseline, Control Group Only

	B	St. Error
Blacks in Untreated Group	4.48***	.82
Blacks × Party Identification	−.72	.50
Whites in Untreated Group	−1.67**	.85
Minorities (not Black) in Untreated Group	−1.08	1.07
Income	.04	.03
Education	.16**	.08
N = 302		
F(7, 294) = 4.98***		
R = squared = .11		

Statistical significance *$p \leq .10$; **$p \leq .05$; ***$p \leq .001$ (two-tailed test)

legitimacy scores drop .72 points [(.36 × 3, for Republicans) minus (.36 × 1, for Democrats)]. This suggests that while Black Democrats and Republicans view the search and seizure decision the same way, white Democrats and Republicans do not.

Finally, we ask whether the three-way interaction terms, party identification x race x treatment (black judge or white judge) together have an impact on one's support for a substantive decision. First, I compare

TABLE 9.8. Weighted Least Squares Regression, Support for Decision Finding an Illegal Search, by Party Identification × Race, Blacks as Baseline, Control Group Only

	B	St. Error
Whites in Untreated Group	2.81***	.46
Whites × Party Identification	–.36**	.16
Blacks in Untreated Group	1.45	1.04
Other Minorities (Not Black) in Untreated Group	.60	.83
Education	.16**	.08
Income	.04	.03
N = 302		
F(7,294) = 4.99***		
R = squared = .11		

Statistical significance *$p \leq .10$; **$p \leq .05$; ***$p \leq .001$ (two-tailed test)

TABLE 9.9. Weighted Least Squares Regression, Support for Decision Finding Illegal Search, by Race of the Judge × Race of the Subject × Party Identification of Subject, Blacks as Baseline

	B	St. Error
Blacks in Untreated Group	5.71***	1.03
Black × Treatment		
Black Judge	–.74	1.71
White Judge	–.42	1.46
Blacks × Party Identification	–.75**	.26
Blacks × Party Identification × Treatment		
Black Judge	–.59	1.50
White Judge	.36	1.73
Whites in Untreated Group	–2.16	1.06
Minorities (not Black) in Untreated Group	–1.14	.97
Education	.17***	.05
Income	–.05**	.02
N = 786		
F(16, 769) = 6.34***		
R-squared = .12		

Statistical significance *$p \leq .10$; **$p \leq .05$; ***$p \leq .001$ (two-tailed test)
Full model set forth in appendix table C.11

TABLE 9.10. Weighted Least Squares Regression, Support for Decision Finding Illegal Search, by Race of the Judge × Race of the Subject × Party Identification of Subject, Whites as Baseline

	B	St. Error
Whites in Untreated Group	3.67***	.35
Whites × Treatments		
Black Judge	.01	.44
White Judge	−.82*	.45
Whites × Party Identification	−.47***	.13
Whites × Party Identification × Treatment		
Black Judge	−.18	.19
White Judge	.27	.20
Blacks in Untreated Group	.77	.62
Minorities (not Black) in Untreated Group	.04	.29
Education	.16***	.05
Income	−.05**	.02
N = 786		
F(16, 769) = 6.21***		
R-squared = .11		

Statistical significance $*p \leq .10$; $**p \leq .05$; $***p \leq .001$ (two-tailed test)
Full model set forth in appendix table C.12

Blacks' and whites' baseline levels of support for the search and seizure decision described in this experiment (the judge excluded evidence against a suspected drug dealer because the police had obtained the contraband via a legally dubious search). The subjects in the control group did not know whether the presiding judge was Black or white because their mock newspaper article did not include a picture; the subjects' only focus was on whether they agreed or disagreed with the substance of the judge's ruling. Tables 9.9 and 9.10 provide the results for each race's support levels of support for the search and seizure decision. Higher numbers indicate more support.

Comparing the results in the two tables, we see that the baseline levels of agreement with the search and seizure decision are much higher for Blacks than for whites (by 2.04 points (5.71 -3.67) on the one to seven agreement scale). Tables 9.9 and 9.10 also reveal that none of the three-way interaction terms are statistically significant. This means that, while party affiliation standing alone has a statistically significant impact on one's agreement with the mock case described in the treatments, party identification combined with the treatment and the subject's race does not have any meaningful impact. But, exactly as we observed in chapter 8, the interaction term white × treatment indicates that whites lose a tremendous amount of support for the search and seizure decision when a white judge rules in a pro-defendant manner.

In the end, for models measuring an individual's agreement with a racialized decision, I cannot reject the null hypotheses presented because none of the treatment × party identification × subject's race interaction terms are statistically significant. Therefore, the findings in chapter 8 concerning descriptive/substantive representation are not altered by virtue of adding the three-way interaction. This means that legitimacy scores (or agreement with the decision scores) do not reflect subjects' beliefs that more Blacks on the court means more Democratic/liberal rulings. Instead, the findings of chapter 8 prevail and subjects' legitimacy scores are driven, in part, by beliefs about descriptive/substantive representation. Blacks responded to the experimental stimuli based on adequate representation on the bench. Because none of the descriptive/substantive representation interaction coefficients are statistically significant, I do not present post-estimate analyses.

Conclusion

From my empirical results it appears that, for descriptive representation, party identification in combination with the experimental treatment conditions does not play much of a role in raising or lowering one's legitimacy for the courts. Standing alone, however, party affiliation is statistically significant. As an individual becomes more Republican, they have less legitimacy for the courts.

I also explored whether party identification was a driving force in calculating one's agreement with the search and seizure decision. As a stand-alone variable, party affiliation has a negative effect, which means that, as you become more Republican, your agreement with the underlying substantive decision (search and seizure) declines. When I interact race and party identification, for Blacks, party identification is not a statistically significant predictor of legitimacy scores. That is not surprising given that an overwhelming percentage of African Americans are Democrats. For whites, however, their levels of agreement with the underlying decision about searches and seizures is affected by the coefficient for race × party identification. But, keep in mind that party identification in these models was also statistically significant for whites, not Blacks.

Conclusion

The Legitimacy of the U.S. Courts Is under Attack

The courts are bulwarks of our Constitution and laws, and they depend on the public to respect their judgments and on officials to obey and enforce their decisions. Fear of personal attacks, public backlash, or enforcement failures should not color judicial decision-making, and public officials have a responsibility to respect courts and judicial decisions. Separation of powers is not a threat to democracy; it is the essence of democracy.
—Brennan Center for Justice 2017[1]

A well-known political scientist once remarked, "why do we [the Law and Courts discipline] worry about the courts' legitimacy so much?" My answer was that judges are unelected and thus do not get the regular infusion of legitimacy an elected congressperson or president would. The second reason, but unbeknownst to the scholar and me at that time, is that we would soon have a president who seriously jeopardized the legitimacy of our courts, leading his followers to feel unsure of the courts' authority.

The first sign that Trump would be hostile to the federal courts came during the 2016 presidential campaign. When a judge born in Indiana, Gonzalo Curiel, ruled against Trump in a class action suit for fraud against Trump University, Trump questioned the judge's ability to remain impartial, given his desire to build a wall between the United States and Mexico. Trump began calling Judge Curiel a "hater" who was being unfair to him because the judge was "Hispanic" (Totenberg 2016).

The Muslim Travel Ban

Then, once in office, Trump denounced the power of the federal courts to declare acts of the president unconstitutional. In a ruling by Judge James L. Robart of the Western District of Washington, Trump's travel ban on Muslim immigrants was stayed (Robbins 2017). President Trump denounced the ruling and referred to the judge as a "so-called judge" (Fuller 2017). He reiterated his hostility toward the courts when he said in a Tweet: "Just cannot believe a judge would put our country in such peril. If something happens, blame him and [the] court system. People pouring in. Bad!" (Bradford and Zeleny, quoting Trump, 2017).

Another judge who lifted the ban on immigration, John Derrick K. Watson of the District of Hawaii, later incurred the wrath of Trump: "Because the ban was lifted by a judge, many very bad and dangerous people may be pouring into our country. A terrible decision" (Ibid.). A subsequent tweet stated: "But courts seem to be so political and it would be so great for our justice system if they would be able to read a statement and do what's right. And that has to do with the security of our country" (Shuham 2017). All of these statements, portraying judges as incompetent and directly responsible for any terrorist attacks on our country by Muslim immigrants, de-legitimize judges and courts and would cause an increase in physical attacks on judges by Trump supporters.

Asylum at the Southern Border Ban

Judge Emmet Sullivan of the D.C. federal district court, also blocked enforcement of Trump's order denying asylum protection to migrants who claim they are fleeing gang violence or domestic abuse; a White House statement blasted Sullivan's decision as "the latest example of judicial activism" (Irons 2019). Irons goes on to state:

> No institution can long survive the gradual erosion and crumbling of its bedrock foundation, the public's perception of its legitimacy. A court seen as overly partisan and result-driven would erode that legitimacy.[2]

In October 2018, Justice Elena Kagan, a reliable "liberal" vote on the bench, made this plea at a Princeton conference: "All of us . . . need to realize how precious the Court's legitimacy is. It's an incredibly important thing for the Court to guard this reputation of being impartial, being neutral and not simply being an extension of a polarizing process" (Speech given at Princeton University, cited in Rubin 2018).

Attacks on the Ninth Circuit

Former President Trump laid the largest blame for his court losses on the Ninth Circuit, which he claimed is out of step with the American public. When a court of appeals judge, Judge Jon S. Tigar of the Northern District of California, stayed enforcement of Trump's asylum ban (those crossing the Southern border into the United States temporarily could not petition for asylum), Trump erupted, tweeting the following: "We need to get rid of chain migration. We need to get rid of catch and release and visa lottery. And we have to do something about asylum. And to be honest with you, you have to get rid of judges." He continued:

> This was an Obama judge. And I'll tell you what, it's not going to happen like this anymore . . . . Everybody that wants to sue the United States, they file their case in—almost—they file their case in the Ninth Circuit. And it means an automatic loss no matter what you do, no matter how good your case is. . . . We will win that case in the Supreme Court of the United States.[3]

This tweet led to a harsh rebuke of Trump by Chief Justice John Roberts: "We do not have Obama judges or Trump judges, Bush judges or Clinton judges. What we have is an extraordinary group of dedicated judges doing their level best to do equal right to those appearing before them." In response, Trump tweeted: "Sorry Chief Justice John Roberts, but you do indeed have 'Obama judges,' and they have a much different point of view than the people who are charged with the safety of our country. It would be great if the Ninth Circuit was indeed an 'independent judiciary.'"

Trump also threatened the Ninth Circuit by hinting he would split the circuit into two or three circuits, thus undermining the independence of the Ninth Circuit: "79 percent of these [Ninth Circuit] decisions have been overturned. . . . It has become a dumping ground for certain lawyers looking for easy wins and delays. Much talk about dividing up the Ninth Circuit into two or three circuits. Too big!"

DACA

The judiciary suffered two separate attacks by Trump, who was trying to undermine the legitimacy of the courts rendering pro-DACA (Deferred Action for Childhood Arrivals Program). In the first instance, in 2018, District Court Judge William Alsup of the Northern District of California held that Trump's plan to dismantle the DACA program would be blocked until a full trial on the merits could be heard.

> It just shows everyone how broken and unfair our court system is when the opposing side in a case (such as DACA) "almost always win[s] before being reversed by higher courts." (Brennan Center 2017, quoting Trump 2018)[4]

But that was not the last word in the DACA case. On June 18, 2020, the Supreme Court ruled that the Trump administration would not be permitted to implement its change to the immigration laws (ending DACA) without following the proper procedures. The case was then sent back to the lower courts for further consideration. To this decision Trump responded:

> These horrible & politically charged decisions coming out of the Supreme Court are shotgun blasts into the face of people that are proud to call themselves Republicans or Conservatives . . . . We need more Justices or we will lose our 2nd. Amendment & everything else. Vote Trump 2020! (Neidig, quoting Trump, 2020)[5]

The Roger Stone Case

In this case, long-time Trump confidante, Roger Stone, was indicted for obstructing a congressional investigation, lying to investigators, and trying to block the testimony of a witness who would testify against him, among other things. On November 15, 2019, Stone was convicted of witness tampering and making false statements to the House Intelligence

Committee, all felony convictions. Here is what Trump had to say on Twitter about the jury's forewoman:

> There has rarely been a juror so tainted as the forewoman in the Roger Stone case. Look at her background. She never revealed her hatred of "Trump" and Stone. She was totally biased, as is the judge. Roger wasn't even working on my campaign. Miscarriage of justice. Sad to watch! (Martin, quoting Trump, 2020)[6]

Legitimacy is just as threatened when the president undermines the fairness of the jury verdict as when the president challenges the decisions of sitting judges. Here, we see the president engage in both of these de-legitimizing acts. After the district court judge, Amy Berman Jackson, sentenced Stone to three years and four months, Trump again turned to Twitter, to undermine the legitimacy of the court, as he implies that Judge Jackson has it in for all Trump advisors:

> Is this the Judge that put Paul Manafort in SOLITARY CONFINEMENT, something that not even mobster Al Capone had to endure? How did she treat Crooked Hillary Clinton? Just asking! (Ruger 2020)

He soon followed up with a series of tweets, quoting a Fox News analyst suggesting that any other judge would acquiesce to calls for a new trial based on alleged statements made by the jury foreperson, but "I'm not so sure about Judge Jackson, I don't know."

* * *

At the outset of the book, I stated several goals I wanted to accomplish. First, answering the overriding question: Why do presidents diversify the courts? The answer to this question is found in three Democratic presidents' own words: They wanted to increase the levels of legitimacy that the U.S. courts enjoy among historically marginalized groups, which presumably accorded lower levels of legitimacy than do whites and white men. Notably, Republican presidents have never argued that diversity increases legitimacy.

This question leads to other related questions. How did diversity become such a partisan issue? Does empirical analyses of the various political claims by Democrats and Republicans confirm or refute the theories of descriptive and descriptive/substantive representation? Do we see a backlash by white men, as Republican presidents have claimed? Finally, does party identification impact one's legitimacy level, standing alone or in combination with the treatment groups?

The Partisan Divide over Diversity Appointment Strategies

Chapters 2 and 3 addressed this initial issue. The findings showed that Democrats and Republicans are sharply divided on the diversity issue. This was not always the case. Earlier in our history, both parties were guilty of ignoring minority and female candidates for the federal bench. And then there was Jimmy Carter, who made great strides in diversifying the U.S. courts. The reason the parties divided the way they did in the post-Carter era has to do with the parties' respective positions on affirmative action. As proponents of diversifying America in all aspects of life, Democrats favored use of affirmative action or any other outreach programs designed to recruit minorities and women, groups that suffer from lower legitimacy scores compared to whites and white men.

How Can Descriptive Representation Help Improve the Courts' Legitimacy?

The concept of descriptive representation is as old as our nation. The theory holds that, for members of formerly marginalized groups—presumed to have lower legitimacy levels because of their outsider status—matching the racial, gender, and ethnic makeup of our U.S. institutions to that of the population has the potential to raise low legitimacy levels. Prior to this study, those that looked at diversity in our political institutions relied on the theory of substantive representation. We know this because the dependent variables used in prior studies of both race (e.g., Gay 2002) and gender (Lawless 2004) relied on survey questions measuring short-term support for the institution (Gibson and Nelson 2015). Moreover, none of the studies previously conducted (but see Scherer and Curry 2010) addressed diversity's capability of raising legitimacy levels of the bench, something we should be concerned about given Trump's and some of his loyal followers' intentions to run for president in 2024.

The good news is that the theory's basic tenet, raising legitimacy levels for marginalized groups, had solid empirical support from the experimental survey responses analyzed here. Not only did we see lower baseline legitimacy levels for minorities and women, thus prompting the need for descriptive and descriptive/substantive representation, but also their legitimacy levels climb when given greater representation. The bad news is that whites, men, and white men all see decreases in legitimacy levels in the presence of higher levels of women and minorities. To those in the in-group, diversity presents a zero-sum game, with gains for minorities and women seen as setbacks for whites, men, and white men, who have long dominated the U.S. courts. That means that we have a diversity dilemma, as greater diversity for minorities and women leads to two polar responses, dependent on whether you are a member of a marginalized out-group or a privileged in-group. At first glance, it appears that a diversity appointment strategy cannot solve the problems of legitimacy for the courts because of the Diversity Dilemma. While the strategy can raise feelings of legitimacy, whites, men, and white men prefer that diversity for women and minorities stays at a low percentage. But, there are two arguments that may hold out hope for more diversity on the bench. In the gender models, men's and white men's legitimacy levels did not change at the mirror- or over-representation treatments. So, theoretically, a president could further diversify the bench and make minorities and women equal to their presence in the population without any backlash from the privileged groups. At the same time, women's legitimacy levels will rise. In addition, if whites and white men were opposing descriptive representation because of bigotry, then their position is illegitimate and diversity would then prevail. It is sometimes difficult to tell whether privileged groups oppose diversity on the grounds usually cited (badge of inferiority, less qualified judges, and reverse discrimination). But, it may be safe to say that Trump is a racist and therefore he did not, and would not, appoint minorities and women to the bench in numbers remotely close to that of white men.

How Can Descriptive/Substantive Representation Help Improve the Courts' Legitimacy?

Scholars have theorized that long-term agreement with the Supreme Court's specific decisions leads to higher legitimacy levels (Mondak 1993). Here, I tried to test whether the race of a judge standing alone can sway public opinion about the correctness of the decision. In other words, could a Black judge raise minorities' agreement when they see that a Black judge presides over the case's decision? At the same time, could a Black judge's decision in a racially-charged case lower whites' level of agreement with the decision as a form of backlash? The empirical findings suggest that the race of the judge is irrelevant to minorities' levels of agreement with a racially charged decision; they care about substantive agreement, but not descriptive/substantive agreement. The race of the judge did not matter to the experimental subjects in terms of assessing the correctness of the mock judge's decision—with one important exception. For whites, we see a precipitous drop in agreement with the racial decision if the judge is Black. As was true for the descriptive representation models, here we see racial backlash, this time caused by a Black judge deciding a search and seizure case and ruling in favor of the minority's interest. For all other combinations for race of the judge/race of the subject, none were statistically significant.

Party Identification and Legitimacy

Finally, I tried to determine how one's party identification influences whether a person feels more or less legitimacy for the courts. Do Democrats in the mass public automatically support diversity the way Democratic elites do; do Republicans automatically reject diversity the way Republican elites do (Scherer 2005)? In order to determine the impact of party identification on legitimacy, I ran several models. First, party identification was included as an independent variable in all of my models. Party identification across the board was a statistically significant coefficient when assessing one's legitimacy. Moreover, party identification as a stand-alone variable told us that as one becomes more Republican, legitimacy levels fall. Given the nature of the experiment, in which subjects read about diversity on the courts, this finding is not surprising as Republicans, by definition, resist diversity on the courts while Democrats embrace it.

ACKNOWLEDGMENTS

I would like to thank the following people for their invaluable assistance on this manuscript: Brett Curry, my original partner in crime, Yaffa Fredrick and Joy Clark, two of the best students I ever had, and David Albert, Sara Benesh, Tom Burke, Lee Epstein, James Gibson, Ken Kersch, Matt Lavalle, Matt Pressman, Amy Steigerwalt, and my editor, Sonia Tsuruoka.

The quantitative research in this manuscript is based on work supported by a grant from the National Science Foundation (Grant No. SES-0960536). Any opinions, findings, conclusions, or recommendations expressed in this material are those of the author and do not necessarily reflect the views of the National Science Foundation.

APPENDIX A

Methods

APPENDIX A1

POPULATION SAMPLES

YouGov panel members are recruited by a number of methods, all designed to ensure diversity in the panel population. Recruiting methods include: Web advertising campaigns (public surveys), permission-based email campaigns, partner-sponsored solicitations, telephone-to-Web recruitment (Random Digit Dialing—RDD)-based sampling, and mail-to-Web recruitment (equivalent to voter registration–based sampling). Additionally, YouGov augments the panel with difficult to recruit respondents by soliciting panelists in telephone and mail surveys. In the fall and winter of 2006, YouGov completed telephone interviews using RDD sampling and invited respondents to join the online panel. Historically, by utilizing different modes of recruitment continuously, YouGov ensures that hard-to-reach populations will be adequately represented in survey samples. Participants were not paid to join the Polling Point panel, but they did receive incentives through a loyalty program to take individual surveys. All surveys are completed online with a computer given to the subjects by YouGov.

The two YouGov experiments (descriptive gender representation and substantive race representation) went into the field July 21–August 4, 2010. In the race/substantive experiment only, I obtained over-samples of African Americans so that I could draw firmer conclusions about Blacks and their feelings about diversity on the bench. The over-sample of 400 African Americans in the race survey was also drawn from YouGov previously recruited panel members, and those who were part of the over-samples were not permitted to participate in any other experiment.

The methods for recruiting the over-sample were the same as those for the principal sample.

The respondents in all experiments were matched on gender, age, race, education, political party identification, ideology and political interest (except for the over-sample of African Americans, who were not matched based on race). YouGov then weighted the matched sets of survey respondents to known marginals for the general population of the United States from the 2006 American Community Survey. The marginals for both data sets are set forth in appendix A2.[1]

APPENDIX A2

MARGINALS

Age: 18–34: 30.21%
   35–54: 39.69 %
   55+: 30.10%
Gender:
Male: 48.27%
Female: 51.73%
Race:
White/Other: 76.17%
Black: 11.06%
Hispanic: 12.77%
Education: HS or less: 46.36%
Some College: 28.63%
College Graduate: 16.15%
Post-graduate: 8.86%

APPENDIX A3

DEBRIEFING DOCUMENT

Principal Investigator: Dr. Nancy Scherer
Thank you for participating in this experiment. The full title of this research experiment is "Citizens' Perceptions of Justice in the U.S. Courts (The Impact of Racial Diversity on Citizens' Perceptions of Justice)." Some people have suggested that certain characteristics may influence the way in which the public evaluates judges and the decisions they make. Specifically, it has been argued that the amount of racial diversity

among U.S. judges may play an important role in structuring how the public views justice in the U.S. My experiment was designed to explore this possibility. The *Chicago Tribune* newspaper article I asked you to read was written in a way that allows me to explore the extent to which differences in the amount of racial diversity among judges may lead individuals to have different opinions about our legal system.

You should know that the *Chicago Tribune* article you read was not real. It was created by me. The actual percentage of African Americans in the U.S. courts today is approximately 8.6 percent, and the percentage of African Americans in the general population of the U.S. is approximately 12.3 percent. While we don't like to mislead people deliberately, in order for an experiment to be an effective form of research, we sometimes need to control the information that participants see. This sometimes means that we have to make up content instead of using real material. I hope you understand why a little deception was necessary here in order for us to conduct the best possible examination of these ideas.

The reason I did not disclose that the experiment was specifically looking at issues dealing with racial diversity among judges is because, if participants are made aware of this fact, it may influence their answers to the survey.

I do not know if people's attitudes affect their perceptions of justice; this experiment will help me find out if this is true.

If you are in any way uncomfortable with participating in this experiment now that you know it was about the impact of racial diversity on citizens' perceptions of justice, you have the right to take back your survey and elect not to participate in the experiment.

Once again, I thank you very much for your willingness to help with this research. If you have any questions about this study, please feel free to contact me at the number below.

Nancy Scherer
Department of Political Science
Wellesley College
781-283-2209

APPENDIX A4

CODING OF SOCIO-DEMOGRAPHIC VARIABLES

FEMALE. This is a dummy variable where one indicates that the respondent identified her gender as female.

MALE. This is a dummy variable where one indicates that the respondent identified his gender as male.

LEVEL OF FEMALE REPRESENTATION ON THE BENCH. The Level of Female Representation on the Bench is a series of variables in which one indicates that the subject was assigned to a particular treatment group. People were randomly assigned to one of the five treatment groups or the control group. The five treatment groups were told that women comprise 12.0 percent, 28 percent, 40.0 percent, 51.0 percent, or 60.0 percent of the bench, and that women comprise 51.0 percent of the population. The sixth group, the control group, is also a dummy variable indicating that the respondent was given no information about diversity on the bench.

BLACK. This is a dummy variable indicating whether the respondent identified their race as Black.

WHITE. This is a dummy variable indicating whether the respondent identified their race as white.

LEVEL OF BLACK REPRESENTATION ON THE BENCH. The Level of Black Representation on the bench is a series of five dummy variables indicating to which of the five treatment groups the respondent was randomly assigned: 3.0 percent (under-representation) or 23.1 percent (over-representation). The third group, the control group, is a dummy variable indicating that the respondent was given no information about diversity on the bench.

PARTY IDENTIFICATION. Party Identification is first measured on a seven-point Likert scale on which one indicates that the subject considers themself to be "strongly Republican" and seven indicates the subject considers themself to be "strongly Democratic." After imputing missing values using the Amelia II program, this variable was then collapsed into three categories: Republican, Independent, or Democrat.

EDUCATION is measured on a six-point scale ranging from no high school to post-graduate work.

INCOME is measured on a 14-point scale ranging from less than $10,000.00 per household to more than $150,000.00 per household.
BLACK JUDGE indicates that a Black judge was pictured in the experimental treatment as having a Black judge preside over a drug case.
WHITE JUDGE indicates that a white judge was pictured in the experimental treatment as having a white judge preside over a drug case.
MINORITY (NOT BLACK) indicates whether a subject identified themself as a member of a minority race, but not African American. African Americans are accounted for in a separate variable in the models. Here, I am not trying to glean information about a particular minority; rather, I use this variable in the model so that minorities other than Blacks do not get aggregated with whites for purpose of the analysis and to avoid dropping any subjects from the analysis.

APPENDIX A5

NOTE ON QUESTION 1 ON GENDER SURVEY

The first question of the descriptive support surveys stated the following: "To what extent do you agree with the following statement: 'Claims of sex discrimination should be settled between employer and employee without involving the courts.'" The purpose of asking this question was to see how litigious the subject was and how useful they believed the courts could be in solving problems. Obviously, my use of "sex" discrimination litigation was not the optimal choice because it had the potential to prime the subjects, leading them to answer the rest of the questions—most important, those to be included in the dependent variable—with racial or feminist tensions on their minds.

In order to test whether this question, in fact, primed the subjects, I conducted an auxiliary experiment using the M-Turk platform available through Amazon. I conducted the exact same experiment as those administered to the national random sample survey, only this time I split the samples into two groups, one having the potential priming question on its survey and the other group not having that question on their survey. I also reduced the number of experimental conditions to three: control, under-representation, mirror-representation and over-representation. I summarize the results as follows. In terms of the gender discrimination experiment, there were no statistically significant differences in the means of the dependent variables with the question and those without the question. The same is true when the four conditions are interacted with gender. This was also true for men, women, white men, white women, Black men, and Black women. From this I conclude that the first question in the gender survey used here did not prime the subjects.

APPENDIX B

Mock Newspaper Articles

APPENDIX B1

Descriptive Gender Representation Experiment

Copyright 2010 Chicago Tribune

Chicago Tribune

chicagotribune.com

January 23, 2010

THE PERCENTAGE OF FEMALE JUDGES IS MUCH LESS THAN THE PERCENTAGE OF WOMEN IN THE U.S. POPULATION

The Administrative Office of the U.S. Courts (AO) yesterday released its annual report on the composition of the federal judiciary. The most notable aspect of this year's report was its finding that women still comprise a mere 12.0% of all judges currently hearing cases in the U.S. court system nationwide. This means that, of 1,284 federal court judges, 154 of them are women. This includes judges on the U.S. Supreme Court, the U.S. Courts of Appeals and the 94 U.S. District Courts.

The number of female federal court judges has remained steady over the past thirty years. As a result, the percentage of women currently serving as federal court judges remains the same as it was in 1980, and falls well below the percentage of women in the general population of the U.S. (which is 51.0%).

When asked to comment on the Report's findings about the current position of African American judges hearing cases in the federal courts, Director of the Administrative Office L. Ralph Mecham observed that, "The Report's results reflect little progress in bringing greater gender diversity to the federal courts."

Copyright 2010 Chicago Tribune

Chicago Tribune

chicagotribune.com

January 23, 2010

THE PERCENTAGE OF FEMALE JUDGES IN THE U.S. COURTS REMAINS LESS THAN THE PERCENTAGE OF WOMEN IN THE U.S. POPULATION

The Administrative Office of the U.S. Courts yesterday released its annual report on the federal courts. One of the most notable aspects of this year's report was its finding that women now comprise only 28.1% of all judges currently hearing cases in the U.S. court system nationwide. This means that, of 1,284 federal court judges, 361 of them are women. This includes judges on the U.S. Supreme Court, the 13 U.S. Courts of Appeals and the 94 U.S. District Courts.

The number of female federal court judges has increased over the past thirty years. Despite some gains, the percentage of women currently serving as federal court judges is still lower than the percentage of women in the general population of the U.S. (which is 51.0%).

When asked to comment on the Report's findings about the current position of female judges hearing cases in the federal courts, Director of the Administrative Office L. Ralph Mecham observed that, "The Report's results reflects some progress in bringing greater gender diversity to the federal courts."

Copyright 2010 Chicago Tribune

Chicago Tribune

chicagotribune.com

January 23, 2010, Monday, Final Edition

THE PERCENTAGE OF FEMALE JUDGES GROWS CLOSER TO THE PERCENTAGE OF WOMEN IN THE U.S. POPULATION

The Administrative Office of the U.S. Courts (AO) yesterday released its annual report on the composition of the federal judiciary. One of the most notable aspects of this year's report was its finding that women now comprise 40.0% of all judges currently hearing cases in the U.S. court system nationwide. This means that, of 1,284 federal court judges, 514 of them are women. This includes judges on the U.S. Supreme Court, the 13 U.S. Courts of Appeals and the 94 U.S. District Courts.

The number of female federal court judges has increased over the past thirty years. Despite some gains, the percentage of women currently serving as federal court judges is still lower than the percentage of women in the general population of the U.S. (which is 51.0%).

When asked to comment on the Report's findings about the current position of female judges hearing cases in the federal courts, Director of the Administrative Office L. Ralph Mecham observed that, "The Report's results reflect the steady progress that has been made in recent years in bringing greater gender diversity to the federal courts."

Copyright 2010 Chicago Tribune

Chicago Tribune

chicagotribune.com

January 23, 2010

THE PERCENTAGE OF FEMALE JUDGES MIRRORS THE PERCENTAGE OF WOMEN IN THE U.S. POPULATION

The Administrative Office of the U.S. Courts (AO) yesterday released its annual report on the composition of the federal judiciary. The most notable aspect of this year's report was its finding that women now comprise a sizable 51.0% of all judges currently hearing cases in the U.S. court system nationwide. This means that, of 1,284 federal court judges, 656 of them are women. This includes judges on the U.S. Supreme Court, the 13 U.S. Courts of Appeals and the 94 U.S. District Courts.

The number of female federal court judges has increased over the past thirty years. As a result of these gains, the percentage of women currently serving as federal court judges is exactly the same percentage of women in the general population of the U.S. (which is 51.0%).

When asked to comment on the Report's findings about the current position of female judges hearing cases in the federal courts, Director of the Administrative Office L. Ralph Mecham observed that, "The Report's results reflect the good progress that has been made in recent years in bringing greater gender diversity to the federal courts."

Copyright 2010 Chicago Tribune

Chicago Tribune

chicagotribune.com

January 23, 2010

THE PERCENTAGE OF FEMALE JUDGES IS MUCH GREATER THAN THE PERCENTAGE OF WOMEN IN THE U.S. POPULATION

The Administrative Office of the U.S. Courts (AO) yesterday released its annual report on the composition of the federal judiciary. The most notable aspect of this year's report was its finding that women now comprise a very sizable 60.0% of all judges currently hearing cases in the U.S. court system nationwide. This means that, of 1,284 federal court judges, 770 of them are women. This includes judges on the U.S. Supreme Court, the 13 U.S. Courts of Appeals and the 94 U.S. District Courts.

The number of female federal court judges has increased over the past thirty years. As a result of these gains, the percentage of women currently serving as federal court judges, for the first time, exceeds the percentage of women in the general population of the U.S. (which is 51.0%).

When asked to comment on the Report's findings about the current position of female judges hearing cases in the federal courts, Director of the Administrative Office L. Ralph Mecham observed that, "The Report's results reflect the great progress that has been made in recent years in bringing greater gender diversity to the federal courts."

APPENDIX B2

Descriptive Race Representation Experiment

Copyright 2010 Chicago Tribune

Chicago Tribune
chicagotribune.com

January 23, 2010, Monday, Final Edition

THE PERCENTAGE OF BLACK JUDGES IS MUCH LESS THAN THE PERCENTAGE OF BLACKS IN THE U.S. POPULATION

The Administrative Office of the U.S. Courts (AO) yesterday released its annual report on the composition of the federal judiciary. The most notable aspect of this year's report was its finding that African Americans still comprise 3.0% of all judges currently hearing cases in the U.S. court system nationwide. This means that, of 1,284 federal court judges, 39 of them are African Americans. This includes judges on the U.S. Supreme Court, the 13 U.S. Courts of Appeals and the 94 U.S. District Courts.

The number of Black federal judges has remained steady over the past thirty years. As a result, the percentage of African Americans currently serving as federal court judges remains the same as it was in 1980, and falls well below the percentage of African Americans in the general population of the U.S. (which is 13.5%).

When asked to comment on the Report's findings about the current position of African American judges hearing cases in the federal courts, Director of the Administrative Office L. Ralph Mecham observed that, "The Report's results reflect little progress in bringing greater racial diversity to the federal courts."

Copyright 2010 Chicago Tribune

Chicago Tribune

chicagotribune.com

January 23, 2010, Monday, Final Edition

THE PERCENTAGE OF BLACK JUDGES IN THE U.S. COURTS REMAINS LESS THAN THE PERCENTAGE OF BLACKS IN THE U.S. POPULATION

The Administrative Office of the U.S. Courts yesterday released its annual report on the federal courts. One of the most notable aspects of this year's report was its finding that African Americans now comprise approximately 8.6% of all judges currently hearing cases in the U.S. court system nationwide. This means that, of 1,284 federal court judges, 111 of them are African American. This includes judges on the U.S. Supreme Court, the 13 U.S. Courts of Appeals and the 94 U.S. District Courts.

The number of Black federal judges has increased over the past thirty years. Despite some gains, the percentage of African Americans currently serving as federal court judges is still lower than the percentage of African Americans in the general population of the U.S. (which is 13.5%).

When asked to comment on the Report's findings about the current position of African American judges hearing cases in the federal courts, Director of the Administrative Office L. Ralph Mecham observed that, "The Report's results reflect little progress in bringing greater racial diversity to the federal courts."

Copyright 2010 Chicago Tribune

Chicago Tribune

chicagotribune.com

January 23, 2010, Monday, Final Edition

THE PERCENTAGE OF BLACK JUDGES MIRRORS THE PERCENTAGE OF BLACKS IN THE U.S. POPULATION

The Administrative Office of the U.S. Courts (AO) yesterday released its annual report on the composition of the federal judiciary. The most notable aspect of this year's report was its finding that African Americans now comprise 13.5% of all judges currently hearing cases in the U.S. court system nationwide. This means that, of 1,284 federal court judges, 173 of them are African Americans. This includes judges on the U.S. Supreme Court, the 13 U.S. Courts of Appeals and the 94 U.S. District Courts.

The number of Black federal judges has increased over the past thirty years. As a result of these gains, the percentage of African Americans currently serving as federal court judges is exactly the same percentage of African Americans in the general population of the U.S. (which is 13.5%).

When asked to comment on the Report's findings about the current position of African American judges hearing cases in the federal courts, Director of the Administrative Office L. Ralph Mecham observed that, "The Report's results reflect the steady progress that has been made in recent years in bringing greater racial diversity to the federal courts."

Copyright 2010 Chicago Tribune

Chicago Tribune
chicagotribune.com

January 23, 2010, Monday, Final Edition

THE PERCENTAGE OF BLACK JUDGES IS MORE THAN THE PERCENTAGE OF BLACKS IN THE U.S. POPULATION

The Administrative Office of the U.S. Courts (AO) yesterday released its annual report on the composition of the federal judiciary. The most notable aspect of this year's report was its finding that African Americans now comprise 18.6% of all judges currently hearing cases in the U.S. court system nationwide. This means that, of 1,284 federal court judges, 239 of them are African Americans. This includes judges on the U.S. Supreme Court, the 13 U.S. Courts of Appeals and the 94 U.S. District Courts.

The number of Black federal judges has increased over the past thirty years. As a result of these gains, the percentage of African Americans currently serving as federal court judges, for the first time, exceeds the percentage of African Americans in the general population of the U.S. (which is 13.5%).

When asked to comment on the Report's findings about the current position of African American judges hearing cases in the federal courts, Director of the Administrative Office L. Ralph Mecham observed that, "The Report's results reflect the good progress that has been made in recent years in bringing greater racial diversity to the federal courts."

Copyright 2010 Chicago Tribune

Chicago Tribune
chicagotribune.com

January 23, 2010, Monday, Final Edition

THE PERCENTAGE OF BLACK JUDGES IS MUCH GREATER THAN THE PERCENTAGE OF BLACKS IN THE U.S. POPULATION

The Administrative Office of the U.S. Courts (AO) yesterday released its annual report on the composition of the federal judiciary. The most notable aspect of this year's report was its finding that African Americans now comprise 23.1% of all judges currently hearing cases in the U.S. court system nationwide. This means that, of 1,284 federal court judges, 297 of them are African Americans. This includes judges on the U.S. Supreme Court, the 13 U.S. Courts of Appeals and the 94 U.S. District Courts.

The number of Black federal judges has increased over the past thirty years. As a result of these gains, the percentage of African Americans currently serving as federal court judges, for the first time, exceeds the percentage of African Americans in the general population of the U.S. (which is 13.5%).

When asked to comment on the Report's findings about the current position of African American judges hearing cases in the federal courts, Director of the Administrative Office L. Ralph Mecham observed that, "The Report's results reflect the great progress that has been made in recent years in bringing greater racial diversity to the federal courts."

APPENDIX B3

DESCRIPTIVE/SUBSTANTIVE EXPERIMENT

Copyright 2010 Chicago Tribune

Chicago Tribune
chicagotribune.com

January 21, 2010, Final Edition

KEY EVIDENCE THROWN OUT IN DRUG CASE

Figure A.1. Photo of Judge A

A federal judge agreed to exclude evidence of 1 pound of cocaine in a local drug trial. The government says it cannot prosecute the case without the key drug evidence.

Two police officers were patrolling an area of Chicago's South Side (known for high rates of drug trafficking), and observed a man, Tyrell Washington, talking in a "huddle" formation with several other men. All of the men made "a lot of hand movements" inside the huddle. The officers claimed that, since they could not see what was in their hands, they decided to walk toward the group to investigate.

When Washington saw the officers coming, he immediately started running away. The officers then called out to Washington "Stop," but he kept running. When the officers finally caught Washington, they searched him and found 1 pound of cocaine in Washington's gym bag. Washington was charged with a federal drug crime.

The arresting officers argued that, considering all the facts available to them at the time they started to approach Washington—the "high crime" neighborhood, the huddled group of men, the suspicious hand movements, and the fact that Washington ran away from them—the officers had reason to believe that Washington was planning to commit a crime.

U.S. District Judge John Ferguson (pictured in figure A.1) ruled that, under the Fourth Amendment of the Constitution (which governs searches and seizures), the facts relied on by the police to justify their actions clearly did not provide a legal basis for searching Washington's gym bag. The judge then made several rulings. First, the drug evidence must be excluded at trial. Second, the government's case without the drug evidence was too weak to go to trial and must be dismissed. Finally, Washington was to be let free.

Copyright 2010 Chicago Tribune

Chicago Tribune
chicagotribune.com

January 21, 2010, Final Edition

KEY EVIDENCE THROWN OUT IN DRUG CASE

Figure A.2. Photo of Judge B

A federal judge agreed to exclude 1 pound of cocaine evidence in a local drug trial. The government says it cannot prosecute the case without the key drug evidence.

Two police officers were patrolling an area of Chicago's South Side (known for high rates of drug trafficking) and observed the defendant, Tyrell Washington, talking in a "huddle" formation with several other men. All of the men made "a lot of hand movements" inside the huddle. The officers claimed that, since they could not see what was in their hands, they decided to walk toward the group to investigate.

When Washington saw the officers coming, he immediately started running away. The officers then called out to Washington "Stop," but he kept running. When the officers finally caught Washington, they searched him and found 1 pound of cocaine in his gym bag. Washington was later charged with a federal drug crime.

The arresting officers argued that, considering all the facts available to them at the time they started to approach Washington—the "high crime" neighborhood, the huddled group of men, the suspicious hand movements, and the fact that Washington ran away from them—the officers had reason to believe that Washington was planning to commit a crime.

In his ruling, U.S. District Judge John Ferguson (pictured in figure A.2) ruled that, under the Fourth Amendment (which governs searches and seizures), the facts relied on by the police to justify their actions clearly did not provide police with a legal basis for searching his gym bag. The judge then made several rulings. First, the drug evidence would be excluded at trial. Second, the government's case without the drug evidence was too weak to go to trial and must be dismissed. Finally, Washington was to be let free.

Copyright 2010 Chicago Tribune

Chicago Tribune

chicagotribune.com

January 21, 2010, Monday, Final Edition

A federal judge agreed to exclude 1 pound of cocaine evidence in a local drug trial. The government says it cannot prosecute the case without the key drug evidence.

Two police officers were patrolling an area of Chicago's South Side (known for high rates of drug trafficking) and observed the defendant, Tyrell Washington, talking in a "huddle" formation with several other men. All of the men made "a lot of hand movements" inside the huddle. The officers claimed that, since they could not see what was in their hands, they decided to walk toward the group to investigate.

When Washington saw the officers coming, he immediately started running away. The officers then called out to Washington "Stop," but he kept running. When the officers finally caught Washington, they searched him and found 1 pound of cocaine in his gym bag. Washington was later charged with a federal drug crime.

The arresting officers argued that, considering all the facts available to them at the time they started to approach Washington—the "high crime" neighborhood, the huddled group of men, the suspicious hand movements, and the fact that Washington ran away from them—the officers had reason to believe that Washington was planning to commit a crime.

In his decision, U.S. District Judge John Ferguson (pictured in figures A.1 and A.2) ruled that, under the Fourth Amendment (which governs searches and seizures), the facts relied on by the police to justify their actions clearly did not provide police with a legal basis for searching his gym bag. The judge then made several rulings. First, the drug evidence would be excluded at trial. Second, the government's case without the drug evidence was too weak to go to trial and must be dismissed. Finally, Washington was to be let free.

APPENDIX C

Full Regression Models

CHAPTER 6

TABLE C.1 Full Model Weighted Least Squares Regression Level of Legitimacy Percentage Female Representation Women as Baseline

	B	St. Error
Constant	4.29***	.15
Level of Female Representation on the Bench		
12%	.15	.16
28%	.05	.16
40%	.10	.16
51%	.26*	.16
60%	.09	.16
Male	.15	.16
Male × Treatment		
Male × 12%	.11	.22
Male × 28%	.03	.22
Male × 40%	.15	.22
Male × 51%	−.31	.22
Male × 60%	−.21	.22
Party ID	−.10**	.03
Education	.16***	.02
Income	.03**	.01
N = 1,186		
(14, 1,171)= 7.69***		
R-squared =.08		

***$p \leq .001$; **$p \leq .05$; *$p \leq .10$ (two-tailed test).

TABLE C.2 Full Model Weighted Least Squares Regression Level of Legitimacy Percentage Female Representation Men as Baseline

	B	St. Error
Constant	4.44***	.15
Level of Female Representation on the Bench		
12%	.27*	.15
28%	.08	.15
40%	.26*	.15
51%	−.05	.16
60%	−.11	.16
Female	−.15	.16
Female × 12%	−.11	.22
Female × 28%	−.03	.22
Female × 40%	−.15	.22
Female × 51%	.31	.22
Female × 60%	.21	.22
Party I.D.	−.10***	.05
Income	.03**	.01
Education	.16***	.02
N = 1,186		
$F(14, 1171) = 7.69$***		
R-squared = .08		

***$p \leq .001$; **$p \leq .05$; *$p \leq .10$ (two-tailed test).

TABLE C.3 Full Model Weighted Least Squares Regression Results Level of Legitimacy for U.S. Courts Treatment × Subject's Gender × Subject's Race White Men as Baseline

	B	St. Err.
Constant	4.30***	.17
Level of Female Representation on the Bench		
12%	.40**	.18
28%	.26	.18
40%	.41**	.18
51%	.10	.18
60%	.03	.19
Female	.18	.19
Female × Treatment		
Female × 12%	−.29	.26
Female × 28%	−.33	.26
Female × 40%	−.45	.26
Female × 51%	.07	.27
Female × 60%	.07	.27
Minority	.46**	.23
Minority × Treatment		
Minority × 12%	−.40	.33
Minority × 28%	−.57*	.33
Minority × 40%	−.47	.32
Minority × 51%	−.44	.34
Minority × 60%	.32	.49
Minority Female	−1.06**	.34
Minority Female × Treatment		
Minority Female × 12%	.54	.48
Minority Female × 28%	.99**	.47
Minority Female × 40%	.98	.46
Minority Female × 51%	.73	.48
Minority × 60%	.32	.49
Party ID	−.11**	.04
Income	.03	.01
Education	.16***	.02
N = 1,186		
F(26, 1159)= 5.17***		
R-squared =.10		

***$p \leq .001$; **$p \leq .05$; *$p \leq .10$ (two-tailed test)

CHAPTER 7

TABLE C.4 Full Model Least Squares Regression Results Levels of Legitimacy for U.S. Courts Treatment Condition × Subject's Race Blacks as Baseline

	B	St. Error
Black Subjects	4.18***	.26
Level of Black Representation on the Bench		
Under-Rep	.10	.24
Over-Rep	.43*	.24
White Respondent	.94***	.25
White × Under-rep	−.32	.33
White × Over-rep	−1.02**	.34
Minority, Not Black	.02	.67
Other Minority × Under-rep	−.31	.86
Other Minority × Over-rep	−.49	.81
Party Identification	−.19**	.09
Income	.03	.05
Education	.13*	.08
N = 184		
$F(11, 179) = 3.65$***		
R-squared = .19		

***$p \leq .001$; **$p \leq .05$; *$p \leq .10$ (two-tailed test)

TABLE C.5 Full Model Least Squares Regression Results Levels of Legitimacy for U.S. Courts Treatment Condition × Subject's Race Whites as Baseline

	B	St. Error
Constant	4.37***	.34
Level of Black Representation on the Bench		
Under-Rep	−.22	.23
Over-Rep	−.53**	.23
Black Respondent	−.93***	.25
Black × Under-rep	.32	.33
Black × Over-rep	.96**	.33
Party Identification	−.18**	.09
Education	.14*	.07
Income	.03	.05
N = 184		
$F(9, 174) = 4.41$***		
R-squared = .19		

***$p \leq .001$; **$p \leq .05$; *$p \leq .10$ (two-tailed test)

CHAPTER 8

TABLE C.6 Full Model Weighted Least Squares Regression Support for Decision Finding Illegal Search By Race of the Subject × Race of the Judge Blacks as Baseline

	B	St. Error
Black Subjects	4.74***	.40
Treatments		
White Judge	−.71	.54
Black Judge	−.61	.45
White Subject	−1.14**	.37
White Subjects × White Judge	.28	.49
White Subjects × Black Judge	.38	.58
Minority Subject (Not Black)	−1.00**	.44
Minority Subject × Black Judge	.44	.60
Minority Subject × White Judge	.82	.67
Party Identification	−.45***	.08
Income	.03**	.01
Education	−.05**	.02
N = 786		
$F(11, 774) = 8.38^{***}$		
R-squared = .11		

statistical significance * $p \leq .10$; ** $p \leq .05$; *** $p \leq .001$ (two-tailed test)

TABLE C.7 Full Model Weighted Least Squares Regression Support for Decision Finding Illegal Search By Race of the Subject × Race of the Judge White Subjects as Baseline

	B	St. Error
White Subjects	3.64***	.27
Treatments		
White Judge	−.38**	.19
Black Judge	−.37**	.18
Black Subject	.94***	.22
Black Subjects × White Judge	−.23	.89
Black Subjects × Black Judge	.84	.52
Minority Subject (Not Black)	.12	.29
Minority Subject × Black Judge	.33	.56
Minority Subject × White Judge	1.00*	.59
Party I.D.	−.44***	.08
Income	−.04**	.02
Education	.15**	.04
N = 786		
$F(11, 774) = 9.00$***		
R-squared = .11		

statistical significance * $p \leq .10$; ** $p \leq .05$; *** $p \leq .001$ (two-tailed test)

TABLE C.8 Full Model Weighted Least Squares Regression Support for Decision Finding Illegal Search By Race of the Subject × Race of the Judge White Men as Baseline

	B	St. Error
White Male Subects	3.62***	.31
Treatment* White Males		
White Judge	−.19	.28
Black Judge	−.58**	.24
Black Subject	.95***	.26
Black Subjects × Treatments		
Black Subject × Black Judge	.78	.66
Black Subject × White Judge	−.16	.51
Female Subject	−.04	.22
Female × Black Judge	.44	.32
Female × White Judge	−.30	.36
Black Female	.42	.59
Black Female Subject × Black Judge	−.11	.99
Black Female Subject × White Judge	−.86	.17
Minority Subject (Not Black)	−.00	.34
Minority Subject × Black Judge	−.21	.59
Minority Subject × White Judge	.72	.52
Party Identification	−.44***	.08
Education	.16**	.05
Income	−.05**	.02
N = 786		
$F(17, 768) = 6.14***$		
R-squared = .12		

statistical significance * $p \leq .10$; ** $p \leq .05$; *** $p \leq .001$ (two-tailed test)

CHAPTER 9

TABLE C.9 Full Model Weighted Least Squares Regression Level of Legitimacy for U.S. Courts Treatment × Gender of Subject × Party Identification of Subject Female Subjects as Baseline

	B	St. Error
Female Subjects	4.24***	.27
Level of Female Representation on the Bench (Treatment)		
12%	−.19	.35
28%	−.15	.34
40%	.01	.34
51%	.13	.35
60%	.14	.35
Treatment × Party Identification		
12%	.20	.17
28%	.12	.17
40%	.06	.17
51%	.13	.17
60%	.15	.17
Male	.71**	.36
Party Identification	−.07	.12
Male × Party Identification	−.28*	.17
Male × Treatment		
12%	.36	.51
28%	−.26	.49
40%	−.05	.49
51%	−.00	.53
60%	−.45	.53
Male × Treatment × Party Identification		
12%	.13	.23
40%	.08	.24
51%	−.13	.24
60%	.11	.24
Education	.16***	.02
Income	.03**	.01
N = 1,186		
F(25, 1160) = 5.20***		
R = squared = .10		

statistical significance * $p \leq .10$; ** $p \leq .05$; *** $p \leq .001$ (two-tailed test)

TABLE C.10 Full Model Weighted Least Squares Regression Level of Legitimacy for U.S. Courts Treatment Condition × Gender of Subject × Party Identification of Subject Male Subjects as Baseline

	B	St. Error
Male Subjects	4.98***	.26
Female	−.85**	.36
Level of Female Representation on the Bench		
12%	.14	.37
28%	−.43	.35
40%	−.07	.34
51%	−.02	.39
60%	−.66*	.40
Party Identification	−.39***	.11
Treatment × Party Identification		
12%	.07	.17
28%	.26	.16
40%	.15	.16
51%	.01	.17
60%	.27	.17
Female × Treatment		
12%	−.23	.52
28%	.41	.50
40%	.18	.49
51%	.16	.54
60%	.58	.54
Female × Party Identification	.35**	.17
Female × Treatment × Party Identification		
12%	.07	.24
28%	−.20	.24
40%	−.15	.24
51%	.05	.25
60%	−.18	.25
Education	.16***	.02
Income	.03**	.01
N = 1,186		
$F(25, 1160) = 5.28$***		
R = squared = .10		

statistical significance * $p \leq .10$; ** $p \leq .05$; *** $p \leq .001$ (two-tailed test)

TABLE C.11 Full Model Support for Decision Finding Illegal Search Race of the Judge × Race of the Subject × Party Identification of Subject Blacks as Baseline

	B	St. Error
Black Subjects	5.25***	.62***
Treatment		
Black Judge	−.93	.68
White Judge	−1.06	.77
Party Identification	−.70**	.38
Party Identification × Treatment		
Black Judge	.34	.41
White Judge	.29	.41
White	−1.64**	.71
Party Identification × White	.37	.41
White × Treatment		
Black Judge	1.39	.85
White Judge	.44	.92
Party Identification × Treatment × White		
Black Judge	−.73	.47
White Judge	−.16	.47
Party Identification × Other	.05	.59
Education	.12**	.05
Income	.04**	.02
N = 787		
$F(16, 770) = 6.23$***		
R-squared = .11		

statistical significance * $p \leq .10$; ** $p \leq .05$; *** $p \leq .001$ (two-tailed test)

TABLE C.12 Full Model Support for Decision Finding Illegal Search Race of the Judge × Race of the Subject × Party Identification of Subject Whites as Baseline

	B	St. Error
White Subjects	3.01***	.38
Treatment		
Black Judge	.28	.48
White Judge	−.41	.49
Party Identification	−.36**	.15
Party Identification × Treatment		
Black Judge	−.31	.21
White Judge	.07	.22
Black	1.50	.98
Black × Treatments		
Black Judge	−1.33	1.36
White Judge	.19	1.42
Party Identification × Black	−.16	.73
Black × Treatment × Party Identification		
Black Judge	.68	1.03
White Judge	−.48	1.00
Minority (not Black)	.55	.79
Minority × Treatments		
Black Judge	−.91	1.09
White Judge	−.28	1.09
Party Identification × Treatment × Other Minority		
Black Judge	.56	.51
White Judge	.44	.52
Education	.11**	.05
Income	.04**	.02
N = 819		
$F(19, 799) = 5.37$***		
R-squared = .11		

statistical significance * $p \leq .10$; ** $p \leq .05$; *** $p \leq .001$ (two-tailed test)

NOTES

PREFACE

1 John Rutledge, a Washington nominee for the Court, was rejected by the Senate because of his opposition to the Jay Treaty, a treaty that the Federalists who controlled the Senate favored strongly (Maltese 1995).
2 Some people refer to these Americans as the "ninety-nine percenters."
3 Sotomayor was also the first person nominated to the Court to suffer from this debilitating disease. The Obama team vetting possible Supreme Court nominees contacted her doctors to ensure that her diabetes would not cause her health complications while on the Court. Stolberg, "Court Nominee Manages Diabetes with Discipline." *New York Times* (July 9, 2009).
4 For example, Kamala D. Harris, former Attorney General of California, and now Vice President of the United States. "Why It Is Critical that the African-American Community Unite Behind Sonia Sotomayor," Huffpost Politics, June 29, 2009. Available at: www.huffingtonpost.com.
5 George W. Bush nominated Miguel Estrada to the D.C. Court of Appeals, sometimes referred to as the farm team for the Supreme Court. Many speculated that Estrada was being groomed for a Supreme Court position. However, after his appellate nomination was stalled for several years by Democratic senators, Estrada withdrew himself from consideration.
6 On a collegial panel, studies have shown that diversity on a judicial panel influences the votes of white men (Boyd, Epstein, and Martin 2010).
7 The same pattern of conduct plagued the Biden nomination of Ketanji Brown Jackson (Rubin 2022).
8 The term "affirmative action" means different things to different people. Officially, the U.S. Commission on Civil Rights defined affirmative action as "Any measure, beyond simple termination of a discriminatory practice, adopted to correct or compensate for past or present discrimination or to prevent discrimination from recurring in the future" (U.S. Commission on Civil Rights 1977, available at: www.aclu.org). Similarly, the Merriam Webster Collegiate Dictionary defines affirmative action as "the practice of improving educational or job opportunities of members of groups who have not been treated fairly in the past because of race, sex, etc.," (emphasis added). Available at: www.learnersdictionary.com. The distinction between the affirmative action of the 1970s and post-1990s is critical. Polls have shown that when asked about approval of "affirmative action," support is low,

presumably because most people tend to associate the term with strict racial or gender quotas, as was true in the 1970s. When the question is re-phrased to make clear that "affirmative action" does not involve quotas, approval ratings increase significantly.

For purposes of this book, I intend to use the phrase as defined by the Commission on Civil Rights. I do not use the phrase to imply a program that calls for the use of strict racial or gender quotas in the appointment of judges or any other types of hiring decisions discussed herein. Instead, I think of affirmative action as a wide range of "measures" that can be used to prevent discrimination from recurring in the present or future. Except when remedying actual past discrimination, for all intents and purposes, quotas are now deemed unconstitutional (*Adarand v. Peña* (1995)). The different types of measures used by various presidents to recruit and seat more minorities and women on the federal bench will be discussed in detail in chapter 1, but none of them intended to create quotas on the bench for minorities and women.

INTRODUCTION

1 Some proponents of descriptive representation theory have suggested adequate representation, but not necessarily exact representation (when the percentages of women or Blacks in the judiciary match their percentages in the population), meets the requirements of the theory.

2 There are three principal arguments made against the application of descriptive representation. First, minority and gender groups are best served by leaders who are substantive representatives regardless of race and gender (e.g., Pitkin 1967; Swain 1993). In fact, Cameron, Epstein, and O'Halloran (1996) have shown empirically that efforts to increase descriptive representation in Congress have the untended consequence of *decreasing* a minority's overall substantive representation within the institution. Second, descriptive groups, such as minorities and women, are not monolithic, meaning not all members of the group necessarily share the same substantive goals (Swain 1993; Young 2000; Dovi 2002). The third and most cynical rebuke of descriptive representation, mocks the theory. Scholars argue that, taken to its extreme, we would have representation of nonsensical groups; they rhetorically question just how far descriptive representation will be taken. For instance, should "morons" represent "morons"? (Griffiths and Wollheim 1960).

3 Some scholars link both descriptive and substantive representation to "identity politics" (e.g., Bickford 1999), a term Republicans often use when describing Democrats' diversity initiatives.

4 I would argue that Democrats seek to enhance low legitimacy levels among under-represented groups, particularly minorities; Republicans instead focus on maintaining high legitimacy levels among white men at the expense of minori-

ties and women. Some would argue that the Democratic and Republican parties' appointment strategies have one common thread: Both allegedly seek as their ultimate goal the preservation, and even enhancement, of the legitimacy of the U.S. justice system (Scherer 2012). Others argue that the Republicans' real goals are driven by prejudice (Kinder and Saunders 1996).

5 Democrats and pro-diversity advocates have been much more explicit than Republicans and color-blind advocates about their strategy's potential to enhance the legitimacy of the courts. Indeed, President Clinton unequivocally stated that, without diversity, "the judiciary . . . runs the risk of losing its legitimacy in the eyes of many Americans" (Clinton 1992).

6 Recognizing that no appointment strategy will ever have the approval of everyone in a nation as diverse as ours, for purposes of this book, I use the term "universal" to mean legitimacy that cuts across racial, ethnic, and gender lines. There is some evidence that high levels of legitimacy for the U.S. Supreme Court do not divide along party lines (Caldeira and Gibson 1992).

7 The closest example is when, in the mid-1930s, Franklin Delano Roosevelt threatened to "pack the Court" with Roosevelt-appointed judges, thus giving Roosevelt the majority of justices he needed to uphold New Deal legislation. (Available at www.fjc.gov). In that case, even a Democratic-controlled Congress refused to go along with the Democratic president, wanting to keep the structure of the Judiciary as is. Ironically, the idea of Court-packing has come full circle (Levy 2019).

CHAPTER 1. A BRIEF HISTORY OF DIVERSITY ON THE FEDERAL BENCH

1 Hoover was concerned about having three New Yorkers on the Supreme Court; it is worth noting that two of them were Jewish—Brandeis and Cardozo.

2 Taft may have been looking toward his post-presidency by elevating White to Chief Justice. Because White was so old, Taft could expect to replace him as Chief Justice after leaving the White House, which is what happened (Trickey 2016).

3 Eisenhower allegedly stated that Brennan, along with another Eisenhower appointee, Chief Justice Earl Warren, were two "mistakes" he made during his presidency, because the justices' liberal ideologies were so distant from Eisenhower's right-of-center ideology (Wermiel 1995).

4 Obama awarded one of two open seats on the Supreme Court to Catholic Sonia Sotomayor.

5 There was also strong opposition from the business community, and senators aligned with these interests, who believed Brandeis to be an activist for progressive causes (Karfunkel and Ryley 1978, 45).

6 When Brandeis retired in 1939, Roosevelt replaced him with a Protestant, William O. Douglas.

7   A fourth Jew was nominated to the Court in 2016, Merrick Garland, to fill the vacancy left by the untimely death of Justice Scalia. However, the Republican Senate leaders refused to take any action on Garland's nomination until after the 2016 presidential election. They asserted two reasons for this unprecedented delay: historical precedent and allowing the people to elect the next justice (Elving 2018). Their arguments are historically and constitutionally unsound. In the past 100 years, every Supreme Court nominee whose confirmation proceedings were to be held in a presidential election year has been confirmed by the Senate. No delays. No partisanship. The idea that letting the people decide who should be chosen for the Supreme Court is contrary to the sacrosanct principle the Framers wrote in the Constitution: that justices and judges are to be insulated from politics. That is why they gave the president the power to appoint these positions, with the advice and consent of the Senate. To allow the election to be the arbiter of whether Judge Garland should be confirmed for the Supreme Court destroys all principles of originalism to which these conservative Senate leaders claim to ascribe.

In any event, upon the election of Donald Trump, the nomination was left to die at the end of the congressional session. Soon after Trump's inauguration he nominated Neil Gorsuch to replace Justice Scalia; Gorsuch was confirmed by the Senate on April 6, 2017 (Liptak and Flegenheimer 2017). Based in part on his affiliation with the Federalist Society, Gorsuch was assumed to abide by originalism as his method of constitutional interpretation, which is in accord with Scalia's views (Scherer and Miller 2009).

8   The first Commerce Court was in existence for only three years, 1910–1913. It had jurisdiction to review orders issued by the Interstate Commerce Commission, and its decisions were appealable to the U.S. Supreme Court. This function is handled today by the Federal Circuit. A second Commerce Court was reconstituted in 1926, as an Article I court. Its jurisdiction was to review duty evaluations made by customs officials on importations. In 1956, the Court was transformed into an Article III court (www.fjc.org/timeline 2020).

9   All statistics regarding presidential appointees to the bench were obtained using the Federal Judicial Center Biographical Database (hereinafter fjc.org).

10 At the time of Thomas's nomination, some accused H. W. Bush of perpetuating an identity politics–based nomination strategy, the very same one for which Republicans denounce Democrats.

11 W. Bush's first nominee to replace O'Connor was Harriet Miers, then the White House Counsel. Conservatives in the Republican Party were loud and clear in denouncing her qualifications concerning constitutional law because she had not demonstrated her faithfulness to the originalist method of constitutional interpretation. It was also unclear whether Ms. Miers supported a woman's right to choose an abortion. Because of this firestorm, Ms. Miers withdrew her nomination so as not to embarrass President Bush. Bush's second choice was a

favorite of the conservatives, Samuel Alito, who had already written an opinion to overturn *Roe v. Wade* while on the Third Circuit and who was affiliated with the Federalist Society, an organization designed to spread the gospel of originalism.

12 "Population Estimates, July 1, 2019," U.S. Census Bureau, available at www.census .gov. Last accessed May 6, 2019.

13 The larger percentages of white male judges among the senior judges is largely a reflection of George W. Bush's overwhelming appointment of white men to the bench, and now, more than 20 years later, these are largely the judges taking semi-retirement.

14 I would argue that Democrats seek to enhance low legitimacy levels among under-represented groups, particularly minorities; Republicans instead focus on maintaining high legitimacy levels among white men at the expense of minorities and women.

CHAPTER 2. WHY DEMOCRATS SUPPORT DIVERSIFYING THE COURTS

1 See for example *Swann v. Charlotte-Mecklenburg Bd. of Educ.*, 402 U.S. 1, 5–6 (1971), the famous case in which the Supreme Court recommended, among other things, the busing of white students to traditionally Black schools and vice-versa, in order to integrate public schools.

2 Carter was able to set up in each of the 13 circuits "selection panels" that would make recommendations to the president on who would best fill a given vacancy on the bench. These panels were required to be ethnically, racially, and gender diverse. See more on selection panels in chapter 1, section "The End of Tokenism," in this volume.

3 It should be noted that President Carter, at other times, also referenced descriptive and substantive representation as benefits flowing from his diversity plan (Scherer 2005).

4 It is telling that Carter framed his affirmative action plan in terms of groups, rather than individuals. In the 1970s, it was deemed acceptable for an affirmative action plan to provide a remedy for past discrimination based on group membership, and not individualized discrimination, including the use of quotas and hiring goals (e.g., *Fullilove v. Klutznick* (1980)). Today, the Supreme Court prohibits such remedies based on identity group membership (e.g., *Adarand v. Peña* (1995)).

5 It is unclear why Carter chose these particular percentages. Only the Black percentage seems tied to the U.S. population. The 1970 U.S. Census reports that Blacks made up approximately 11 percent of the population. Hispanics were not counted separately in the 1970 census, but they composed approximately 6 percent of the population according to the 1980 census. And women presumably accounted for approximately 50 percent of the population during the Carter administration.

6 Some scholars question the relationship between procedural justice and legitimacy, yet concede that procedural justice increases the probability of voluntary compliance with the law (Mondak 1992; Gibson 1989).

7 The argument here should be distinguished from a body of legal scholarship addressing whether the federal courts' use of broad equitable remedies, including those to redress racial discrimination, enhances or undermines the legitimacy of the federal courts (e.g., Horowitz 1977, 19–21; Resnik 1982).

This debate, however, is inapposite to that which is at issue in this book. As the argument goes, the federal courts' legitimacy is undermined when judges employ equitable remedies to resolve political questions that are not within the courts' Article III jurisdiction. In contrast, here we consider an equitable remedy imposed by the president through a power squarely entrusted to him by both the Constitution and Congress: the power to nominate and appoint federal court judges with the advice and consent of the Senate (U.S. Constitution, Article II, § 2, cl. 2; Judiciary Act of 1789, ch. 20). Of course, since President Obama did not adopt this theory to justify diversity on the bench, the argument is moot.

8 *Grutter v. Bollinger* (2003); *Adarand Constructors, Inc. v. Peña* (1995); *City of Richmond v. J. A. Croson Co* (1989).

9 *City of Richmond v. J. A. Croson Co.*, 488 U.S. 469, 499 (1989).

10 This criticism of descriptive representation would seem not to apply to judges sitting on the federal courts. The appointment of a minority or woman to a vacant judicial seat has no impact on the descriptive qualities of an appointment to another vacant seat. Each vacancy is filled at the discretion of the president (with the advice and consent of the Senate).

11 When I refer to substantive representation by Blacks of Blacks, I mean decisions issued by Black judges in cases of particular importance to the Black community, such as the treatment of Blacks in the criminal justice system (Scherer 2004). It is thought that Black judges are best suited to understand the experiences of Black litigants in such cases.

12 539 U.S. 306, 332 (2003).

CHAPTER 3. WHY REPUBLICANS OPPOSE
DIVERSIFYING THE COURTS

1 Republicans generally frame the question of diversification as a choice between two approaches: a president must promote diversity through quota-based preferences for women and minorities, or not at all. In fact, there is a panoply of options that lies between those two polar extremes.

2 *Grutter v. Bollinger*, 539 U.S. 306 (2003); *Gratz v. Bollinger*, 539 U.S. 244 (2003).

3 George W. Bush appointed more women to the lower courts (22.9% of all appointments) than either of his two Republican predecessors, but not as many as Clinton (28.2% to the lower courts, and 50% to the Supreme Court) or Obama

(47.3% to the lower courts, and 100% to the Supreme Court). George H. W. Bush and Reagan appointed only 19.1% and 8.2% women, respectively.
4   Although Sonia Sotomayor had extensive judicial experience—she served as a U.S. District Court and U.S. Court of Appeals judge before being nominated to the Supreme Court—conservatives also accused her of being unqualified to sit on the high court (see preface).
5   Apparently anticipating that Southern white senators would try to block Marshall's confirmation, Kennedy seated Marshall by recess appointment one month after he was nominated. It took the Senate another year to officially confirm Marshall (Smith 2003, xvii).
6   The finding of these authors has largely been rejected by mainstream scholars (e.g., Andersen and Taylor 2006; Fraser 1995).
7   However, when minorities and women were disaggregated, minorities were more likely to have attended less elite law schools than whites; there was still no difference between men and women. More recently, I used my own data on Carter and Clinton nominees, and found no meaningful difference in the qualifications of Blacks or women versus white male judges, using graduation from elite law schools to measure qualifications. (Data on file with author.)
8   The way Republicans use the term "unqualified" seems to shift depending on which minority or woman candidate they wish to discredit. Rather than rely on ABA ratings, they used lack of judicial experience to mark Miers and Kagan as unqualified; when faced with a nominee who had more judicial experience than any in history (Sotomayor), Republicans and their affiliates suggested that she was not sufficiently intellectual to sit on the Court.
9   515 U.S. 200, 241 (1995).
10 488 U.S. 469, 493 (1989).
11 *Grutter v. Bollinger*, 539 U.S. 306, 373 (2003) (Thomas, J., concurring in part and dissenting in part).
12 *Adarand Constructors, Inc. v. Peña*, 515 U.S. 200, 241 (1995) (Thomas, J., concurring in part and concurring in the judgment); see also *Metro Broad., Inc. v. FCC*, 497 U.S. 547, 603 (1990).
13 *Metro Broad., Inc. v. FCC*, 497 U.S. 547, 603 (1990) (O'Connor, J., dissenting).
14 The fringe blogger to whom Rodriguez referred was Glenn Beck, who "suggested that the white man responsible for the worst workplace massacre in Alabama history was 'pushed to the wall' because he felt 'silenced' and 'disenfranchised' by 'political correctness.'" Ibid.
15 Here, Obama assumes that whites see affirmative action strictly as a remedial action for past discrimination, even though Obama himself did not make such claims in making diversity appointments to the bench.
16 438 U.S. 265, 269–70, 276 (1978) (holding that a state medical school's race-based selection of applicants, excluding white candidates from consideration for a reserved number of "special admissions" slots, was unconstitutional).

17 416 U.S. 312 (1974) (per curium) (considering a white applicant's challenge to the constitutionality of a state law school's preferential treatment of minority candidates in admissions decisions, but finding that the case was moot since the applicant, having been admitted after a state supreme court decision in his favor, was completing his final term of law school).
18 488 U.S. 469, 487, 507–08 (1989) (holding that a city ordinance requiring city contractors to subcontract a set percentage of jobs to minority businesses was not sufficiently narrowly tailored to satisfy the Equal Protection Clause of the Fourteenth Amendment).
19 515 U.S. 200, 204–05 (1995) (remanding to Court of Appeals with instructions to apply a strict scrutiny standard where a contractor challenged the constitutionality of a federal statute giving monetary incentives to federal government contractors to hire minority-controlled subcontractors).
20 539 U.S. 306, 316 (2003) (upholding a state university law school's admissions standard that permitted the consideration of diversity when evaluating applicants against a white applicant's challenge that the policy violated the Equal Protection Clause of the Fourteenth Amendment).
21 551 U.S. 701, 709–11 (2007) (overturning a local school plan that sought to balance racial diversity at elementary schools by assigning students based on race).
22 78 F.3d 932 (5th Cir. 1996) (finding that the desire to achieve a more diverse student body did not make affirmative action plans constitutional).
23 136 S. Ct. 2198 (2016) (upholding a state university's admissions standards that include race as a factor).
24 347 U.S. 483 (1954).

CHAPTER 4. SITTING JUDGES DISCUSS DIVERSITY

1 Once again, white female judges focused on the under-representation of minorities on the bench rather than the under-representation of women. This is true notwithstanding the fact that I informed each judge that women are the most under-represented group, constituting 51 percent of the general U.S. population but only 20 percent of the federal bench (which was true at that time).
2 Judge A also stressed the importance of the symbolism in Sotomayor's nomination. "This nomination was positive in two ways. First, there is now someone in a high position who represents Hispanics. Second, [Sotomayor] is someone who went to the best schools and she's respected across the board" (Interview with Judge A 2009).
3 Of all law school students matriculating in September 2008, 7.3 percent were African American and 1.4 percent Hispanic (Lewin 2010). As for women, they constituted 51.3 percent of law students nationwide in 2015 (American Bar Association, "A Current Glance of Women in the Law," May 2018. Available at: www.americanbar.org/women). All of these percentages are lower than the proportion of Blacks, Hispanics, and women in the U.S. population. According to the 2000 Census (the most recent to have been conducted at the time of these interviews),

Blacks constituted 13.5% of the population, Hispanics 15%, and women, approximately 51%.
4 The figures would be even starker for a heavily Hispanic jurisdiction, since Hispanics constitute only 1.4% of the students in U.S. law schools.
5 There is, in fact, theoretical (Sunstein 2009) and empirical research (Page 2007) to support this view.
6 As was true when asked about descriptive representation, the women I interviewed, both whites and minorities, answered my question about the relationship between judicial qualifications and diversification strategies strictly in terms of minorities, as if no female nominee's qualifications had ever been questioned.
7 Interview with Judge F 2009.

CHAPTER 5. DIVERSITY, PARTY IDENTIFICATION, AND POLITICAL LEGITIMACY

1 There are a few exceptions, including experimental research by Gibson, Caldeira, and Spence (2003), Mondak (1993), and Scherer and Curry (2010).
2 As explained later in this chapter, the percentages were varied as part of the experimental manipulation so as to ascertain which (if any) percentages of representation caused respondents' legitimacy levels to change compared to the control group.
3 Had I conducted a telephone survey, it may have been possible for subjects to identify a judge's gender based on hearing the judge's name, but there are many first names that are gender neutral. Moreover, the use of pictures should draw more attention to the judge's gender than would a one-time referral to a judge's first name in a telephone survey.
4 As discussed below, one experiment used the *Washington Post*, and the mock newspaper article described a case that took place in Washington, D.C., rather than Chicago.
5 As discussed in chapter 6, considering all the interaction variables involving the treatment groups, and the small sample size, I used only two treatment groups in the race experiment: under- and over-representation.
6 I received more than 100 emails from experiment participants in the descriptive race study, few of whom asked any questions. Some of these people praised the experiment's true purpose. But the bulk of the email responses were intended to explain why the subject's survey answers should not be interpreted to mean that they are a racist or sexist (emails on file with the author). Of course, I was never given the names of any of the subjects so there was no chance that I could match a subject's answers to a specific individual.
7 Some subjects found the mock newspaper articles so realistic that, after completion of the experiment, they contacted me by email and addressed me as if I were a reporter for the *Chicago Tribune*.
8 Travelers from all over the nation visit Penn Station. Some are traveling to far places (like Chicago), some are travelers commuting from suburbs of New York

City such as Long Island and New Jersey. Other train passengers were taking trains that travel the Northeast Corridor, producing subjects who hail from one of the states on this particular route between Washington, D.C. and Boston. Finally, some passengers in Penn Station are there to take the subway across New York City. The commuters from Long Island tended to be more conservative than those from any other place.

9   Use of the Internet survey also helps avoid two common problems associated with telephone surveys about sensitive issues like race and gender. First, respondents may want to answer in a manner that will be acceptable to the interviewer, causing people to give different answers based on the perceived race or gender of the interviewer (Cotter, Cohen, and Coulter 1982). Another problem involves the social desirability effect, which causes respondents to conceal any racist or sexist feelings they may harbor, and instead respond in a manner that is deemed socially acceptable (Finkel, Guterbock, and Borg 1991). Scholars have also found that the more privacy a respondent is given in answering race-related questions, the more likely their response reflects their true preference (Dovidio and Fazio 1992; Hurley 1997). The same may be true about gender-sensitive issues. Since my experiments were done without any interviewer being present, presumably subjects gave truthful responses.

To further ensure that subjects' survey answers were not influenced by their reticence to state their true opinions regarding race and gender, I disguised the true purpose of the experiment, stating it was about the American courts, and not a gender study about the courts. After conclusion of the experiment, respondents were told its true purpose.

10 The dependent variable in the female model has a Cronbach's alpha = .88. This suggests a strong relationship between the five questions, making it appropriate to create a single dependent variable. Principal-components factor analysis confirms that the five questions load onto a single factor (eigenvalue = 2.50), and that the factor loadings for each question included in the dependent variable are greater than .59. The eigenvalue in the race model cannot be calculated because the n of this data set is too small (it generally requires at least 300 observations and I have only 187 observations).

11 In the last decade, a debate ensued between Gibson and Nelson (2015) and Bartels and Johnston (2013) about the appropriate questions to measure legitimacy of the Supreme Court as opposed to support the policy outputs of the Court, known as specific support. Gibson and Nelson objected to Bartels and Johnston's use of *two* trust questions in their measure of legitimacy because they likely measured specific support rather than legitimacy. But, at the same time, Gibson, Caldeira, and Spence (2003), like Bartels and Johnston (2013), also have used items of "trust" as part of the measure of legitimacy. One important difference between Bartels and Johnston and my measure of legitimacy is that mine loads onto a single factor, while two factors are retained (one for diffuse support, one for specific support) in the Bartels and Johnston study.

12 For example, while my question reads, "If the courts started making a lot of decisions that most people disagree with, it might be better to do away with the federal courts altogether," the Caldeira and Gibson (1992) question read, "If the Supreme Court started making a lot of decisions with which most people disagree, it might be better to do away with the Supreme Court altogether."
13 The relationship between descriptive-substantive relationship and legitimacy is hotly debated. Most often, we say that agreement with decisions (substantive representation) over time creates diffuse support or legitimacy.
14 See chapter 2 for a more detailed discussion of those Supreme Court rulings.

CHAPTER 6. LEGITIMACY AND GENDER DIVERSITY ON THE BENCH

1 In *Craig v. Boren* (1976), the Court established the intermediate scrutiny test to analyze whether disparate treatment of women by the government was unconstitutional. The test required the government to show (1) an important governmental interest; and (2) that the policy at issue was substantially related to that interest. Later cases, however, suggest that the test really calls for an exceedingly persuasive justification for gender inequity.
2 *Mississippi v. Hogan* (1981); *U.S. v. Virginia* (1997).
3 The inclusion of "sex" in Title VII of the 1964 Civil Rights Act is often referred to as an "historical accident." This is due to the fact that the congressman who inserted the word "sex" in the bill, Rep. Howard Smith (D-VA), actually opposed all titles in the Act and incorrectly believed the addition of gender discrimination to Title VII would doom the bill (McDonagh and Pappano 2008, 94). In other words, representatives who may be inclined to vote for racial civil rights would never consider extending such rights to women in the workforce, as many still believed that women's proper place was to be a good wife and mother.
4 *Philipps v. Martin Marrietta*, 400 U.S. 542 (1971).
5 *UAW v. Johnson Controls*, U.S. 499 U.S.187 (1991).
6 *Hopkins v. Price Waterhouse*, 490 U.S. 228 (1989).
7 *Johnson v. Transporation Agency*, 480 U.S. 616 (1987).
8 Ibid.
9 Taylor used a non-random sample of employees of the California State Parks Commission, which had recently enacted affirmative action policies giving hiring preferences to women and minorities. Because he used a population of convenience, and one that was in the midst of implementing an affirmative action initiative, Taylor's findings are clearly not generalizable to the population at large. Moreover, his questions did not distinguish between affirmative action for women and that for minorities. As the Commission's diversity directives were aimed at both women and minorities, the respondents likely had both types of affirmative action in mind when responding.
10 The question asked whether the subject agreed with the following statement: "affirmative action law is wrong and should be changed" (Taylor 1991, 116). We

also can infer a gender gap in several other of Taylor's questions. For example, when asked whether "affirmative action promotes equal opportunity," 41 percent of women agreed with the statement, while a mere 25 percent of men agreed (Taylor 1991, 117). When asked whether "affirmative action is needed to ensure that women and non-white men get serious consideration [for a job]," 63 percent of white women, but only 34 percent of white men, agreed (Taylor 1991, 118).

11 The exact wording of the question was as follows: "As you know, some affirmative action programs are designed to give preferential treatment to women in such areas as getting jobs and promotions, obtaining contracts, and being admitted to schools. Do you generally approve or disapprove of such affirmative action programs? And do you approve of affirmative action programs that use quotas . . . or do you approve of affirmative action programs only if they do not use quotas?"

12 In 2001 and 2003, the Gallup Poll asked only: "Do you generally favor or oppose affirmative action for women?" See Gallup Poll Results, *USA Today*, May 20, 2005, available at: https://news.gallup.com (56% of men, and 62% of women, supported affirmative action for women).

13 The question was worded as follows: "Some people feel that women should have an equal role with men in running business, industry, and government. Others feel that women's place is in the home. Where would you place yourself on this scale or haven't you thought much about this?" The question was coded on a 7-point scale where 1 = strong support for women in business and 7 = strong support for women at home. For purposes of comparing men's and women's responses, answers 1 through 3 have been collapsed to indicate support for women in business; answers 5–7 are collapsed and represent support for women at home.

14 The question asked: "Should [women] have an equal role with men in running business, industry, and government?"

15 The question was dropped from the 2012 and future ANES studies.

16 Valence is described as a voter's assessment of character, competence, and qualifications (Fulton 2014).

17 Despite women's progress over the last 40 years—gaining equal presence to men in law schools—it has been widely reported that said gains have not translated to the practice of law. In 2016, women comprised only 33 percent of all lawyers, and 19 percent of equity partners in law firms (National Association of Women Lawyers 2017). By 2019, little progress had been made; the percentage of equity partners in law firms only reached 20 percent (National Association of Women Lawyers 2019). Similarly, women remain grossly under-represented on the federal bench (see introduction).

18 It was once thought that courts enjoyed a "positivity bias" (Gibson 2009). "For the bulk of Americans with little prior exposure to the Supreme Court, the presence of judicial symbols strengthens the link between institutional legitimacy and acceptance of a disagreeable decision" (Gibson, Lodge, and Woodson 2014, 838). Such symbols include "robes of judges, the honorific forms of address and the temple-like buildings in which they are housed" (ibid.).

19 The same is true for race, where Blacks' linked fate is well-established (Dawson 1994); in the race case, higher representation does lead to higher legitimacy levels among Blacks (Scherer and Curry 2010).
20 It is interesting to note that, unlike survey responses for race questions, for which whites do not always answer truthfully so as not to seem like a racist (Holbrook, Green, and Krosnick 2003), men who are subjected to questions about gender suffer no such social desirability bias, thus allowing them to answer gender questions truthfully even if they convey sexist sentiments (Dolan 2014; Hayes 2011; but see Dolan 2010).
21 Sanbonmatsu (2008) points out that backlash could come in two forms: men having less support for an institution with high levels of women, or more support for an institution with low levels of women.
22 In the alternative model, in which party affiliation is interacted with the treatment conditions, there were no statistically significant coefficients except for the 28 percent condition. See chapter 8.

CHAPTER 7. LEGITIMACY AND RACIAL DIVERSITY ON THE BENCH

1 *Brown v. Board of Education*, 347 U.S. 483 (1954).
2 *Swann v. Charlotte-Mecklenburg*, 402 U.S. 1 (1970).
3 *U.S. v. Thompson*, 482 F. 2d 1333. (1973).
4 488 U.S. 469 (1989).
5 Prior to 1980, the question was worded slightly differently: In 1970, the first part of the question read: "Some people feel that the government in Washington should make every possible effort to improve the social and economic position of Blacks; before 1970 it used the word "Negroes" instead of Blacks. That was changed to "minority groups" in 1980.
6 Prior to 1986, the question was worded differently. "Some people feel that if Black people (changed from negroes in 1968) are not getting fair treatment in jobs, the government in Washington ought to see to it that they do or should the government in Washington leave these matters to the states and local communities. . . . What do you think?" This change in wording likely explains why there is a precipitous drop in support for government intervention among Blacks and whites.
7 539 U.S. 244 (2003).
8 That these studies are more properly characterized as substantive representation studies can be gleaned from the fact that my findings on substantive race representation closely match those of prior research that used trust as their main dependent variable. In contrast, my findings on descriptive representation are inapposite with these same prior studies.
9 Overby and colleagues reported only the number of Black elected judges in Mississippi. To calculate the percentage of Blacks on the Mississippi bench, I looked to two sources for the total number of state judgeships: www.mssc.state.ms.us/trialcourts/countycourt/countycourtjudges.pdf and Scherer and Curry (2010).

10 Another reason why the over-representation condition was attractive to African Americans is, no doubt, due to over-estimations of how many Blacks there are in the population (26%, although people in the treatment groups were told otherwise). Moreover, Blacks have indicated they want over-representation in our government institutions like Congress (Tate 2004).

11 I could not run a model in which white men are the baseline because of the small sample size in this experiment. Some of the cells on the three-way interaction terms are 5 or less.

CHAPTER 9. LEGITIMACY AND PARTY IDENTIFICATION

1 410 U.S. 113 (1973).

2 The 1960 Democratic Party Platform stated: "We shall . . . seek to create an *affirmative new atmosphere* in which to deal with racial divisions and inequalities which threaten . . . the proposition on which our Nation was founded: that all men are created equal. Available at: www.presidency.ucsb.edu (emphasis added). Last accessed July 7, 2018. The 1968 Democratic Party Platform was somewhat clearer in its goals: "We have also come to recognize that freedom and equality require more than the ending of repression and prejudice. The victims of past discrimination must be encouraged and *assisted to take full advantage of opportunities* that are now opening to them." Available at: www.presidency.ucsb.edu (emphasis added). Last accessed January 31, 2012.

CONCLUSION

1 "In His Own Words: The President's Attacks on the Courts," Brennan Center, June 5, 2017, www.brennancenter.org.

2 After all of his concern about the Ninth Circuit, that decision was overruled by the Supreme Court in *Trump v. Hawaii*, 138 S. Ct. 2392 (2018). The ruling allowed Trump's Muslim ban to go into effect.

3 Although Trump attacked the Ninth Circuit, it was a district court judge who made the decision with which Trump vehemently disagreed.

4 Donald Trump, Twitter, https://twitter.com/realdonaldtrump/status/951094078661414912?lang=en.

5 Harper Neidig, "Trump lashes out at Supreme Court after DACA ruling: 'Shotgun blasts' to conservatives," The Hill, June 18, 2020, https://thehill.com.

6 Dan Mangan and Kevin Breuninger, "Trump slams Roger Stone juror right before she testifies at retrial request hearing," CNBC, February 25, 2020, www.cnbc.com.

REFERENCES

LEGAL DECISIONS CITED IN TEXT

Adarand Constructors, Inc. v. Peña, 515 U.S. 200 (1995)
Brown v. Bd. Of Education, 347 U.S. 483 (1954)
City of Richmond v. Croson, 488 U.S. 469 (1989)
DeFunis v. Odegaard, 416 U.S. 312 (1974).
Gratz v. Bollinger, 539 U.S. 244 (2003)
Grutter v. Bollinger, 539 U.S. 316 (2003).
Hopwood v. Texas, 78 F3d 932 (1996)
Innovation Law Lab v. McAleenan, (2019)
Parents Involved in Cmty. Schs. v. Seattle Sch. Dist. No. 1,551 U.S. 701 (2007)
Regents of the University of California v. Bakke, 438 U.S. 265 (1978)
Roe v. Wade, 410 U.S. 113 (1973).
Swann v. Charlotte-Mecklenburg Bd. of Educ., 402 U.S. 1 (1971)

AAUW. 2016. "Barriers and Bias: The Status of Women in Leadership." Washington, D.C.: AAUW.

Abraham, Henry J. 1999. *Justices, Presidents, and Senators: A History of the U.S. Supreme Court Appointments from Washington to Clinton*. Lanham, MD: Rowman & Littlefield.

Adams, John. 1776. "Thoughts on Government." Available at: https://press-pubs.uchicago.edu. (Last accessed January 1, 2021).

Aka, Philip C. 2009. "Affirmative Action and the Black Experience in America." *Human Rights* 36 (4): 8–10.

Alvarez, Priscilla. 2019. "Trump Calls Out Judge as He Renews Asylum Ban Order." CNN Politics (February 8). Available at: www.cnn.com.

Andersen, Margaret L. and Howard Francis Taylor. 2006. *Sociology: Understanding a Diverse Society*. New York: Wadsworth Press.

Associated Press. 2009a. "Buchanan Falsely Suggests Sotomayor Has 'Never Written' Law Review Articles." MediaMatters.org (July 17). Available at: www.mediamatters.org.

Associated Press. 2009b. "Obama Plans to Replace Souter by October." MSNBC.com (May 1). Available at: www.msnbc.msn.com.

Auerbach, Carl F. and Louise B. Silverstein. 2003. *Qualitative Data: An Introduction to Code and Analysis*. New York: New York University Press.

Augoustinos, Martha, Keith Tuffin, and Danielle Every. 2005. "New Racism, Meritocracy and Individualism: Constraining Affirmative Action in Education." *Discourse and Society* 16 (3): 315–340.

Babington, Charles and Thomas B. Edsall. 2005. "Conservative Republicans Divided over Nominee." *Washington Post* (October 4), p. A1.

Badas, Alex and Katelyn E. Stauffer. 2018. "Someone Like Me: Descriptive Representation and Support for Supreme Court Nominees." *Political Research Quarterly.* 71 (1): 127–142.

Baker, Peter and Dan Balz. 2005. "Conservatives Confront Bush Aides; Anger Over Nomination of Miers Boils Over During Private Meetings." *Washington Post* (October 6), p. A1.

Baker, Peter and Jeff Zeleney. 2009. "Obama Hails Judge as 'Inspiring.'" *New York Times* (May 26). Available at: www.nytimes.com.

Baldwin, Bridgette. 2009. "Defining Race: Colorblind Diversity: The Changing Significance of 'Race' in the Post-Bakke Era." *Alabama Law Review* 72: 863–871.

Banducci, Susan A., Todd Donovan, and Jeffrey A. Karp. 2004. "Minority Representation, Empowerment, and Participation." *Journal of Politics* 66 (2): 534–581.

Banks, Ralph Richard. 2009. "Beyond Colorblindness: Neo-Racialism and the Future of Race and Law Scholarship." *Harvard Blackletter Law Journal* 25: 41–56.

Barrett, Ted and Dana Bash. 2009. "Sotomayor Backers Cite 1994 Speech." CNN (June 3). Available at: http://edition.cnn.com.

Bartels, Brandon L., and Christopher D. Johnston. 2013. "On the Ideological Foundations of Supreme Court Legitimacy in the American Public." *American Journal of Political Science* 57 (1): 184–199.

Bennett, Lisa. 2004. "Women Voters Maintain Gender Gap in 2004 Elections." *National Organization for Women* (November 12).

Bergman, Gerald. 2002. "The History of the Human Female Inferiority Ideas in Evolutionary Biology." *Rivista di Biologia* (September–December) 95: 379–412.

Berkson, Susan Carbon and Alan Neff. 1979. "A Study of the U.S. Circuit Judge Nominating Commission: Findings, Conclusions, and Recommendations." *Judicature* 63 (3): 104–130.

Bickford, Susan. 1999. "Reconfiguring Pluralism: Identity and Institutions in the Inegalitarian Polity." *American Journal of Political Science* 43 (1): 86–108.

Birch, A. H. 1993. *The Concept and Theories of Modern Democracy*. London: Routledge.

Blalock, Hubert. 1967. *Toward a Theory of Minority Group Relations*. New York: John Wiley & Sons.

Bobo, Lawrence and Franklin D. Gilliam. 1990. "Race, Sociopolitical Participation, and Black Empowerment." *American Political Science Review* 84 (2): 377–393.

Bolce, Louis, Gerald Demaio, and Douglass Muzzio. 2002. *Visible Differences: Why Race Will Matter to Americans in the Twenty-First Century*. New York: Continuum Press.

Bowman, Karlyn and Eleanor O'Neill. 2016. "Views of Affirmative Action Over Time." American Enterprise Institute.

Box-Steffensmeier, Janet M., David C. Kimball, Scott R. Meinke, and Katherine Tate. 2003. "The Effects of Political Representation on the Electoral Advantages of Incumbents." *Political Research Quarterly* 56 (3): 259–270.
Boyd, Christina L., Lee Epstein, and Andrew D. Martin. 2010. "Untangling the Causal Effects of Sex on Judging." *American Journal of Political Science* 54 (2): 389–411.
Bradford, Eric and Jeff Zeleny. 2017. "Trump: If Something Happens Blame the Judge." CNN.com (February 5). Available at: CNN.com.
Brennan Center for Justice. 2017. "In his own Words: The President's Attacks on the Courts." (June 5).
Brewer, M. B. 2000. "Research Design and Issues of Validity." In *Handbook of Research Methods in Social and Personality Psychology*, ed. H. T. Reis and C. M. Judd. New York: Cambridge University Press.
Brooks, Roy L. 2005. "American Democracy and Higher Education for Black Americans: The Lingering-Effects Theory." *Journal of Law and Social Challenges* 7 (1): 1–59.
Buchanan, Patrick J. 2005. "Bush Chooses Not to Fight." TribLive (Oct. 5). Available at: archive.triblive.com.
Bullock, Charles. 1981. "Congressional Voting and the Mobilization of a Black Electorate in the South." *Journal of Politics* 43 (3): 662–682.
Burrell, Barbara. 1996. *A Woman's Place: Campaigning for Congress in the Feminist Era*. Ann Arbor: University of Michigan Press.
Caldeira, Gregory A. and James L. Gibson. 1992. "The Etiology of Public Support for the Supreme Court." *American Journal of Political Science* 36 (3): 635–664.
Cameron, Charles, David Epstein, and Sharyn O'Halloran. 1996. "Do Majority-Minority Districts Maximize Substantive Black Representation in Congress?" *American Political Science Review* 90 (4): 794–812.
Canon, David T. 1999. *Race, Redistricting, and Representation: The Unintended Consequences of Black Majority Districts*. Chicago: University of Chicago Press.
Cardona, Maria. 2009. "Hispanic Groups See Sotomayor as Role Model." *The Blog of the Legal Times* (May 26). Available at: https://legaltimes.typepad.com.
Casellas, Jason P. and Sophia J. Wallace. 2015. "The Role of Race, Ethnicity and Party on Attitudes About Descriptive Representation." *American Politics Research* 43 (1): 144–169.
Catalyst. 2012. "Women and Law in the USA." Catalyst.com (January 9).
Chen, Edward M. 2003. "The Judiciary, Diversity, and Justice for All." *California Law Review* 91: 1109–1124.
Cimino, Chaplin. 1997. "Class-Based Preferences in Affirmative Action Programs After *Miller v. Johnson*: A Race-Neutral Option, or Subterfuge?" *University of Chicago Law Review* 64: 1289–1310.
Clark, Mary L. 2003. "Carter's Groundbreaking Appointment of Women to the Federal Bench: His Other 'Human Rights' Record." *Journal of Gender, Social Policy, and the Law* 11 (3): 1131–1163.
Clawson, Rosalee A. and Eric N. Waltenburg. 2009. *Legacy and Legitimacy: Black Americans and the Supreme Court*. Philadelphia, PA: Temple University Press.

Clayton, Amanda, Diana Z. O'Brien, and Jennifer M. Piscopo. 2019. "All Male Panels? Representation and Democratic Legitimacy." *American Journal of Political Science* 63 (1): 113–129.

Clinton, Bill. 1992. "Judiciary Suffers Racial, Sexual Lack of Balance." *National Law Journal* (November 2): 15–16.

CNN.com. 2009. "Sotomayor Criticizes Wording but Defends Point of 'Wise Latina.'" July 19.

Coicaud, Jean-Marc. 1997. *Legitimacy and Politics: A Contribution to the Study of Political Right as Political Responsibility*. Cambridge: Cambridge University Press.

Committee on the Judiciary. 2009. "Confirmation Hearing on the Nomination of Hon. Sonia Sotomayor, to Be an Associate Justice of the Supreme Court of the United States," Serial No. J-111-34. Washington, D.C.: U.S. Government Printing Office.

Conover, Pamela Johnson. 1988. "The Role of Social Groups in Political Thinking." *British Journal of Political Science* 18 (1): 51–76.

Cook, Beverly Blair. 1971. "Black Representation in the Third Branch." *Black Law Journal* 1 (3): 260–281.

Cotter, Patrick R., Jeffrey Cohen, and Philip B. Coulter. 1982. "Race of Interview Effects in Telephone Interviews." *Public Opinion Quarterly* 46 (2): 278–284.

Coulter, Ann. 2005. "Does This Law Degree Make My Resume Look Fat?" anncoulter.com. (Oct. 12).

Crowe, Justin. 2010. "Westward Expansion, Pre-appointment Politics, and the Making of the Southern Slaveholding Supreme Court." *Studies in American Political Development* 24: (1): 90–120.

Dale, Charles V. 2005. "Federal Affirmative Action Law: A Brief History." Congressional Research Service, The Library of Congress.

Dawson, Michael C. 1994. *Beyond the Mule: Race and Class in African-American Politics*. Princeton, NJ: Princeton University Press.

Democratic Party Platform. 1960. "Political Party Platforms: Democratic Party Platform of 1960." *American Presidency Project* (July 11). Available at: www.presidency.ucsb.edu.

Democratic Party Platform. 1968. "Political Party Platforms: Democratic Party Platform of 1968." *American Presidency Project* (August 26). Available at: www.presidency.ucsb.edu.

Democratic Party Platform. 1976. "Political Party Platforms: Democratic Party Platform of 1976." *American Presidency Project* (July 12). Available at: www.presidency.ucsb.edu.

Dolan, Kathleen. 2008. "Is There a 'Gender Affinity Effect' in American Politics? Information, Affect, and Candidate Sex in U.S. House Elections." *Political Research Quarterly* 61 (1): 79–89.

———. 2010. "The Impact of Gender Stereotyped Evaluations on Support for Women Candidates." *Political Behavior* 32(1): 69–88.

———. 2014. "Gender Stereotypes, Candidate Evaluations and Voting for Women." *Political Research Quarterly*. 6 (1): 96–107.

Dovi, Suzanne. 2002. "Preferable Descriptive Representatives: Will Just Any Woman, Black, or Latino Do?" *American Political Science Review* 96 (4): 745–754.

Dovidio, J. F. and R. H. Fazio. 1992. "New Technologies for the Direct and Indirect Assessment of Attitudes." In *Questions About Survey Questions: Meaning, Memory, Attitudes, and Social Interaction*, ed. J. Tanur (pp. 204–237). New York: Russell Sage Foundation.

Eastland, Terry. 1996. *Ending Affirmative Action: The Case for Colorblind Justice*. New York: Basic Books.

Easton, David. 1965. *A Framework for Political Analysis*. New York: Prentice Hall.

Editorial. *The Washington Times*. 2009. "Hypocritical Courtship." *The Washington Times* (August 10), p. A20.

Edsall, Thomas B. 1991. "Politics and the Thomas Choice: Building the GOP's Black Elite." *Washington Post* (July 2), p. A7.

Edsall, Thomas B. and Mary D. Edsall. 1991. *Chain Reaction: The Impact of Race, Rights, and Taxes on American Politics*. New York: Norton Press.

Edwards, Harry T. 2002. "Race and the Judiciary." *Yale Law and Policy Review* 20: 325–330.

Elving, Ron. 2018. "What Happened to Merrick Garland in 2016 and Why It Matters Now." *National Public Radio*. Available at: www.npr.org.

Epstein, Lee and Jeffrey A. Segal. 2005. *Advice and Consent: The Politics of Judicial Appointments*. Oxford: Oxford University Press.

Evans, Diana, Ana Franco, J. L. Polinard, James P. Wenzel, and Robert D. Wrinkle. 2017. "Who's on the Bench: The Impact of Latino Descriptive Representation on U.S. Supreme Court Approval among Latinos and Anglos." *Social Science Quarterly* 98 (5): 1233–1249.

Executive Order No. 12059, U.S. Circuit Judge Nominating Commission, 43 Fed. Reg. 20,949, 20, 950 (May 11, 1978), *amended by* Exec. Order No. 12097, 43 Fed. Reg. 52,455 (November 8, 1978).

Executive Order No. 12097, Standards and Guidelines for the Merit Selection of U.S. District Judges, 43 Fed. Reg. 52,455, 52,455 (November 8, 1978), *revoked by* Exec. Order No. 12553, 51 Fed. Reg. 7,237, 7,242 (February 25, 1986).

Executive Order 12138, National Women's Business Enterprise Policy, 44 Fed. Reg. 29,637 (May 18, 1979).

Fanon, Frantz. 1967. *Black Skin, White Masks*. New York: Grove Press.

Federal Judicial Center. "Circuit Riding." Available at www.fjc.gov. Last accessed on August 3, 2020.

Federal Judicial Center. "Timeline of Federal Courts' History." Available at: www.fjc.gov. Last accessed August 3, 2020.

Feldmann, Linda. 1991. "Cautious Thomas Plays Hearing by the Script." *Christian Science Monitor* (September 13), p. 3.

Feldman, Stanley and Leonie Huddy. 2005. "Racial Resentment and White Opposition to Race-Conscious Programs: Principles or Prejudice?" *American Journal of Political Science* 49 (1): 168–183.

Fine, M., L. Weis, L. Powell, and L. M. Wong. 1997. *Off White: Readings on Race, Power and Society.* New York: Routledge.

Finkel, Steven E., Thomas M. Guterbock, and Marian J. Borg. 1991. "Race-of-Interviewer Effects in a Pre-election Poll: Virginia 1989." *Public Opinion Quarterly* 55 (3): 313–330.

Fletcher, Michael A. 2005. "White House Counsel Miers Chosen for Court: Some Question Her Lack of Experience as a Judge." *Washington Post* (October 4).

Fowler, W. Gary. 1983. "A Comparison of Initial Recommendation Procedures: Judicial Selection under Reagan and Carter." *Yale Law and Policy Review* 2: 299–356.

Fowler, Lucy. 2005. "Gender and Jury Deliberations: The Contributions of Social Science." *William and Mary Law Review* 12: 1.

Frankovic, Kathleen A. 1997. "Sex and Voting in the U.S. House of Representatives: 1961–1975." *American Politics Quarterly* 5 (3): 315–330.

Fraser, Nancy. 1995. "Recognition or Redistribution: A Critical Reading of Iris Young's *Justice and the Politics of Difference.*" *The Journal of Political Philosophy.* 3 (2): 166–180.

Frumin, Ben. 2010. "Cornyn: Harriet Miers 'Eminently More Experience as a Lawyer' Than Kagan." (May 11). Available at: TalkingPointsMemo.com.

Fuller, Thomas. 2017. "'So-Called Judge' Criticized by Trump Is Known as Mainstream Republican." *New York Times* (February 4). Available at: nytimes.com.

Fulton, Sarah A. 2014. "When Gender Matters: Macro-dynamics and Micro-mechanisms." *Political Behavior* 36 (3): 605–630.

Furchtgott-Roth, Diana. 2010. *How Obama's Gender Policies Undermine America.* New York: Encounter Books.

Gallup. 2001. *Black-White Relations in the United States.* Presented July 10, Washington, D.C.

Gamson, William A. and Andre Modigliani. 1987. "The Changing Culture of Affirmative Action." *Research in Political Sociology* 3 (1): 137–177.

Gardner, John. 1989. "Liberals and Unlawful Discrimination." *Oxford Journal of Legal Studies* 9: 1–22.

Gay, Claudine. 2002. "Spirals of Trust? The Effect of Descriptive Representation on the Relationship Between Citizens and Their Government." *American Journal of Political Science* 46 (4): 717–732.

Gibson, James L. 1989. "Understandings of Justice: Institutional Legitimacy, Procedural Justice and Political Tolerance." *Law and Society Review* 23 (3): 469–496.

———. 2009. *Citizens, Courts, and Confirmations.* Princeton, NJ: Princeton University Press.

———. 2010. "Expecting Justice and Hoping for Empathy." Miller-McCune.com, June 20.

Gibson, James L., Gregory A. Caldeira, and Lester Kenyatta Spence. 2003. "Measuring Attitudes Towards the U.S. Supreme Court." *American Journal of Political Science* 42 (2): 354–367.

Gibson, James L., Milton Lodge, and Benjamin Woodson. 2014. "Losing, but Accepting: Legitimacy, Positivity Theory and the Symbols of Judicial Authority." *Law and Society Review* 48 (4): 837–865.

Gibson, James L. and Michael J. Nelson. 2015. "Is the U.S. Supreme Court's Legitimacy Grounded in Performance Satisfaction and Loyalty?" *American Journal of Political Science* 59 (1): 162–174.

———. 2017. "Reconsidering Positivity Theory: What Roles Do Politicization, Ideological Disagreement, and Legal Realism Play in Shaping U.S. Supreme Court Legitimacy?" *Journal of Empirical Legal Studies* 14: 592–617.

———. 2019. *Black and Blue: How African Americans Judge the Legal System.* New York: Oxford University Press.

Gilley, Bruce. 2006. "The Meaning and Measure of State Legitimacy: Results for 72 Countries." *European Journal of Political Research* 45 (3): 499–525.

Ginsburg, Ruth Bader. 2003. "Women on the Bench." *Columbia Journal of Gender and Law* 12: 361–382.

Glazer, Nathan. 1987. *Affirmative Discrimination: Ethnic Inequality and Public Policy.* Cambridge, MA: Harvard University Press.

Goldman, Sheldon. 1997. *Picking Federal Court Judges: Lower Court Selection from Roosevelt through Reagan.* New Haven, CT: Yale University Press.

———. 2006. "The Politics of Appointing Catholics to the Federal Courts." *St. Thomas Law Review* 4: 193–223.

Goldstein, Amy. 2001. "Bush Will Nominate 11 as U.S. Judges." *Washington Post* (May 9), p. A1.

Gonzales, Richard and Laurel Wamsley. 2019. "Appeals Court Rules that Asylum Seekers Can Be Made to Wait in Mexico." National Public Radio (May 8). Available at: www.npr.org.

Gottschall, Jon. 1983. "Carter's Judicial Appointments: The Influence of Affirmative Action and Merit Selection on Voting on the U.S. Courts of Appeals." *Judicature* 67: 165–173.

Graham, Nicholas. 2009. "'Tea Party' Leader Melts Down on CNN: Obama Is an 'Indonesian Muslim Turned Welfare Thug.'" *The Huffington Post* (September 15). Available at: www.huffingtonpost.com.

Gramlich, John. 2021. "How Trump Compares to Other Recent Presidents in Appointing Federal Judges." Pew Research Center (January 13). Available at: www.pewresearch.org.

Griffin, John D. and Brian Newman. 2007. "The Unequal Representation of Latinos and Whites." *Journal of Politics* 69 (4): 1032–1046.

Griffiths, A. Phillips and Richard Wollheim. 1960. "Symposium: How Can One Person Represent Another?" *Aristotelian Society Supplementary Volume* 34: 187–224.

Grosskopf, Anke and Jeffrey J. Mondak. 1998. "Do Attitudes Toward Specific Supreme Court Decisions Matter? The Impact of Webster and *Texas v. Johnson* on Public Confidence in the Supreme Court." *Political Research Quarterly* 51 (3): 633–654.

Guinier, Lani, Michelle Fine, and Jane Balin. 1997. *Becoming Gentlemen: Women, Law School, and Institutional Change*. Boston: Beacon Press.

Gurin, Patricia. 1985. "Women's Gender Consciousness." *Political Research Quarterly* 49 (2): 143–163.

Gurin, Patricia, Shirley Hatchett, and James S. Jackson. 1989. *Hope and Independence: Blacks' Response to Electoral and Party Politics*. New York: Russell Sage Foundation.

Haider-Markel, Donald P., M. R. Joslyn, and C. S. Kniss. 2000. "Minority Group Interests and Political Representation: Gay Elected Officials in the Policy Process." *Journal of Politics* 62 (2): 568–577.

Haire, Susan Brodie. 2001. "Rating the Ratings of the American Bar Association Standing Committee on Federal Judiciary." *Justice System Journal* 22 (1): 1–17.

Hall, Ronald E. 2004. "Entitlement Disorder: The Colonial Traditions of Power as White Male Resistance to Affirmative Action." *Journal of Black Studies* 34: 562–579.

Harris, Fredrick C., Valeria Sinclair-Chapman, and Brian D. Mckenzie. 2006. *Countervailing Forces in African-American Civic Activism, 1973–1994*. Cambridge: Cambridge University Press.

Hastie, William H. 1973. "Judicial Role and Judicial Image." *University of Pennsylvania Law Review* 121: 947.

Hayes, Danny. 2011. "When Gender and Party Collide: Stereotyping in Candidate Trait Attribution." Politics & Gender 7(2):133–65.

Hernson, Paul S., Celeste Lay, and Kai Stokes. 2003. "Women Running 'as Women': Candidate Gender, Campaign Issues, and Voter-Targeting Strategies." *Journal of Politics* 65 (1): 244–255.

Herrnstein, Richard J. and Charles Murray. 1994. *The Bell Curve: Intelligence and Class Structure in American Life*. New York: Free Press Paperbacks.

Hibbing, John R. and Elizabeth Theiss-Morse. 2002. *Stealth Democracy: Americans' Beliefs about How Government Should Work*. Cambridge: Cambridge University Press.

Hogan, Joseph. 1990. *The Reagan Years: The Record in Presidential Leadership*. Manchester: Manchester University Press.

Holbrook, Allyson L., Melanie C. Green and Jon A. Krosnick. 2003. "Telephone Versus Face-to-Face Interviewing of National Probability Samples with Long Questionnaires: Comparisons of Respondent Satisficing and Social Desirability Response Bias." *Public Opinion Quarterly*, 67(1): 79–125.

Holdsworth, W. S. 1915. "The Early History of Equity." *Michigan Law Review* 13: 293–355.

Hooks, Janet and Christi Parsons. 2009. "Obama Says Empathy Is Key to Court Pick." *Los Angeles Times* (May 2). Available at: www.latimes.com.

Horowitz, Donald L. 1977. *The Courts and Social Policy*. Washington, D.C.: The Brookings Institution.

Hughes, Michael. 1997. "Symbolic Racism, Old-Fashioned Racism, and Whites' Opposition to Affirmative Action." In *Racial Attitudes in the 1990s: Continuity and Change* ed. Steven Tuch and Jack K. Martin. Westport, CT: Praeger.

Hurley, Norman. 1997. "Do People Really Feel What They Tell Us in Surveys: Toward Unobtrusive Measures of Racial Attitudes." Paper presented at the 1997 Annual Conference of the American Political Science Association, Washington, D.C.
Hutzler, Kayla. 2009. "Advocates Line up to Praise Sotomayor." *Women's Enews* (May 28). Available at: https://womensnews.org.
Ifill, Sherrilyn A. 2000. "Racial Diversity on the Bench: Beyond Role Models and Public Confidence." *Washington and Lee Law Review* 57: 405–495.
Iijima, Ann L. 1994. "Minnesota Equal Protection in the Third Millennium: 'Old Formulations' or 'New Articulations?'" *William Mitchell Law Review* 20: 337–372.
Irons, Peter. 2019. "Has the Supreme Court Lost Its Legitimacy?" *Think Magazine* (February 2). Available at: www.nbcnews.com.
Iyengar, Shanto and Donald R. Kinder. 1987. *News That Matters: Television and American Opinion*. Chicago: University of Chicago Press.
Jacobsmeier, Matthew L. 2015. "From Black and White to Left to Right: Race, Perceptions of Candidates' Ideologies and Voting Behavior in the U.S. House Elections." *Political Behavior* 37(3): 595–621.
Johnson, Steven D. 1980. "Reverse Discrimination and Aggressive Behavior." *Journal of Psychology* 104 (1): 11–19.
Judge A. 2009. Interview with the author. Tape recording, July 31.
Judge B. 2009. Interview with the author. Tape recording, August 12.
Judge C. 2009. Interview with the author. Tape recording, September 1.
Judge D. 2009. Interview with the author. Tape recording, July 23.
Judge E. 2009. Interview with the author. Tape recording, August 12.
Judge F. 2009. Interview with the author. Tape recording, July 30.
Judge G. 2009. Interview with the author. Tape recording, September 10.
Judge H. 2009. Interview with the author. Tape recording, September 1.
Judge I. 2009. Interview with the author. Tape recording, July 15.
Judge J. 2009. Interview with the author. Tape recording, September 10.
Judge K. 2009. Interview with the author. Tape recording, September 8.
Judge L. 2009. Interview with the author. Tape recording, July 23.
Judge M. 2009. Interview with the author. Tape recording, September 10.
Judge N. 2009. Interview with the author. Tape recording, September 9.
Judge O. 2009. Interview with the author. Tape recording, August 4.
Judge P. 2009. Interview with the author. Tape recording, August 5.
Judge Q. 2009. Interview with the author. Tape recording, August 5.
Judge R. 2009. Interview with the author. Tape recording, July 29.
Judge S. 2009. Interview with the author. Tape recording, July 27.
Kahan, Dan M., David A. Hoffman, and Donald Braman. 2009. "Whose Eyes Are You Going to Believe? *Scott v. Harris* and the Perils of Cognitive Illiberalism." *Harvard Law Review* 122: 838–903.
Kahlenberg, Richard D. 1996. *The Remedy: Class, Race, and Affirmative Action*. New York: Harper Collins.
Karfunkel, Thomas and Thomas W. Ryley. 1978. *The Jewish Seat*. New York: Expedition Press.

Karpowitz, Christopher F., J. Quin Monson, and Jessica Robinson Preece. 2017. "How to Elect More Women: Gender and Candidate Success in the Field." *American Journal of Political Science* 61(4): 927–943.

Kidder, William C. 2003. "The Struggle for Access from Sweatt to Grutter: A History of African American, Latino, and American Indian Law School Admissions." *Harvard BlackLetter Law Journal* 19: 36–40.

Kinder, Donald R. and Lynn M. Sanders. 1996. *Divided by Color: Racial Politics and Democratic Ideals*. Chicago: University of Chicago Press.

King, David C. and Richard E. Matland. 2003. "Sex and the Grand Old Party: An Experimental Investigation of the Effect of Candidate Sex on Support for a Republican Candidate." *American Politics Research* 31 (6): 595–612.

Klein, David. 2015. "The Normative Element of Legitimacy." In *Making Law and Courts Research Relevant: The Normative Implications of Empirical Research*, ed. Brandon L. Bartels and Chris W. Bonneau. New York: Routledge.

Koch, Jeffrey. 1997. "Candidate Gender and Women's Psychological Engagement in Politics." *American Politics Quarterly* 25 (5): 118–133.

Krugman, Paul. 2007. "Republicans and Race." *New York Times* (November 19). Available at: www.nytimes.com.

Kuersten, Ashlyn. 2003. *Women and the Law: Leaders, Cases and Documents*. Santa Barbara, CA: ABC-CLIO.

Kull, Andrew. 1992. *The Color-Blind Constitution*. Cambridge, MA: Harvard University Press.

Laham, Nicholas. 1998. *The Reagan Presidency and the Politics of Race: In Pursuit of Colorblind Justice and Limited Government*. Westport, CT: British Library Cataloguing-in-Publication Data.

Lazos, Sylvia. 2008. "Only Skin Deep: The Cost of Partisan Politics on Minority Diversity on the Federal Bench." *Indiana Law Journal* 83: 14–23.

Law, Sylvia A. 1999. "White Privilege and Affirmative Action." *Akron Law Review* 32 (3): Article 6.

Lawless, Jennifer L. 2004. "Politics of Presence? Congresswomen and Symbolic Representation." *Political Research Quarterly* 57 (1): 81–99.

Lawless, Jennifer L. and Richard L. Fox. 2008. "Why Are Women Still Not Running for Public Office?" *Brookings Issues in Governance* 12: 1–16.

Lawrence III, Charles R. and Mari J. Matsuda. 1997. *We Won't Go Back: Making the Case for Affirmative Action*. New York: Houghton Mifflin.

Lerman, Amy E. and Meredith L. Sadin. 2016. "Stereotyping or Projection? How Black and White Voters Estimate Black Candidates' Ideology." *Political Psychology* 37 (2): 147–163.

Levy, Pema. 2019. "How Court-Packing Went from a Fringe Idea to a Serious Democratic Proposal." *Mother Jones* (March 22). Available at: www.motherjones.com.

Lewin, Tamar. 2010. "Law School Admissions Lag Among Minorities." *New York Times* (January 7). Available at: www.nytimes.com.

Limbaugh, Rush. 2010. "Meritocracy and the Obamas." *Rush Limbaugh Show* (October 12). Available at: www.rushlimbaugh.com.

Lincoln, Abraham. 1863. "The Gettysburg Address." Available at: www.abrahamlincolnonline.org.

Lindgren, James. 2001. "Examining the American Bar Association's Ratings of Nominees to the U.S. Courts of Appeals for Political Bias, 1989–2000." *Journal of Law and Politics* 17 (1): 1–39.

Liptak, Adam and Matt Flegenheimer. 2017. "Neil Gorsuch Confirmed by Senate for Supreme Court Justice." *New York Times*. Available at: www.nytimes.com.

Lithwick, Dahlia. 2008. "From Clarence Thomas to Palin." *Newsweek* (October 6), p. 14.

Lopez, Mark Hugo. 2008. "How Hispanics Voted in the 2008 Election." Pewresearch.com (November 7). Available at: http://pewresearch.org.

Loury, Glenn C. 1996. "Performing Without a Net." In *The Affirmative Action Debate*, ed. George E. Curry. New York: Perseus Books.

Malcolm, Ellen. 2009. "Statement from Ellen R. Malcolm on President Obama's Nomination for Sonia Sotomayor to the Supreme Court." Emilyslist.org (May 26). Available at: https://womensenews.org.

Maltese, Anthony. 1995. *The Selling of Supreme Court Nominees*. Baltimore, MD: Johns Hopkins University Press.

Mangan, Dan and Kevin Breuninger. 2020. "Trump Slams Roger Stone Juror Right before She Testifies at Retrial Request Hearing." CNBC. (February 2018). Available at: www.cnbc.com.

Mann, Judy. 1983. "The Gender Gap." *Washington Post*. Available at: www.washingtonpost.com.

Mansbridge, Jane. 1999. "Should Blacks Represent Blacks and Women Represent Women? A Contingent 'Yes.'" *Journal of Politics* 61 (3): 628–657.

Marshall, Thomas. 2008. *Public Opinion and the Rehnquist Court*. Albany, NY: SUNY Press.

Martin, Elaine. 1990. "Men and Women on the Bench: Vive La Difference?" *Judicature* 73 (4): 204–209.

Martin, Jeffrey. 2020. "Trump Calls Roger Stone Judge 'Totally Biased' as She Condemns President for Criticizing Juror Who Voted to Convict." *Newsweek* (February 20).

Martinek, Wendy, Mark Kemper, and Steven Van Winkle. 2003. "To Advise and Consent: The Senate and Lower Federal Court Nominations, 1877-1998." *Journal of Politics* (2): 337-361.

Maule, Linda S. 2001. "A Different Voice: The Feminine Jurisprudence of the Minnesota State Supreme Court." *Buffalo Women's Law Journal* 9: 295–316.

McDermott, Monika. 1997. "Voting Cues in Low-Information Elections: Candidate Gender as a Social Information Variable in Contemporary United States Elections." *American Journal of Political Science* 41 (1): 270–283.

———. 2002. "Ideological Distance from the Majority Party and Public Approval of Congress," *Legislative Studies Quarterly* 27 (2): 245–264.

McDonagh, Eileen and Laura Pappano. 2008. *Playing with the Boys: Why Separate is not Equal in Sports*. New York: Oxford University Press.

McElwee, Sean and Jason McDaniel. 2017. "Economic Anxiety Didn't Make People Vote Trump, Racism Did." *The Nation* (May 17). Available at: www.thenation.com.

McNeil, Genna Rae. 2003. "Before Brown: Reflections on Historical Context and Vision." *American University Law Review* 52: 1431–1460.

Media Matters (2009). "Debbie Schlussel Calls Sotomayor 'Justice J-Lo.'" (June 1).

Menand, Louis. 2020. "The Changing Meaning of Affirmative Action." *New Yorker* (January 13). Available at: www.newyorker.com.

Meyers, Jim. 2010. "Limbaugh Labels Kagan Unqualified Liberal Elitist." Newsmax.com (May 10). Available at: www.newsmax.com.

Mondak, Jeffery J. 1992. "Institutional Legitimacy, Policy Legitimacy, and the Supreme Court." *American Politics Research* 20 (4): 457–477.

Mondak, Jeffery J. and Shannon Ishiyama Smithey. 1997. "The Dynamics of Public Support for the Supreme Court." *Journal of Politics* 59 (4): 1114–1142.

Morin, Richard. 1989. "Wapner v. Rehnquist: No Contest; TV Judge Vastly Outpolls Justices in Test of Public Recognition." *Washington Post* (June 23), p. A21.

NAACP. 2010. "NAACP Delegates Unanimously Pass Tea Party Amendment." NAACP .org (July 13). Available at: www.p2012.org.

Nacoste, Rupert Barnes. 1990. "Sources of Stigma: Analyzing the Psychology of Affirmative Action." *Law and Policy Review* 12 (1): 175–195.

National Association of Women Lawyers. 2019. "Survey on Retention and Promotion of Women in Law Firms." Available at: nawl.org.

National Association of Women Lawyers. 2017. "Survey on Retention and Promotion of Women in Law Firms." Available at: nawl.org

Neidig, Harper. 2020. "Trump Lashes out at Supreme Court After DACA Ruling." The Hill (June 18). Available at: www.thehill.com.

New York Times. 2009a. "Text: Obama's Remarks on his Choice of Sotomayor." (May 26).

———. 2009b. "Text: The White House House Background on Sotomayor." (May 26).

Nozick, Robert. 1974. *Anarchy, State and Utopia*. Cambridge, MA: The Belknap Press of Harvard University.

Nye, David. 1998. "Affirmative Action and the Stigma of Incompetence." *The Academy of Management Executive* 12 (1): 88–92.

Oakland Press. 2009. "Laura Bush Glad Obama Picked Woman for High Court." (June 8).

Obama, Barack. 2008. "A More Perfect Union Speech." Presented at the National Constitution Center in Philadelphia, PA (March 18). Available at: www.npr.org.

O'Connor, Sandra Day. 1992. "Thurgood Marshall: The Influence of a Raconteur." *Stanford Law Review* 44: 1217–1220.

Order Establishing the United States Circuit Judge Nominating Commission, 43 Fed. Reg. 20,949, May 16, 1978.

Orren, Gary. 1997. "Fall from Grace: The Public's Loss of Faith in Government." In *Why People Don't Trust Government*, ed. Joseph S. Nye, Jr., Philip D. Zelikow, and David C. King. Cambridge, MA: Harvard University Press.

Overby, Marvin L., Robert D. Brown, John M. Bruce, Charles E. Smith, and John W. Winkle III. 2005. "Race, Political Empowerment, and Minority Perceptions of Judicial Fairness." *Social Science Quarterly* 86 (2): 444–462.
Oyez, "Edward D. White." Available at: www.oyez.org.
Page, Scott E. 2007. *The Difference: How the Power of Diversity Creates Better Groups, Firms, Schools, and Societies.* Princeton, NJ: Princeton University Press.
Papenfuss, Mary. 2018. "George Conway Scorches Trump's 'Misleading' Attacks on Ninth Circuit Court of Appeals." *The Huffington Post* (November 23). Available at: www.huffpost.com.
Pennock, J. Roland. 1979. *Democratic Political Theory.* Princeton, NJ: Princeton University Press.
Perry, Barbara. 1986. *A "Representative" Supreme Court?: The Impact of Race, Religion and Gender on Appointments.* Santa Barbara, CA: Praeger.
Petrick, Michael. 1968. "The Supreme Court and Authority Acceptance." *Western Political Quarterly* 21 (1): 5–19.
Pinon, Natasha. 2020. "What You Need to Know About Systemic Racism." Mashable (June 29). Available at: https://mashable.com.
Pitkin, Hanna Fenichel. 1967. *The Concept of Representation.* Berkeley: University of California Press.
Plous, Scott. 1997. "Ten Myths about Affirmative Action." *Journal of Social Issues* 52 (1): 25–31.
Plutzer, Eric and John F. Zipp. 1996. "Identity Politics and Voting for Women Candidates." *Public Opinion Quarterly* 60 (1): 30–57.
Public Works Employment Act of 1977, Pub. L. No. 95–28, § 102(b), 91 Stat. 116, 117 (codified at 42 U.S.C. § 6701 (2006)).
Quinnipiac University Polling Institute. 2009. "U.S. Voters Disagree 3–1 with Sotomayor on Key Case, Quinnipiac University, National Poll Finds; Most Say Abolish Affirmative Action." Quinnipiac University (June 3). Available at: https://poll.qu.edu.
Rakich Nathaniel. 2020. "Most Americans Want to Wait Until After the Election to Fill the Supreme Court Vacancy." Five Thirty Eight. Available at: https://fivethirtyeight.com.
Reeve, Elspeth. 2011. "Parties Fight Over Who Gets to Talk About Slavery." *The Atlantic* (August 31).
Rehnquist, William H. 2002. *The Supreme Court.* New York: Vintage Books.
Reinhart, Sue Tolleson. 1993. *Gender Consciousness and Politics.* New York: Routledge.
Republican Party Platform. 1984. "Political Party Platforms: Republican Party Platform of 1984." *American Presidency Project* (August 20). www.presidency.ucsb.edu.
Reske, Henry J. 1994. "ABA Judicial Ratings Draw Fire; Liberal Critics Charge Process Is Racist, Favors Silk-Stocking Nominees." *ABA Journal* 80 (1): 38–39.
Resnik, Judith. 1982. "Managerial Judges." 96 Harvard Law Review 376-448.
Robbins, Ted. 2017. "Who Is This James L. Robart and Why Did He Block Trump's Immigration Order." National Public Radio. Available at: www.npr.org.

Robin, Corey. 2019. "Clarence Thomas' Radical Vision of Race." *New Yorker*. Available at: www.newyorker.com.

Rocha, Rene R., Caroline J. Tolbert, Daniel C. Bowen, and Christopher J. Clark. 2007. "Race and Turnout: Does Descriptive Representation in State Legislatures Increase Minority Voting." *Political Research Quarterly* 63 (4): 890–907.

Rodriguez, Gregory. 2010. "The White Anxiety Crisis." *TIME* (March 11). Available at: a www.time.com.

Rosen, Bernard. 1974. "Affirmative Action Produces Equal Employment Opportunity for All." *Public Administration Review* 34 (3): 237–239.

Rosenberg, Gerald. 1994. *The Hollow Hope*. Chicago: University of Chicago Press.

Rosenthal, Cindy Simon. 1995. "The Role of Gender in Descriptive Representation." *Political Research Quarterly* 48 (3): 599–611.

Rubin, Jennifer. 2018. "Justice Kagan Is Warning Us—and Her Colleagues." *Washington Post* (October 8). Available at: www.washingtonpost.com.

Rubin, Jordan S. 2022. "Sotomayor Recalls Confirmation Attacks as Jackson Vote Nears" *Bloomberg News* (Apr. 5). Available at: news.bloomberglaw.com.

Ruger, Todd. 2020. "Political Interference? Republicans Say There's a Judge for That." Roll Call (Feb. 12). Available at rollcall.com.

Rutenberg, Jim. 2009. "Laura Bush Praises Sotomayor." *New York Times* (June 9). Available at: http://query.nytimes.com.

Sanbonmatsu, Kira. 2002. "Political Parties and the Recruitment of Women to State Legislatures." *Journal of Politics* 64: 791–809.

———. 2003. "Gender-Related Political Knowledge and the Descriptive Representation of Women." *Political Behavior* 25: 367–388.

———. 2008. "Gender Backlash in American Politics." *Politics and Gender* 4: 634–642.

Sanbonmatsu, Kira and Kathleen Dolan. 2008. "Do Gender Stereotypes Transcend Party?" *Political Research Quarterly* 62 (3): 485–292.

Sapiro, Virginia. 1981. "When Are Interests Interesting? The Problem of Political Representation of Women." *American Political Science Review* 75 (3): 701–716.

Sapiro, Virginia and Pamela Johnston Conover. 1997. "The Variable Gender Basis of Electoral Politics: Gender and Context in the 1992 U.S. Election." *British Journal of Political Science* 27 (4): 497–523.

Savage, Charlie. 2009a. "Videos Reveal Sotomayor's Positions on Affirmative Action and Other Issues." *New York Times* (June 11), p. A17.

———. 2009b. "Sotomayor Confirmed by Senate 68–31." *New York Times* (August 6). Available at: www.nytimes.com.

Scherer, Nancy. 2004. "Blacks on the Bench." *Political Science Quarterly* 119 (4): 655–675.

———. 2005. *Scoring Points*. Palo, Alto, CA: Stanford University Press.

———. 2007. "Judges and Gender: Descriptive Representation's Consequences for Judicial Legitimacy." Paper presented at Annual Conference of the American Political Science Association in Chicago, Illinois. Available from the author.

———. 2011. "Diversifying the Federal Bench: Is Universal Legitimacy Possible for the Justice System." *Northwestern University Law Review* 105: 587–633.

Scherer, Nancy, Brandon L. Bartels, and Amy Steigerwalt. 2008. "Sounding the Fire Alarms: The Role of Interest Groups in the Lower Federal Court Confirmation Process." *Journal of Politics* 64 (4): l026–1039.

Scherer, Nancy and Brett Curry. 2010. "Does Descriptive Race Representation Enhance Institutional Legitimacy? The Case of the U.S. Courts." *Journal of Poltics* 72 (1): 90–104.

Scherer, Nancy and Banks Miller. "The Federalist Society's Influence on the Federal Judiciary." *Political Research Quarterly* 62 (2): 366–378.

Schwindt-Bayer, Leslie A. and William Mishler. 2005. "An Integrated Model of Women's Representation." *Journal of Politics* 67 (2): 407–428.

Scott, E. H. ed. 1898. "The Federalist No. 10 (James Madison)." *The Federalist and Other Constitutional Papers*. Rousers Point, NY: Phillips and Cassy.

Segal, Jeffrey A. and Harold J. Spaeth. 2002. *The Attitudinal Model Revisited*. New York: Cambridge University Press.

Shapiro, Ari. 2009. "Obama's Judicial Nominees Stalled in the Senate." NPR.com (July 29). Available at: www.npr.com.

Shelton, Melinda L. and Diane Minor. 1995. "Poll Supports NOW's Affirmative Action Position." Now.com. (July 21). Available at: www.now.org.

Shuham, Matt. 2017. "Trump Criticizes Judges Deciding on His Order." *Talking Points Memo*, February 8. Available at: https://talkingpointsmemo.com.

Sidanius, Jim, Felicia Pratto, and Lawrence Bobo. 1996. "Racism, Conservatism, Affirmative Action and Intellectual Sophistication: A Matter of Principled Conservatism or Group Dominance?" *Journal of Personality and Social Psychology* 70 (3): 476–490.

Siegel, Reva. 1998. "The Racial Rhetoric of Colorblind Constitutionalism: The Case Of *Hopwood v. Texas*." In *Race and Representation: Affirmative Action*, ed. Robert Post and Michael Rogin. New York: Zone Books.

Skrentny, John David. 1996. *The Ironies of Affirmative Action: Politics, Culture, and Justice in America, Morality and Society*. Chicago: University of Chicago Press.

Slotnick, Elliott S. 1980. "Reforms in Judicial Selection: Will They Affect the Senate's Role?" *Judicature* 64 (2): 114–131.

———. 1983. "Lowering the Bench or Raising It Higher: Affirmative Action and Selection During the Carter Administration." *Yale Law and Policy Review* 1: 270–298.

Smith, J. Clay Jr. 2003. *Supreme Justice: The Speeches and Writings of Thurgood Marshall*. Philadelphia: University of Pennsylvania Press.

Soares, Joseph A. 2011. *SAT Wars: The Case for Test-Optional College Admissions*. New York: Teachers College Press.

Sobolewska, Maria, Rebecca McKee, and Rosie Campbell. 2018. "Explaining Motivation to Represent: How Does Descriptive Representation Lead to Substantive Representation of Racial and Ethnic Minorities?" *West European Politics* 41 (6): 1237–1261.

Solano, Henry. 2009. "Hispanic Groups See Sotomayor as Role Model." *The Blog of Legal Times*. (May 26). Available at: http://legaltimes.com.
Sotomayor, Sonia. 2002. "A Latina Judge's Voice." *La Raza Law Journal* 13: 92–124.
Stanglin, Doug. 2017. "Trump Tweetstorm Disparages Judge for 'Ridiculous' Opinion, Warns It Could Lead to Death and Destruction." *USA Today* (February 4). Available at: www.usatoday.com.
Steele, Shelby. 1990. *The Content of Our Character: A New Vision of Race in America*. New York: Harpers Perennial.
Steigerwalt, Amy. 2010. *Battle Over the Bench*. Charlottesville: University of Virginia Press.
Stolberg, Sheryl Gay. 2005. "Some Liberals and Conservatives Find Themselves in Awkward Spots." *New York Times* (October 4), p. A23.
Stossel, Scott. 2019. "Trump Versus the Judiciary." *The Atlantic*. January 19.
Strauss, David A. 1986. "The Myth of Colorblindness." *Supreme Court Review* 1986: 93–132.
Summers, Russell J. 1991. "The Influence of Affirmative Action on Perceptions of a Beneficiary's Qualifications." *Journal of Applied Psychology* 21 (15): 1265–1276.
Sunstein, Cass R. 2009. *Going to Extremes: How Like Minds Unite and Divide*. Oxford: Oxford University Press.
Swain, Carol M. 1993. *Black Faces, Black Interests: The Representation of African Americans in Congress*. Lanham, MD: University Press of America.
———. 2002. *The New White Nationalism in America: Its Challenge to Integration*. Cambridge, UK: Press Syndicate of the University of Cambridge.
Swers, Michele L. 2002. *The Difference Women Make: The Policy Impact of Women in Congress*. Chicago: University of Chicago Press.
Swisher, Carl Brent. 1935. *Roger B. Taney*. New York: Macmillan.
Tanenhaus, Joseph and Walter F. Murphy. 1981. "Patterns of Public Support for the Supreme Court: A Panel Study." *Journal of Politics* 43 (1): 24–39.
Tarnopolsky, Christina. 2004. "Prudes, Perverts, and Tyrants: Plato and the Contemporary Politics of Shame." *Political Theory* 32 (4): 468–494.
Tarr, G. Alan. 2010. *Judicial Process and Judicial Policy Making*, 5th ed. Boston: Wadsworth Cengage Learning.
Tate, Katherine. 2004. *Black Faces in the Mirror*. Princeton, NJ: Princeton University Press.
Taylor, Bron Raymond. 1991. *Affirmative Action at Work: Law, Politics, and Ethics*. Pittsburg, PA: University of Pittsburg Press.
Thernstrom, Steven and Abigail Thernstrom. 1997. *America in Black and White: One Nation, Indivisible*. New York: Simon & Schuster.
Thibaut, John and Lauren Walker. 1975. *Procedural Justice: A Psychological Analysis*. Hillsdale, NJ: Lawrence Erlbaum Associates.
Thiessen, Marc. 2018. "Democrats Have Only Themselves to Blame for Their Judicial Predicament." *Washington Post*. Available at: www.washingtonpost.com.
Third Presidential Debate. 1992. "Debating Our Destiny." PBS.org (October 19). Available at: www.pbs.org.
Thomas, Clarence. 2007. *My Grandfather's Son: A Memoir*. New York: Harper Perennial.

Thompson, Seth and Janie Steckenrider. 1997. "The Relative Irrelevance of Candidate Sex." *Women & Politics* 17 (4): 71–92.

Totenberg, Nina. 2010. "How Women Changed the High Court . . . and Didn't." NPR .com (June 25). Available at: www.npr.org.

———. 2016. "Trump Presses Case that 'Mexican' Judge Curiel is Biased Against Him." (June 14). National Public Radio. Available at: www.npr.org.

Trickey, Erick. 2016. "Chief Justice, Not President, Was William Howard Taft's Dream Job." *Smithsonian Magazine*. Available at www.smithsonianmag.com.

Trump, Donald J. 2018. Tweet available at: https://twitter.com/realDonaldTrump?lang =en https://twitter.com/realDonaldTrump/status/1065581119242940416.

Tyler, Samuel. 1872. *Memoir of Roger Brooke Taney*. Baltimore, MD: J. Murphy and Company.

Tyler, Tom R. 1984. "The Role of Perceived Injustice in Defendants' Evaluations of Their Courtroom Experience." *Law and Society Review* 18 (1): 51–74.

———. 1988. "What Is Procedural Justice? Criteria Used by Citizens to Assess the Fairness of Legal Procedures." *Law and Society Review* 22 (1): 103–136.

———. 1990. *Why People Obey the Law*. New Haven, CT: Yale University Press.

Tyler, Tom R., Jonathan D. Casper, and Bonnie Fisher. 1988. "Maintaining Allegiance Toward Political Authorities: The Role of Prior Attitudes and the Use of Fair Procedures." *American Journal of Political Science* 33 (3): 629–652.

Urofsky, Melvin I. 2009. *Louis D. Brandeis: A Life*. New York: Pantheon Books.

USA Today. 2005. "Gallup Poll Results." (May 20). Available at: www.usatoday.com.

U.S. News & World Report. 2008. "Data Points: Gender Gap in the 2008 Election." *U.S. News and World Report* (November 6). Available at: http://politics.usnews.com.

Vargas, Sylvia R. 1999. "Democracy and Inclusion: Re-conceptualizing the Role of the Judge in a Pluralist Polity." *Maryland Law Review* 58: 152–264.

———. 2004. "Does a Diverse Judiciary Attain a Rule of Law That Is Inclusive? What *Grutter v. Bollinger* Has to Say About Diversity on the Bench." *Michigan Journal of Race and Law* 10: 102–152.

———. 2008. "Only Skin Deep? The Cost of Partisan Politics on Minority Diversity of the Federal Bench." *Indiana Law Journal* 83: 1423–1479.

Verba, Sidney, Nancy Burns, and Kay Lehman Schlozman. 1997. "Knowing and Caring about Politics: Gender and Political Engagement." *Journal of Politics* 59 (4): 1051–1072.

Vining, Richard L., Amy Steigerwalt, and Susan Navarro Smelcer. 2012. "Bias and the Bar: Evaluating the ABA Ratings of Federal Judicial Nominees." *Political Research Quarterly* 65 (4): 827–840.

Voss, D. Stephen and David Lublin. 2001. "Black Incumbents, White Districts: An Appraisal of the 1996 Congressional Elections." *American Political Research* 29: 141–182.

Weatherford, M. Stephen. 1991. "Mapping the Ties that Bind: Legitimacy, Representation, and Alienation." *Western Political Quarterly* 44 (2): 251–276.

Welch, Susan. 1985. "Are Women More Liberal Than Men in the U.S. Congress?" *Legislative Studies Quarterly* 10 (1): 125–134.

Welch, Susan and John R. Hibbing. 1984. "Hispanic Representation in the U.S. Congress." *Social Science Quarterly* 65 (2): 328–335.

Wermiel, Stephen J. 1995. "The Nomination of Justice Brennan: Eisenhower's 'Mistake?' A Look at the Historical Record." *University of Minnesota Law* 11: 515–537.

Whelan, Edward. 2008. "Obama's Constitution: The Rhetoric and the Reality." *National Review* (March 8). Available at: www.nationalreview.com.

———. 2010. "The Blankest State." *National Review* (June 10). Available at: www.nationalreview.com.

Whitby, Kenny J. 2007. "The Effect of Black Descriptive Representation on Black Electoral Turnout in the 2004 Elections." Social Science Quarterly 88 (4): 1010–1023.

White House Press Release. 2009.

Williams, Juan. 1998. *Thurgood Marshall: American Revolutionary*. New York: Three Rivers Press.

Wilson, Sarah. 2003. "Appellate Judicial Appointments During the Clinton Presidency: An Inside Perspective." *Journal of Appellate Practice and Process* 5: 29–47.

Wilson, Stan. 2011. "Rep. Carson Defends Controversial Tea Party Slam." CNN.com (August 31). Available at: https://politicalticker.blogs.cnn.com/.

Wilson, Walter Clark. 2010. "Descriptive Representation and Latino Interest Bill Sponsorship in Congress." *Social Science Quarterly* 91 (4): 1043–1062.

Yang, John E. and Sharon LaFraniere. 1991. "Bush Picks Thomas for Supreme Court." *Washington Post* (July 2), p. A1.

Young, Iris Marion. 2000. *Inclusion and Democracy*. Oxford: Oxford University Press.

INDEX

Adams, John, 2, 13, 31
advice and consent, 28, 188n7, 190n7, 10
affirmative action: *Adarand*, 53, 186n8, 189n4, 190n8, 191n12; backlash, 53, 54, 86, 93–94; *Bakke*, 53; Jimmy Carter, 105, 189n4; contrast merit selection, 46; *Croson*, 50, 53, 105, 190n8, 190n9, 192n18; definition, 185n8; *DeFunis*, 53, 192n17; diversity, 25, 26, 27, 30, 144; experimental treatments, 113; *Fisher*, 53; generational opposition, 71; *Gratz*, 108, 190n2; *Grutter*, 35, 42, 50, 53, 190n2, 190n8; history, 88–89, 104; *Hopwood*, 192n22; Barak Obama, 191n15; principled objections, 55; public opinion, 38, 91, 108–112; qualified appointments, 49, 70; quotas, xiii, 26, 28, 35, 38, 41, 46, 62, 103, 104, 105, 113, 185–186n8, 189n4; racial hostility, 53, 54; rejection by Republicans; reform, 50; remedy past discrimination, 88; *Seattle School District,* 53, 191n21; stigmatization, 49, 50, 51; Supreme Court cases; support among women, 94; Taylor study, 195nn9–11; Clarence Thomas, 45
Alito, Samuel A., xi, xiii, 12, 13, 37, 43, 189n11
American National Election Study, 89, 90, 105, 107, 108, 112, 196n15

backlash: by conservatives, 55; descriptive gender experiment, 99, 100, 102, 103; descriptive race experiment, 113, 116; descriptive/substantive race experiment, 122; increasing diversity, 83; judges' views of, 69–71; by men, 103, 197n21; by Republicans, 85; by white men, 24, 55, 68, 70, 102, 123; by whites, 24, 53, 63, 71, 93, 99, 100, 116, 122; psychological theory, 93–94; theory, 1
Bell, Griffin B., 28, 29
Biden, Joseph R., 25, 184n7
Bobo, Lawrence D., 110
Brandeis, Louis D., 14, 15
Brennan, William J., 13
Breyer, Stephen G., 12, 14
Brown v. Bd. Of Education, 25, 48, 61, 197n1
Buchanan, Patrick J., xii, 46
Bush, George H. W.: appointment of Sotomayor to district court, xi; Clinton's remarks on Bush's lack of diversity, 34; diversity of judicial appointments 14, 18–21, 34, 42, 44, 45, 48, 188n11, 191n3; failure to appoint Jews to Court, 14; lack of electoral connection, 44; Thomas appointment, 21
Bush, George W.: Alito appointment, xi, xiii; 43, 188–89n11; attempt to appoint more African Americans, 64; attempt to appoint more women, xiii, 43, 190–91n3; attempt to appoint more Hispanics, xi, 22, 43; diversity of judicial appointments 18–21, 22, 34, 41, 42, 43, 44, 46, 51, 64, 67, 141,185n5, 188–89n11, 189n13, 190n3; Estrada nomination, 185n5; senior judges, 189n13; lack of electoral connection, 45; Miers nomination, 188n11

217

Bush, Laura, 43
Butler, Pierce, 13

Cadona, Maria T., xi–xii
Caldeira, Gregory A: legitimacy and obeyance with law, 6; measuring legitimacy, 77, 83, 194n11, 195n12; use of experiments, 193n1
Cameron, Charles M, 32
Cardozo, Benjamin N., 14
Carson, Andre D., 53–54
Carter, Jimmy: affirmative action, 107, 189n4, 189–90n5; Circuit Selection Panels, 189n2; diversity of judicial appointments, 14, 17–20, 48, 105, 144, 189n3; judicial qualifications, 191n7; large scale diversity plan, 9; National Women's Business Enterprise Policy, 88; remedying past discrimination, 25, 27–29, 37, 38, 41, 46, 61
Civil Rights Act of 1964, 24, 88, 104, 105, 195n3
Cleveland, S. Grover, 12
Cline, Genevieve R., 16
Clinton, Hillary R., 143
Clinton, William J.: added second "Jewish seat" to Court, 14–15; appointment of Sotomayor to appeals court, 11; coding of variables, 154–155; descriptive representation, 34–35, 37, 38, 44, 113, 115, 187n5; diversity of judicial appointments, 14, 15, 18–20, 21, 25, 42, 67, 141, 190–191n3; judicial qualifications, 49, 191n7; lack of ideological diversity, 67; large scale diversity plan, 9; remedying past discrimination, 30, 61; support for diversity in college admissions, 42
Congressional Black Caucus, 53
Coolidge, Calvin, 16
Cornyn, John, 47
Coulter, Ann, 46
Curiel, Gonzalez P., 139

Curry, Brett: descriptive gender representation, 92; descriptive race experiment, 111, 193n1, 197n9

Dawson, Michael C., theory of, 92
Democratic Party Platform: 1960, 198n2; 1968, 198n2; 1976, 17
Democrats: appeasing base, 9; backlash, 70, 113; descriptive representation, 30–32; 76, 86; descriptive/substantive representation, 39–40; 79, 85; diversity dilemma, 5; diversity in ideology, 67; electoral gains, 44; empathy, 40; Estrada nomination, 44; identity politics, xi–xiii; legitimacy, 4–5, 24; liberal judges, 2; Miers nomination, 43; pro-diversity, 4, 7–9, 25–40, 41, 114, 186n3, 189n15; party platforms, 17, 198n2; remedying past discrimination, 25–29; stigmatization, 49, 68–69
descriptive gender experiment: backlash, 100–102; descriptive gender studies, 91–93; gender in the workplace, 88–91; hypotheses, 95; results, 95–102
descriptive race experiment: backlash, 116–17; descriptive race studies, 91–92, 110–112; hypotheses, 113; results 114–117
descriptive representation: Adams' views, 31; affirmative action, 37, 38, 91; backlash, 93, 146; Clinton, 35; connection with legitimacy, 35, 39, 40, 146; critics, 31–32, 186n2, 190n10; difference from elected representatives, 32, 33; difference from substantive representation, 3, 9; gender experiment, 73–77, 81, 83; instrumental purpose, 2, 31; judges as representatives, 33–35, 193n6; judges' views, 62–68; mirror representation, 22–23, 188n11; normative theory, 2, 36, 39, 40, 102; Pitkin view, 35; political parties, positions of, 4–5; race experiment, 113–17; symbolic purpose, 2, 31

INDEX | 219

descriptive/substantive representation: definition, 3, 8–9, 36, 39; diversity dilemma, 5; empirical studies, 118–20; experiment, 74, 79–80, 86, 118; legitimacy, 39, 146; judges as representatives, 58–59; Obama, 37; party identification, 132; raising legitimacy, 1, 5–6, 39–40; specific support, 73; support by Democrats, 4; symbolic message, 3

descriptive/substantive experiment: empirical studies, 118–20; hypotheticals, 120; hypotheticals on party identification, 133; improves legitimacy, 146–47; party identification results, 135–137; results, 120–24; sample, 81

descriptive race study: empirical studies, 118–19; hypotheses, 127; results, 121–25

diversity dilemma: affirmative action, 26; backlash against women, 100, 101; backlash against minorities, 145; definition, 5–6; implications, 6

Dovi, Suzanne, 32

education: need for affirmative action, 26; independent predictor of legitimacy, 76, 97, 98, 99, 101, 114–16, 117, 120–22, 123, 124; matching, 80

Edwards, Harry T., on views of Black judges, 36

Eisenhower, Dwight D.: diversity of judicial appointments, 13, 15, 16, 18, 19, 187n3

Ellinwood, Florence Allen, 16

empathy of judges, ix, x, 8, 38, 40, 65

Epstein, Lee, 186n2

Estrada, Miguel A., 43

experiments, benefits of, 74, 79–80, 86

Fanon, Frantz, 54

The Federalist Papers: No. 10, 39; No. 39, 30

Ford, Gerald R.: diversity of judicial appointents, 16, 17, 18, 19

Fortas, Abraham, 14
Frankfurter, Felix, 14
Frist, William H., 47
Furchtgott-Roth, Diana, 51

Garza, Reynaldo G., 17
Gay, Claudine, 110, 118, 119
geographic diversity, idea of, 11–12
Gibson, James L.: legitimacy and the Supreme Court, 6, 38, 39, 83, 193n1; measuring legitimacy, 77, 127, 194n11, 195n2
Gilliam, Franklin D., 110
Ginsburg, Ruth Bader: descriptive representation, 60; Jewish seat, 14; opposition to affirmative action for women, 71, 94; substantive representation, 37
Goldberg, Arthur J., 14
Gonzales, Alberto R., 43
Guinier, Lani, 92

Haider-Markel, Donald P., 31
Haire, Susan B., 48
Harding, Warren G., 13
Harper, Samuel H., 14
Hastie, William H., 15
Hoover, Herbert C., 11, 14
Horowitz, Lisa, xii

Jackson, Amy Berman, 143
Jackson, Andrew, 12, 14, 110
Jackson, Ketanji Brown, 185n7
Jefferson, Thomas, 14
Johnson, Lyndon B.: and affirmative action, 26, 104; diversity of judicial appointments, 15, 16, 17, 18, 19
Joslyn, Mark R., 31
judges as symbols, 2, 3, 31, 32, 34, 62, 71, 192n2
Judiciary Act of 1789, 11
Judiciary Act of 1801, 13
Judiciary Act of 1891, 11

Kagan, Elena, 12, 14, 38, 47, 67, 140, 191n8
Kahlenberg, Richard D., 54
Kathleen Dolan A., 119
Kavanaugh, Brett M., 12, 13
Kennedy, John F.: diversity of judicial appointments, 13, 16, 17, 18, 19, 191n5
Key, Philip B., 13, 14
Kniss, Chad J., 31

legitimacy: acquiescence in the law, 4, 6, 7, 24; backlash, 1, 56; Clinton, 189n14; colorblind judicial selection, 55; court under attack, 139–44; defined, 3, 4, 52; Democrats, 4, 5, 25, 186n4, 187n5; descriptive gender experiment, 88, 95–102; descriptive representation, 1, 30, 35, 144, 147; descriptive race experiment, 113–117; descriptive/substantive race experiment, 118, 120–25; descriptive/substantive representation, 36, 39; diversity dilemma, 5–6; diversity raises, 1, 2, 24, 144–45; judges' beliefs on diversity, 62, 67, 68; linked fate of Blacks, 197n19; marginalized groups, 25, 39; measurement, 73, 81–84, 194n11, 195n13; normative goal, 3, 24; party identification, 1, 86, 126, 130–31, 135–37, 146; political questions, 190n7; procedural justice, 190n6; reasons for diversifying, 1; remedying past discrimination, 29–30; Republicans, 4, 6, 52, 186n4, 187n5; role of symbols, 196n18; Trump, 7, 139–44; universal legitimacy, 187n6
Lipschutz, Robert, 27
Loury, Glen C., 50

Mack, Julian K., 15
Madison, James, 2, 30, 39
Malcolm, Ellen R., xii
Manafort, Paul, 143
Mansbridge, Jane J., 111, 119

marginalized groups: appointments to federal courts, 18–20; empathy, 38; *Grutter* decision, 35; identity groups, 3; impact on judging, 2, 17, 37, 65, 66; judicial selection, xi, xiii, 18, 19, 22, 35, 38, 42, 46, 54, 72, 189n2; legitimacy, 1; non-meritorious judicial selection, 46, 68, 93, 109; Reagan's refusal to diversify, 42; reverse discrimination, 52; Supreme Court's aid, ix
Marshall, Thurgood, 16, 21, 32, 45, 48, 66, 191n5
Martin, Jack K., 36
Matthews, Burnita Shelton, 16
McCree, Wade H., 16
McKenna, Joseph D., 12, 13, 27
McKenna, Margaret A, 27
McKinley, William, 12, 15
Miers, Harriet E., 43, 44, 46, 47, 188n11, 191n8
Motley, Constance Baker, 16
Murphy, William F., 13, 39

Nelson, Michael J., 39, 127, 194n11
Nixon, Richard M., diversity of judicial appointments, 14, 15, 16, 17, 18, 19

Obama, Barak: affirmative action, 37, 38; backlash, 53, 54, 71; and Democrats' diversity strategy, 25; diversity of judicial appointments, 9, 14, 18, 19, 20, 21, 22, 47, 67; empathy ix, x, 38, 40, 65, 125; nomination of Sotomayor, xi, xii, xiii; remedying past discrimination, 30
O'Connor, Sandra Day, xi, xiii, 21; backlash, 52; *Croson* decision, 50; first woman on the Supreme Court 42, 44; gender's impact on decisions 37, 66; *Grutter* decision, 35, 36; replacement, 188n11; substantive representation, 65

Omnibus Judgeship Act of 1978, 28
Overby, Marvin L., 111, 197n9

Parsons, James B., 16
party identification: freestanding independent variable, 76, 97, 98, 99, 101, 115, 117, 122, 123, 124; hypotheticals, 127, 133; legitimacy, 1, 8, 126, 127, 128, 146–47; matching, 80
Pelosi, Nancy P., 32
Philadelphia Plan, 26
Pitkin, Hannah F., 35
prejudice, 71, 186–87, 198n2
procedural justice, 29, 35, 52, 190n6

race and ethnicity: affirmative action, 54, 60, 108; backlash, 52; descriptive representation, 30, 31, 34, 62, 63, 144; impact on judging, ix, 2, 17, 37, 66; judicial qualifications, 68, 93, 109; judicial selection, xi, xiii, 18, 19, 22, 35, 38, 42, 46, 72, 189n2; substantive representation, 40, 65, 67
racism, 54, 55, 57, 70, 93, 94
Reagan, Ronald W.: diversity of judicial appointments, 13, 18, 19, 20, 21, 34, 190–91n3;
religious diversity, Catholics 12–14; Jews, 14–15
remedying past discrimination: Carter, 27; Clinton, 61
Republican Party Platform: 1960, 198n2; 1968, 198n2; 1976, 17; 1984, 41
Republicans: affirmative action, 2, 75, 190n1; arguments against diversity, 4, 7, 24, 41–56, 143, 190n1; backlash, 55–56, 69–72, 85, 86, 87, 94, 95, 99, 100, 103, 113, 126; Catholics, 13; colorblind selection of judges, 6, 9, 40; criticism of Sotomayor, xi–xiv; diversity dilemma, 6, 9; female appointments, 21, 22, 190n3; Merrick Garland, 188n7; Hispanic judges, xiii; identity politics, xii, 186n3; Ketanji Brown Jackson, 186–187n4; judicial ideology, 1; judicial qualifications, 48, 191n8; lack of diversity, 18; legitimacy, 122, 127, 146–47, 187n5, 189n15; Harriet Miers, 188n11; Obama appointees, 38; partisanship, 1, 6, 8, 144; Clarence Thomas, 188n7
reverse discrimination, 41, 71, 85, 126, 145; backlash, 52–54; delegitimizing of political institutions, 55–56
Richardson, Scovel, 15
Robart, James L., 140
Roberts, John G., xii, 13, 47, 141
Rodriguez, Gregory, 53
Roosevelt, Franklin D., 13, 14, 15, 16, 18, 19, 20, 187n6; packing of the Court, 187n7
Rosen, Bernard, 26

Sanbonmatsu, Kira, 91–92, 119, 197n21
Savage, Michael, xiii, xiv
Scalia, Antonin G., 13, 188n7
Schlussel, Debbie, xiii
Segal, Jeffrey A., 45
senatorial courtesy concept, 27, 28, 35, 46
sexism, 47, 70
Slotnick, Elliot E., 48, 49
Solano, Henry, xii
Sotomayor, Sonia M.: and descriptive representation, 61, 70, 71, 74, 192n2; ethnicity and gender in decision-making, 37; and judicial diversity, 12, 13, 185n3, 185n4, 187n4; and nomination process, ix, xii, xiii, xiv
Souter, David H., ix
Spellman, Cardinal Francis, 13
Spence, Lester Kenyatta, 6, 192n1, 194n11
Stone, Roger J., 142–43
Strauss, David A., 56
substantive representation: Carter on, 189n3; definition, 2; descriptive representation decreases substantive

substantive representation (*cont.*)
representation, 32, 186n2; descriptive representation increases substantive representation, 3, 39, 98, 118; experiment, 118, 119; female Supreme Court justices' views, 36; identity politics, 186n3; judges' motivation to represent, 7; judges' views, 65–67; measurement, 111, 144; minority voices, 40; Pitkin view, 35; public support of decisions, 195n13; short term policy agreement, 39; theory, 36; use of experiments, 75;
Sullivan, Emmet G., 140

Taft, William H., 13, 15, 187n2
Taney, Roger B., 12
Tate, Katherine, 110, 111
Taylor Greene, Marjorie, 32
Thibaut, John W., 29
Thomas, Clarence: *Adarand* decision, 51, 191n11; affirmative action, 49, 50; backlash, 52; *Grutter* decision, 51; ideology, 45; judicial diversity, 13, 21, 188n10; qualifications, 43, 44, 69; substantive representation, 32, 42
Tigar, Jon S., 141
Truman, Harry S: diversity of judicial appointments, 13, 15, 16, 18, 19
Trump, Donald J.: attacking the judiciary, 7, 8, 139, 140, 141, 142, 143, 145; diversity of judicial appointments, 18, 19, 20, 21, 22, 198nn1–6; Merrick Garland, 188n7; rebuke by Justice Roberts, 141
Tyler, Tom R., 29

U.S. Census 2019, updated, 22

Walker, Lauren, 29
Washington, George, ix, xv, 11, 45
Watson, John Derrick K., 140
White, Edward D., 12
Wilson, Woodrow, 14
Wilson, Walter C., 118

ABOUT THE AUTHOR

NANCY SCHERER is Associate Professor of Political Science at Wellesley College. She is the author of *Scoring Points: Politicians, Political Activists and the Lower Federal Court Appointment Process.*

www.ingramcontent.com/pod-product-compliance
Lightning Source LLC
Chambersburg PA
CBHW020251030426
42336CB00010B/715